Post - Conservative
AMERICA

Post-Conservative AMERICA

People, Politics and Ideology in a Time of Crisis

KEVIN P. PHILLIPS

Vintage Books
A Division of Random House
New York

For Andrew and Alexander

Grateful acknowledgment is made to the following for permission
to reprint previously published material:

Commentary: Excerpt from "Reagan and the Republican Revival" by James Q. Wilson, *Commentary* (October 1980). Excerpt from "Is There A New Republican Majority?" by Andrew Hacker, *Commentary* (November 1969). Excerpt from "Ideology and Supply-Side Economics" by Irving Kristol, *Commentary* (April 1981). Excerpt from "The Exposed American Jew" by Nathan Glazer, *Commentary* (June 1975). Reprinted from *Commentary* by permission; all rights reserved.

Foreign Affairs: Excerpt from "To Form a Government" by Lloyd Cutler. Published in *Foreign Affairs* (Fall, 1980). Copyright© 1980 by the Council on Foreign Relations, Inc.

Harper and Row Publishers, Inc.: Specified excerpt from *The Counter Reformation: 1559–1610* by Marvin R. O'Connell. Copyright© 1974 by Marvin R. O'Connell. Excerpts from pages 151, 152–53 of *Only Yesterday: An Informal History of the Nineteen-Twenties* by Frederick Lewis Allen. A Perennial Library book. Copyright 1931 by Frederick Lewis Allen. Copyright© 1959 by Agnes Rogers Allen. Reprinted by permission of Harper & Row Publishers, Inc.

King Features Syndicate, Inc.: Excerpt from syndicated column by Nicholas Von Hoffman. Copyright© 1975 by King Features Syndicate, Inc.

New York. Excerpt from "Nixon as Dreyfus" from *New York* magazine (September 6, 1976). Copyright© 1976 by News Group Publications, Inc. Reprinted by permission.

Public Opinion Quarterly: Excerpt from "Ideological Complexity and Middle American Rationality." Reprinted by permission of the publisher from *Public Opinion Quarterly* (Fall 1973), p. 320. Copyright© 1973 by the Trustees of Columbia University.

Library of Congress Cataloging in Publication Data
Phillips, Kevin P.
Post-conservative America.
Reprint. Originally published: New York:
Random House © 1982. With new introd.
Includes bibliographical references and index.
1. United States—Economic policy—1981–
2. United States—Politics and government—1981–
3. United States—Social policy—1980–
I. Title.
HC106.8.P48   1983   338.973   82-48898
ISBN 0-394-71438-5

PREFACE TO THE
PAPERBACK EDITION

IN THE SPRING OF 1981, WHEN I SET OUT TO PLUMB THE impact of Ronald Reagan on U.S. politics, the prospect seemed quite different than the "Reagan Revolution"—the bold new conservative era—being heralded by others. So *Post-Conservative America* expressed the notion that the economic and political decline of the United States over the previous two decades had simply created too great a strain to be resolved by traditional conservatism. Crisis circumstances were generating a more unsettled and radical response. As of January 1983, sixteen months after writing the book and the original introduction, that thesis seems to have held up fairly well. Very little requires change. If anything, the predicted processes of Reagan Administration institutional frustration and metamorphosis are farther along than I expected.

By the November 1982 elections, President Reagan's thrust of trying to restore the economic beliefs of the Coolidge Era and the U.S. military supremacy of the Eisenhower Era had slowed markedly. Then, by early 1983, observers again began to perceive the flaws in the political system and to fear yet another recurrence of the stalemate and disarray prevalent in the 1973—74 Watergate Era and then in the Carter trauma of 1979—80. The pro-Republican "rolling realignment" invoked by the administration in mid-1981 had already come to naught in 1982, and no new realignment seems imminent. Likewise, in mid-1982, independent 1980 presidential candidate John Anderson escalated his talk about starting a new party for another run in 1984, basically confirming Chapter 17's thesis of dealignment and fragmentation, although the two-party system may intermittently seem resurgent.

Furthermore, 1983 began with a substantial Washington consensus that first-stage Reaganomics had been a disappointment—a conclusion justifying Chapter 10's hypothesis that the original Reagnomics of 1981 was a mass of unworkable contradictions between the incompatible supply-side, monetarist and balanced-budget wings of the Republican Party. Even as this is written, harsh 1982—83 circumstances are producing a major modification of Reaganomics.

As for *Post-Conservative America's* speculation on the possible rise of a right-tilted populism or "Middle American Radicalism," that trend, too, seems to have been even stronger by 1983 than in 1981. In October, key leaders of the New Right announced that they henceforth wanted to be known under the label of the "New Populist Coalition," and the Associated Press linked their attempted transformation to the analyses in *Post-Conservative America*. At the same time, politicians of all hues—New Right, conservative, AFL-CIO loyalist and liberal Democrat—have been increasingly prone to draw from among populist themes like economic nationalism, control of immigration, direct democracy (initiative and referendum) and opposition to special-interest-group control of national politics. Smack in the historical mainstream of Middle American Radicalism, these issues could be the stuff of a volatile politics indeed if hard times linger. Let me underscore that it's difficult to characterize this kind of "center extremism" as being either left or right in the traditional sense, as Chapter 15 amplifies. Yet particularly in the context of recent political history, these themes and frustrations have a more "rightist" than "leftist" set of advocates, vehicles and implications. In economic policy, of course, middle-class frustration is clearly *not* conservative—interventionism is its usual thrust. Consequently, as predicted in the book (p. 221), the Democrats' middling unemployment-based gains in the 1982 Congressional elections have confused discussion of the ideological tilt of 1983—1984 frustration politics.

PREFACE

Will the faster-than-expected modification of Reaganomics in 1982 – 83 help put the U.S. economy back on an expansive enough course to suppress and subordinate the forces and issues breeding frustration, fragmentation and Balkanization? Possibly, but ongoing stagflation is global in scope and origin, and the economic future still remains as ambiguous in 1983 as it was in 1981. Four years into the nineteen eighties, it appears we are still in a decade of turmoil and crisis.

K.P.P.
Washington, January 1983

Acknowledgments

This book would not have been possible without the assistance of a number of people. Lewis Lapham, then editor of *Harper's,* commissioned the articles that have been substantially reproduced as chapters 6 and 16; thanks are due my secretary, Michelle Moore, for her long hours at the typewriter; my agent, Liz Darhansoff; Jason Epstein of Random House for his support and encouragement; and—most of all—my editor, Grant Ujifusa, for his pivotal role in launching and then helping shape the project. And, of course, any author owes a debt to his wife for putting up with it all.

Contents

Contents

INTRODUCTION

MY OWN POLITICAL PREFERENCE AND PARTISAN
temptations aside, this book is not a paean to the conservative trend
in our country. The convolutions of the early 1980s are too complicated to accommodate that. One way or another, this country is
going to move *beyond* conservatism as it is now understood. Which
means that despite Ronald Reagan's triumph in 1980, the chances for
a historical 28-to-36-year cycle of Republican dominance are slim.

To say that the book is about the national rightward trend comes
somewhat closer to what I want to say. But the two phenomena—
traditional conservatism and a shift to the political right—are by no
means identical.

To say that what we have been seeing is a radicalization of the
electorate of the old center—a center no longer "vital"—comes closest of all, especially when considered with the kindred notion that
"conservatism" has become a vehicle for radical ideas. Much of the
volatile populist component of the Reagan coalition and the New
Right is not "of the right" in any classic or traditional sense. Dakota

wheat farmers, New York City Orthodox Jews and the poor white Baptists of the Southern pineywoods—three especially notable pro-Reagan trend groups of 1980—epitomize the "conservative" radicalization of voting streams almost never found embracing conservatism or moving toward the right in the European sense of the word. The same can be said for supporters of the tax revolt. Thus, the coalition empowered in 1980 contains major elements of instability.

Of course, our political coalitions have never made sense by the thinking employed in London, Paris or Berlin—and have never needed to, thank you. Hitherto we have done well enough with unique electoral aggregations, to say nothing of leaders, that could never pass muster on the other side of the Atlantic. But I have a certain reservation about the structure of the Reagan constituency of 1980. Inherent cultural and ideological contradictions are not the problem. Past coalitions have survived them, though no lasting electoral watersheds have taken place since television began circumscribing the ability of parties to be different things to mutually contradictory constituencies. My skepticism about the durability of the Reagan revolution runs deeper. Unlike prior groupings, the new coalition empowered in 1980 seems to be one whose constituencies are conjoined more by various nostalgias and backward-looking vistas than by shared philosophies for the *future*. If so, and given that the United States has never before tried revolutionary conservatism, I doubt whether this coalition can launch a full-fledged, generation-long, deep-rooted party realignment of the sort the country has seen five times before in its political history—certainly not unless the new supply-side (deep tax cut) economics achieves a widely unpredicted success. Electorally the new coalition looks plausible, but if the policies coming out of it turn out to be the stuff of ideological nostalgia and not of a national renaissance, the impact on American confidence, institutions and parties could be explosive. So the political cycle getting under way could be a short one.

The shame, the great shame, is that the conservative trend—the move to the right in American politics—has taken so long to come to political power, or so long to be able to *hold* power, if one thinks of 1972 and Watergate as a bloodless political countercoup. The passage of fourteen disruptive years between the first convincing electoral evidence, in 1966, of popular reaction against 1960s liberalism and the first effective repudiation of that credo in the political upheaval of 1980 may have bred a Reagan coalition with an unstable dependence on cultural and economic frustration, revisionism and reaction. The "establishment" may have left the popular trend to the right—the public's radical disaffection with liberalism—unheeded for too long. Problems, and frustrations, may have gotten too big for any governing political coalition to handle.

I don't see how any serious observer of our politics can fail to recognize, at least in retrospect, that the ideological shift that recently crested had its origins in the mid-to-late 1960s and gained strength across a broad spectrum of politics, culture, economics, religion and geography. Let us sum up symbolically by saying that for the country of the late 1960s—of urban riots, the Woodstock Nation and Charles Reich's *The Greening of America*—to become instead a nation of Sun Belt ascendancy, supply-side economics, the computerized New Right, electronic revivalism, neoconservatism, resurgent campus ROTC and even Grand Ole Opry performances on public television bespeaks an extraordinary political and ideological metamorphosis. Such change doesn't occur overnight. At the same time, many of the conservative counterforces provoked in the 1960s have been around for quite a while now. New dynamics and leaders have been emerging, some of them quite radical. Everything I see suggests that the 1980s will not be remembered as a placid era of Coolidge or Eisenhower restoration, fond presidential evocation notwithstanding.

To shed some light on what should be rather precarious times ahead, I have used an unusual approach to American political analysis. My earlier books (in particular *The Emerging Republican Majority*, written after looking at the 1966 election returns) pretty much confined themselves to analysis of American voting patterns and related socioeconomic trends. Frankly, I don't think that kind of analysis can be used to deal with the volatilities of the 1980s. Bear in mind that from the early nineteenth century through World War II—the period encompassing each and every U.S. watershed election and party realignment to date—the major nations of the West, notably Britain and the United States, have been living through what historians have called the Industrial Era—one that gave rise to the mass-based party system, the alignment of which in the United States has followed a pattern of changing every 28–36 years.

That pattern isn't in place any longer. The old politico-economic era exhausted itself during the 1960s and 1970s, and a transition into a new global political and economic regime appears to be occurring

—a regime in which the role and influence of the United States is on the wane. If this capsule theory is correct, our politics are no longer operating in their old sequence of 28–36-year political realignments by which we could assume, and look for, a nice, neat, new and cyclical political majority taking shape.

Academicians like to talk about *de-alignment,* which is fair enough, but the underlying dynamics of electoral de-alignment go beyond politics. What I am suggesting is that for the first time, American party upheaval is part and parcel of a global economic realignment—a historical process by which a post-industrial era replaces the industrial era in one of those epochal structural and inflationary upheavals history calls "price revolution." If we are now in a period of price revolution—and the supporting evidence of this is fairly strong—it is a situation with which our politics has never before had to cope. Likewise, political realignment in this country has never had to face, save for the time before the Civil War, a breakdown of public faith in our institutions, a partial loss of belief in the future, a gnawing fear that our children will not live as well as we do, and in general, a fear that America may now be traversing the downslope of history. So public perceptions have created a whole new group of psychologies and radical frustrations that lie beyond traditional American politics, historically based on optimism.

Thus, while the first seven-chapter section of this book opens with an examination of the purely national context of our political behavior and potential change during the 1980s, the two middle sections go further afield. The second section (chapters 8 to 11) postulates that the West is caught up in a major economic shift, with the global nature of the price revolution likely to frustrate any clear solution, or clear party realignment, in the United States. If these chapters seem like an odd lurch away from an analysis of American politics, they are not. Likewise, the third section of the book (chapters 12 to 15) looks at the possibility that the demise of the American Dream, and in general, the malaise of the West, could lead to political radicalism and institutional upheaval. In short, must our electoral and party-cycle analysis now consider Arnold Toynbee and Oswald Spengler along with V. O. Key and Walter Dean Burnham?

The opening chapters of the book can be compared to one-dimensional chess. American politics is examined on American terms. In chapters 8 to 15 I try to make the game multidimensional by looking at the interplay of American and global trends before returning, in

INTRODUCTION

chapters 16 to 18, to a second look at the probable shape of political and social upheaval in the United States during the coming decade. My thesis, really, is that old, purely American patterns, relationships and institutions are breaking down in a way that requires reference to larger global and historical forces.

If my analysis of these trends doesn't sound very "conservative," it probably isn't. And one of my hopes is that this book can help explain some insufficiently appreciated aspects of the forces at work in the economy and polity under the label (or guise) of "conservatism." Traditional liberal interpretations are demonstrably obsolete, but traditional conservative interpretations are perhaps less useful than many imagine. And the old "center" merely reflects the interaction and analytical compromises of a position midway between these two pasts. A dynamic, vital center has yet to be re-established.

Traditional conservatism, for its part, has chroniclers aplenty. George Nash, in his perceptive and well-crafted volume *The Conservative Intellectual Movement in America Since 1945,* has analyzed growing conservative strength in intellectual and literary terms. Fair enough. No one can deny the impact of the conservative books and ideas marketed in the United States since World War II, whether they have launched a thousand activists or helped nominate a presidential candidate, as with Barry Goldwater's *The Conscience of a Conservative.* However, to me American "conservatism" as a political and grass-roots electoral force of the 1980s—precisely the subject of this book—owes less to intellectual trends of a "classical" renaissance and more to the forces of cultural anomie, religious fundamentalism, economics (including economic apprehension), nationalism and even frustration. Ideas count, yes. But they are only one factor in a list that also includes population change, economics, ethnic and religious tribalisms and sheer voter frustration. In this none too ideological country of ours, doctrine, by itself, is an entirely insufficient explanation of why things happen in politics.

I intend to offer a more eclectic thesis. Without embracing historical or economic determinism, grasping at runes or conjuring up some trans-Appalachian *volk,* I'm inclined to explain the recent emergence of what we call "conservatism" using a number of nonintellectual variables: the rise of the Sun Belt and the shift of national power South and West; longstanding Southern and Western opposition to the politics of Eastern elites; traditionalist Middle America's reaction against the social, moral and racial upheavals of the 1960s; popular frustration with the revolution of rising prices; apprehension that America's hour may be passing and a feeling that a restoration of old values and circumstances is somehow needed; the rise of the activist, nonintellectual (some would say *anti-*intellectual) New Right; and the dramatic growth of religious fundamentalism, so dramatic that some observers see a fourth "Great Awakening." To conservative theorists enamored of triumphant philosophical truths based on Adam Smith or Saint Augustine, these factors and interpretations— some more populist than conservative, others more national than universal, still others verging on determinism—are too often ignored or relegated to the less important.

My own view is admittedly rather populistic, a vaguely neo-Marxian brand of conservative analysis. Concerned with elites, regional antagonisms and popular frustrations, my framework attaches somewhat less importance to forces like the conservative intellectual movement, neoconservatism and supply-side economic theory than the other schemes might. Quite obviously, political implications exist in such an interpretation, and my analysis suggests that there was less conservative doctrinal mandate in the 1980 election results, and rather more popular restiveness, though that restiveness was linked to basic conservative perceptions of reality and human nature.

Another caveat is in order. I can hardly pretend to be a totally disinterested commentator. My book *The Emerging Republican Majority* (written in 1967, used in the 1968 Nixon campaign, and then published in 1969) laid out the new Southern-Western geography of a populist-tilting conservatism. It *did not,* as some observers said, initiate the so-called Southern Strategy; however, it *did* coin the term "Sun Belt" and predict that therein lay the political future. The truth of that forecast has become more apparent with every passing year, and my Sun Belt thesis is updated in Chapter 18.

My second book, *Mediacracy: American Parties and Politics in the Communications Age* (published in 1975), suggested that the Watergate debacle had derailed the various forces moving toward the consolidation of a new coalition—one temporarily achieved in 1972. But beyond that, the book speculated that Watergate's warping of trends, alignments, parties and popular confidence in institutions, aggravated by the economic, foreign and energy policy dislocations of 1972–76, might well mean that the future held a larger upheaval, possibly one that would go beyond the framework of a decreasingly viable two-party system. I'm still inclined to think so. The clear possibility of a new party in 1984 based on John Anderson's 1980 splinter electorate of students, affluent professionals, old Yankee progressives, Midwest Scandinavians and Pacific avant-guardists, spurred by negative reaction to the populist, fundamentalist and supply-side ascendancy in the GOP, could fit the bill. Moreover, just as the decaying Democratic coalition of the 1960s and 1970s underwent a bilateral disintegration, with mutually hostile Wallaceite populist conservatives on one side and McGovernite Northern middle-class activists on the other, the Republican coalition may well be undergoing a similar twin-pressured narrowing. The Anderson element and the New Right are just as incompatible. As Chapter 17 will show, the old coalitions appear to encompass unbridgeable sociological disparities. Since the Watergate scandal smashed the political framework under construction in 1972 and intensified popular institutional distrust, I have been inclined to expect a new party system, possibly containing three or more parties, to take shape around new ideological-cultural fault lines. The existing Republican-Democratic party system was first spawned in the industrial 1850s and was then given clear shape by the coming of the Civil War. No other major country has such an ancient—and obsolescent—pair of parties.

The emergence of one new ideological-cultural force, the New Right, was a major political phenomenon of the late 1970s and early 1980s. In his book *The New Right: We're Ready to Lead,* Richard Viguerie, the principal fund raiser of the movement, credits me with being the first, back in 1974–75, to apply the term to the right-wing social-issue groups in which he and his allies played a central role. At first such groups emphasized issues like the Panama Canal treaties, busing and education. But by 1980–81 the focus of the New Right, working with the Moral Majority, the Religious Roundtable and the right-to-life movement, had clearly shifted to religious, moral and family-related issues. As late as 1977–78, the "Old Right" —the conservative element principally concerned with economics, foreign/defense policy and internal security—took issue with the concept of a genuinely "new" right with a substantially distinct agenda, constituency and goal. *Congressional Quarterly* once quoted, sans attribution, several conservative spokesmen as saying that the New Right existed only in the mind of Kevin Phillips. The 1980 elections appear to have disposed of that semantic quibble.

Nevertheless, I wouldn't be surprised if the New Right was pretty much a spent force by the end of the 1980s, at least in its moral, religious and family-issue positions. Movements of this sort usually only last a decade or so, until their causes are acknowledged and partially accepted. In the meantime, however, its moral and religious agenda is likely to have a substantial effect on the national culture and polity. Like Ronald Reagan, the religious right was underestimated up until November 1980.

The current political importance of religious and moral issues has a *second* implication. Beyond their single-issue focal points, many Southern fundamentalist and Northern right-to-life voters have been historically associated with a politics whose economics is more populist and activist than doctrinally conservative. In short, much of the social-issue constituency has a New Deal economic past. The voting blocs represented have often cheered such opponents of the prevailing power elite as Andrew Jackson, William Jennings Bryan, Franklin D. Roosevelt and George C. Wallace. So there's no avoiding the fact that the new "conservatism" has important populist and radical roots, and that's exactly why it has achieved a mass of potential watershed significance. In many ways, populism, *not* conservatism, is *the* electoral force unique to our politics. In one form or another, American populism has gathered force and helped to give ideological direction to the nation when it confronted various historical crossroads.

I had underscored the populist aspect of the conservative electoral opportunity as early as 1969 (in *The Emerging Republican Majority*) but these caveats were generally ignored. By the mid-1970s, however, my further analyses in these directions had begun to make a number of conservative purists and theorists unhappy. William F. Buckley Jr. penned a newspaper column calling me "the voice of Philistia," and his magazine *National Review* later followed suit with a critique called "To the Nashville Station," lamenting my economic and populist interpretation of conservatism as "country and western Marxism." Others also picked up the idea of conservatism-as-radicalism, though often in error-studded diatribes that undermined their own goals. As late as 1978 and 1979, most observers dismissed the factionalism on the right as politically meaningless. But since 1980, the divisions on the right, like the factions of early 1930s left-liberalism, have become—to use that tired word—considerably more "relevant."

Enough about context. Individual book chapters will soon put meat on these theoretical, historical and factional bones. Structurally, my approach is to lay out political, economic and institutional theses, stating them first in basic terms and then interrelating and amplifying the ideas in subsequent chapters.

The volume is arranged as follows: Chapter 1, an overview, tries to assess the dynamics of the Reagan revolution launched by the election of 1980—the implications of the nostalgic "Coolidge restoration" convergence of conservatism and de facto radicalism, one result of which is the sweeping, revolutionary White House blueprint for disassembling federal power and restoring business, the private sector, to its pre-1929 primacy.

The sense of national frustration that paved the way for that risky and massive turn in our collective lives is the subject matter of Chapter 2—a look at the "Two-Decade Breakdown" of the United States as a society, economy and polity during the 1960s and 1970s. "Breakdown" may be too extreme a word, but "trauma" would be fair. And historically, the major American social and economic traumas have been followed by watershed political upheavals. That has almost certainly happened again.

With the upheaval, class and ideology have been turned on their heads. We have seen the partial transition of American liberalism to an out-of-touch *elite* credo while conservatism, for its part, shifted gears and moved toward the *populist* constituencies of East Texas and South Boston. These transitions are explained in Chapter 3 as being two sides of the same coin. The bulk of the chapter is a chronicle of how American conservatism has radicalized itself over the last two decades—geographically, ideologically, institutionally, and by way of economic theology.

The first possible conservative resolution of the politics of the 1960s, "The Emerging Republican Majority" of 1968–72, is revisited in Chapter 4: the realignment that could have happened in 1972 but for Watergate (and probably no longer can). Thus, Chapter 5 looks at "The Watergate Warp"—the impact of the scandal and its dislocation of American party politics and policy making. Absent Richard Nixon's premature exit, things might have turned out differently; moreover, there are reasons to believe that the whole truth about Watergate may never be known—too much mythology and history is already in place. Another phenomenon of the 1970s was the breakdown of old loyalties, the fragmentation of the country into narrower communities, interest groups and tribes. I deal with it in Chapter 6 as "The Balkanization of America." And Chapter 7 profiles the current balance of power in the nation—regional, cultural, religious, economic and political—after two decades of upheaval. Measurements of the present decade's trends may confirm a rightward dynamic, but they also suggest potential left counterforces. There is a lot of yeast and instability—some of it produced by the right, some of it not—in our economic and political demography.

Instability might easily come to preoccupy us if conservative economics is not the success its advocates hope. For the Western world, inflation is the great challenge, and history suggests a dangerous parallel. Since World War II, the price level in much of Europe and North America has soared by 400–500 percent, not unlike the pattern of the last similar surge, Europe's sixteenth-century "price revolution." That economic transformation worked enormous hardship on politics and politicians: kings, cardinals and chancellors had trouble keeping their seats of power; parliaments lost headway; the peasantry's standard of living fell, in some cases substantially. The evidence that the West is caught up in another price revolution, one that spotlights (but also transcends) the failure of liberal/welfare-state economics, is, I think, considerable. The political and institutional implications of ongoing inflation are weighed in chapters 8 to II. Historically, price revolutions have generated *profound* political and social upheaval.

Cultural and social frustration is *already* a major force. Indeed, one can argue that the circa-1980 United States bore at least a superficial relationship to the German Weimar Republic in the multiple legacy of a lost war, diminished faith in institutions, the gap between an elite "cabaret culture" and the beliefs of the more traditional masses, with the middle class strapped by inflation. This is the thrust of Chapter 12. Embellishing that thesis, Chapter 13 discusses our habit of refighting our wars in later political campaigns, a precedent that may suggest a 1980s revisionist refighting of the conflict in Vietnam, the frustrations and miscalculations of the first major war Americans have ever lost. Chapter 14 inspects yet another potential framework for radicalization. The "religious right," shaped by reaction to the moral upheaval of the 1960s and 1970s, can be usefully compared with past religious waves of subsequent political importance: the so-called Great Awakenings of the mid-eighteenth century and the early nineteenth century, and the late-nineteenth-century time of William Jennings Bryan. Summarizing those three themes,

Chapter 15 looks at *majority*-type constituencies as the pivotal seedbeds of recent American political alienation, and ponders the overall extent of middle-class radicalization. The extent to which it is radicalized may very well define the decade.

Finally, chapters 16, 17 and 18 consider our political institutions—the Constitution and its separation of powers, the Republican and Democratic party system, the federal system and the general belief in limited state power—and weigh their capacity (or lack of it) to reaggregate American productivity, competition and power. We may well approach the two-hundredth anniversary of the U.S. Constitution in 1987 with a renewed national awareness of the need for some structural overhaul. A decade ago Watergate generated considerable attention to the shortcomings of our basic political institutions. Then Nixon's resignation solved the problem, or appeared to. From 1975 to 1978, public and academic interest in institutional reform ebbed. Nobody expected much from interim, appointive President Gerald Ford, but by 1979, when Jimmy Carter, too, could not handle Washington's separation of powers and special interests, institutional reform once again began to receive attention. By 1980, both presidential counsel Lloyd N. Cutler and White House domestic policy chief Stuart E. Eizenstat were suggesting that we might do well to move in the direction of a parliamentary system. The new Reagan Administration provided a new hiatus, with analysts once again confident that the system—and the presidency—was proving itself. This writer is less optimistic. I believe we have been ignoring basic, underlying institutional problems.

Before concluding my introduction, I want to say that I have avoided elaborate documentation of collateral matters taken up in the book. My discussions of subjects like the failure of Great Society social legislation, the role of the CIA in Watergate, the rise of fundamentalist religion, the possibility of a twentieth-century price revolution, the excesses of welfare-state economics, the vagaries of "supply-side" restatement of Adam Smith and Jean-Baptiste Say, the parallels between the United States and Weimar Germany, a historical look at recrimination against wartime defeatism, and so forth, are not intended to be comprehensive analyses or statements. I have generally stated my theses with much less documentation than would be necessary to fend off critics. Limited space was one factor; so was a desire not to spend too much time on the peripheral. In some cases—the Watergate and Vietnam chapters—I have set forth arguments not to prove their accuracy but to establish their potential political potency. For my limited purposes, I believe the collateral ideas are sufficiently stated and supported. But I recognize that specialists will sometimes feel otherwise.

All in all, the probable dynamics of the 1980s seem to me to be the stuff of which convulsions are made. If revolutionary conservatism prevails, or if it fails, the changes wrought in American politics and political institutions are likely to exceed anyone's expectations.

KEVIN P. PHILLIPS
Washington, October 1981

Part One

AMERICA'S TWO-DECADE BREAKDOWN AND THE TRANSFORMATION OF AMERICAN POLITICS

1

CALVIN COOLIDGE AND THE "SHADOW EMPIRE" OF NOSTALGIC CONSERVATISM

"Can't repeat the past," he cried incredulously.
"Why of course you can."

—Jay Gatsby in *The Great Gatsby* (1925)

NO SOONER WAS RONALD REAGAN INAUGURATED AS president in 1981 than the era of F. Scott Fitzgerald became fashionable again, invoked by White House aides paying great tribute to Andrew Mellon's economics or applauding Calvin Coolidge's refusal to tolerate strikes by public employees. The Gatsby years were a decade when politicians and preachers extolled the lost virtues of the kerosene lamp as they confronted the revolution produced by radio, transatlantic flights and the vote for women. The nostalgia of the 1980s is even bolder.

The trouble is, the early 1980s attempt to bring back elements of Mellon's theories of taxation, William Jennings Bryan's views on evolution, and Coolidge's preferences on business regulation amounts to a leap *past* conservatism. Bluntly put, we may live in a time in which conservatism cannot conserve, and so must reach back for *lost* truths and practices. The greater the problems and popular frustration, the further back the politicians try to reach, and the greater the risk.

The politics of nostalgia is especially appealing to conservatives, of course. Self-made men, like those in Ronald Reagan's "kitchen cabinet," believe that because they became very rich and lived lives based on values of decades long departed, all Americans would profit from re-establishing those circumstances and entrepreneurial opportunities. Yet in the last fifteen years or so, moderates and liberals have also begun to evoke the past. If Ronald Reagan invoked Calvin Coolidge and if Richard Nixon conjured up parallels with Woodrow Wilson and Benjamin Disraeli, Jimmy Carter sought to picture himself as a second Harry S. Truman. Somehow, since the late 1960s, not one President has been able to tag his Administration with a "new" image theme like those of yore—New Deal and New Frontier. Unable to sell the future, they have instead begun to market an implicit rerun of a greater and more prideful past.

I cannot disagree with the historians (Richard Hofstadter, Peter Viereck, among others) who have labeled such politics "pseudoconservatism." But their critique would be sounder if it were less one-dimensional. Pseudoconservatism has a chicken-or-egg relationship to pseudoliberalism: Which ideological mutation came first, and are word games worth the trouble? Down through the years, numerous observers have cautioned us that our most important historical periods also tend to be the most confused, and not least when it comes to descriptive terminology. Surely this applies to the 1980s. A historical theory of semantic confusion can contain a sophisticated rationale for the extent to which commentators are currently floundering in a sea of prefixes: neoconservative, New Right, pseudoconservative, post-Keynesian, neopopulist, post-industrial, etc. All hope soon to come ashore on conceptual terra firma. When that will be, nobody knows.

Certainly existing political word concepts fail to describe the political, economic and social experiment launched in the United States in November 1980. Meanwhile, nothing about the Reagan constituency or revolution is monolithic. Reaction stands with populism; conservatism finds itself allied with the idea of economic and social progress; quasi-religious faith in capitalism finds itself in bed with a fundamentalist religious apprehension of the Biblical "End Times." But the politics of watershed periods in our history have rarely fit pre-existing one-word ideologies; more often such politics create the ideologies and the ideologues.

Have we, then, experienced a conservative revolution? No and yes. No, in the sense that the term logically fails almost by definition. No revolution *conserves*. Yes, however, in the sense that the term "conservative revolution" has been used to describe the late-nineteenth- and early-twentieth-century movements in Europe antagonistic to liberalism, secularism, rationalism and universalism. Then, as now, change had gone too far too fast. In France, Italy and Germany, conservative revolutionaries—unlike the more adjustment-inclined power elite—sought to roll back the liberal tide with a contrary credo of nationalism, religion and Social Darwinism. Whatever their validity, these critiques ultimately helped lay the groundwork for the fascist upheavals of the 1920s and 1930s. Elements of the Reagan coalition bear some latter-day resemblance to these conservative revolutionaries. The parallel should not be overstated, but it should be noted.*

More precisely, the 1980s must be considered a decade following a twenty-year period of turbulence in which the American people lost their first war, saw a number of prominent leaders assassinated, their first President forced from office, their currency at one point lose 95 percent of its value against gold, and generally came to feel that their "Heaven-bless'd nation" was somehow no longer favored. The fact that these statements have become clichéd only underscores the pervasiveness of their national absorption. This context supplies little of the cultural placidity needed to nurture either the establishment variety of conservatism or a genuine traditionalist renaissance. By contrast, there has been a superabundance of the frustration and anomie needed to nurture a kindred, but different, politics: call it nostalgic nationalism, shadow imperialism or merely an attempt to re-create bygone halcyon days, but the process is one Arnold Toynbee describes as a nationalist "archaism" of a fading, apprehensive civilization.† Politicians often find a body politic willing and even

---

*See Chapter 15 for a more detailed comparison.

†In *A Study of History,* Toynbee describes the proclivity of declining civilizations to try to return to some past "Golden Age" of the society in question: "The archaistic version may be defined as a reversion from the mimesis of contemporary creative personalities to a mimesis of ancestors . . . alternatively, it may be defined as an attempt to arrest a society at a given stage, or forestall a threatening change, by immobilizing the dynamic factors of social growth—and this, as we have seen, is an invariably catastrophic reaction to social challenges . . . In its social and political institutions, in its aesthetic culture and its religion, [a community] will try

eager to reach back into prouder times. Sometimes the process turns into plebiscitary democracy—orchestrated populism—and then into Caesarism. These days, I imagine Caesarism could make a more triumphal entry through television than was ever possible by chariot.

Knowing the skepticism it will engender, I will nevertheless cite the precedents of several European nations indulging kindred psychologies and apprehensions during the 1930s: Italy's Benito Mussolini, with his Roman symbols and salutes, his attempts to equate minor and not even very skillful military conquests in Libya, Eritrea and Ethiopia with the reconstruction of the empire of Trajan; and most of all, Hitler's Germany, with its notion of Germanic racialism, emotive restoration of Frederick the Great's Prussia, and reversion to Teutonic mythology. France, for its part, had pursued a Shadow Empire two generations earlier, seeking to re-create the glories of the Napoleonic era with the "Second Empire" of Louis Napoleon. Countries do these things, in different ways and at different evolutionary stages. Europe's archaisms would not be America's.

This is probably the appropriate point to state and then underscore a caveat I will refashion and restate in several other segments of this book. A number of the dynamics, psychologies and pathologies of U.S. politics in the early 1980s bear some relation to the dynamics, psychologies and pathologies that have caused some of modern European history's most aberrant regimes, along with many lesser transformations. To cite these is not to suggest or even hint that "it could happen here." The lesson to be taken, no less and no more, is that circumstances somewhat similar to those now confronting the United States have bred substantial degrees of political turmoil in many nations.

So despite theories of American "exceptionalism," I'm inclined to think Shadow Empire dynamics may well be at work in the United States. We do not like to entertain such thoughts, and few scholars profess them. Even so, William Appleton Williams, chief historian of the end-of-America-as-empire school, makes an enormously important point when he insists that "our intellectual, political and psychological confusion is the result of our *a*historical faith that we are not now and never have been an empire. Yet there is *no way* to

---

to recapture the ostensible purity of an age of national independence prior to the one in which it finds itself incorporated in the larger society of a supranational civilization." See Toynbee, *A Study of History,* abridged ed. (Barre, Mass., Weathervane, 1972), p. 245.

understand the nature of our predicament except by confronting our history *as* an empire."[1] Williams' thesis is crucial to any understanding of an America in decline: *the great historical precedents are all imperial.* Nevertheless, the United States, reacting to decline, could be drawn to not a man on horseback but a Norman Rockwell figure from the front cover of the *Saturday Evening Post.* If we are a nostalgizing empire, we are a uniquely republican one, a modern commercial state trying to re-create the period of its most ebullient capitalism, its Rotarian zenith, and its middle-class *Happy Days.* In its early stages, such a politics might be difficult to distinguish from a genuine national renaissance. A number of critics—from John Kenneth Galbraith to Lester Thurow and Albert Wojnilower—have dismissed the new conservative economics as a reversion to Coolidge-era policies. They all seem to miss the *larger* sociocultural context of 1980s restorationism.

Chronologically and psychologically, recent history offers contemporary Americans two obvious choices for imitation-cum-restoration: the eras following shortly after the two world wars in which the United States accumulated worldwide military, political and economic hegemony. Both periods were reasonably similar in politics and culture—and in longevity. The 1920s, of course, is one. If we omit the immediate post–World War I years of soaring inflation, anti-Bolshevik witch hunting, the deep 1921–22 recession and the 1923 Teapot Dome scandal, the presumed golden era encompasses the years 1923 to 1929, and so coincides very neatly with the presidency of Calvin Coolidge. The second halcyon era, following World War II, can also be said to have begun after a brief delay encompassing the early postwar years of inflation, Communist scandals, McCarthyism and the Korean War. So defined, it would run from, say, 1953, to the end of the decade, again conveniently overlapping with a single presidency—that of Dwight D. Eisenhower. Both the "Roaring Twenties" and the "Fabulous Fifties" were eras of peak American inventiveness, technological advance and middle-class consumer gains, both periods when the United States came closest to embracing the comfortable self-assurance of George F. Babbitt.

If time is a healer, it is also a conjurer. The space of a generation, born and come to some maturity, must occur before a decade can become mythologized, and the 1950s seem to have been so transformed in the late 1970s. Nostalgia flowered. Let future cultural historians chart the various social indices: television programs about the decade's *Happy Days* moving to the top of the ratings; pasteboard baseball cards of Mickey Mantle, Willie Mays and Ted Williams climbing to values of from $700 to $1,700 each; the emergence of societies for the preservation of mid-century commercial archeology symbolized by the original McDonald's Golden Arch and the orange abomination of Howard Johnson's; and—perhaps most symptomatic of all—the proliferation of sympathetic Eisenhower biographies. In the six months around the election and inauguration of Ronald Reagan as President, over half a dozen studies of the Eisenhower era were published. The May 9, 1981, book section of the *New Republic* —a magazine once stereotypically liberal—featured a sympathetic review by Professor Stephen E. Ambrose of the University of New Orleans (himself "currently at work on a full-scale biography of Eisenhower") of five other benign new Eisenhower assessments.* By 1980, 1950s revisionism had become an established major force.

What was at work in colleges was even more vividly at work in the American electorate. Political nostalgia for the America of a more powerful, less sophisticated and less cynical yesteryear played an undoubted role in the 1980 presidential election. Yet inasmuch as Americans shun Spenglerian national pessimism, Ronald Reagan, both during his campaign and after his inauguration, took pains to characterize his politics as optimistic and forward-looking—continued belief in America's ongoing "rendezvous with destiny." Not for Ronald Reagan was there any admission that the American era was over. "I don't agree that our nation must resign itself to inevitable decline," he proclaimed in his November 1979 presidential announcement speech.[2] Instead, he promised a national *renaissance.*

In doing so, he picked up on a theme advanced by a number of conservative politicians and thinkers. Jack Kemp, who was the chief congressional advocate in 1978–80 of national renewal through federal tax reduction, entitled his 1979 book *An American Renaissance,* and conservative ideologist Russell Kirk took up the same theme in a 1980 symposium on "The Conservative Movement: Then and

---

* *The Eisenhower Diaries,* by Robert H. Ferrill; *Eisenhower the President,* by William Bragg Ewald; *Eisenhower and the Cold War,* by Robert Divine; *Trade and Aid: Eisenhower's Foreign Economic Policy,* by Burton Kaufman; and *The Declassified Eisenhower,* by Blanche Cook.

No better measure is available of how far intellectuals—and even college professors—traveled in the late 1960s and early 1970s. Back in the late 1950s, Professor Eric Goldman proclaimed the Eisenhower era possibly the dullest in history.

Now": "It has happened from time to time in the history of civilization that a period of decadence and discouragement has been followed by a period of renewal and hope. It can be so with our American civilization."[3]

No sooner was Reagan installed in the White House than he hung the portraits of the Presidents whose policies exemplified the dynamics of his renaissance: Calvin Coolidge and Dwight Eisenhower. And therein lay the great irony. Answering a reporter's question about the two men, Reagan said, "If you go back, I don't know if the country has ever had a higher level of prosperity than it did under Coolidge. And he actually reduced the national debt, he cut taxes several times across the board. And maybe the criticism was . . . that [he wasn't] activist enough. Well, maybe there's a lesson in that. Maybe we've had instances of government being too active, intervening, interfering."[4] Queried about this, Treasury Secretary Donald Regan amplified Reagan's remarks by saying, "We're not going back to high-button shoes and celluloid collars. But the President does want to go back to many of the financial methods and economic incentives that brought about the prosperity of the Coolidge period."[5] Many, many more Coolidge citations were to follow.* By contrast, defense and foreign policy drew on a hoped-for Eisenhower-era parallel: strength through preparedness, Pax Americana, the return of American greatness. Note that here restorationists find the Coolidge years unattractive—the Republican Administration of the 1920s pursued disarmament and naval limitation treaties, eschewing military expansion.

Taxes and global strategy aside, the overall similarity between the times of Eisenhower and Coolidge is considerable. Both were prosperous, conservative peacetime interludes—lulls between storms, really—guided by Republican Presidents who admired the business community and kept company with its leaders. Yet one would have to say that while the public was wallowing in nostalgia for the more recent era, Ronald Reagan and his advisers were mostly looking back a full half-century to the 1920s.

There are a number of explanations. Some of them, possibly the most important, flow from Ronald Reagan's own experiences and

*Probably the ultimate came in mid-1981 when the monthly magazine of the Republican National Committee published an analysis linking the Reagan tax cuts to the Coolidge tax cuts under the headline "It Worked Before. It Will Work Again."

predilections. In his autobiography, Reagan describes his Coolidge-era boyhood in a succession of Illinois towns as an ideal existence, "a rare Tom Sawyer–Huck Finn idyll." Biographers invariably emphasize Reagan's deep psychological roots in the Midwest of the 1920s, although he has spent most of his life in California. Some academicians also see a significance in Reagan's coming to the presidency from the Sun Belt, a region especially inclined to a mythical interpretation of the American past. Still others suggest that Reagan, influenced by his Hollywood career, came into office determined to recapture the white picket fences of "Movie America."[6]

Over the last two decades or so, a number of academicians began to undertake studies of presidential personalities and pathologies. Lyndon Johnson, Richard Nixon and Jimmy Carter were subjected to analysis several times, with results that were less than reassuring. Surprisingly little of that has been done with Ronald Reagan, but I suspect we will see more of it⁻ in later years, with his Midwest boyhood, Hollywood experience and Sun Belt ideological metamorphosis probably receiving analytical emphasis.

Psychology aside, the Coolidge era was the only imitative choice in economics for policy reasons. The Eisenhower years were pedestrian in their balanced-budget Republicanism. The Coolidge years, by contrast—and the difference was enormously important to key Reagan theorists and advisers—were years when the federal income tax was only a decade old, and high rates were a World War I emergency phenomenon. Republican financiers and economic policy makers had no compunction about slashing the high upper-bracket levies imposed temporarily during hostilities.* The results, as we shall see in Chapter 10, were ambiguous: rather more money for the rich to spend and speculate with, too much investment and excessive productive capacity in some sectors of industry, and a precarious, narrow-based prosperity. However, to some of the leading economic advisers in the campaign and the early Reagan Administration, men like New York Representative Jack Kemp, Budget Director David Stockman and California Professor Arthur Laffer, tax cuts and "supply" were part of a theology of national economic revitalization. So the 1920s came to be admired and emulated. Treasury Secretary Andrew Mellon, against whom impeachment was brought in mid-

---

*Authority to tax incomes was granted to Congress by the Sixteenth Amendment to the U.S. Constitution in 1913. Low at first, the maximum rate shot up to 77 percent during World War I. It was reduced in four stages, to 25 percent by 1925.

Depression 1932, re-emerged among highly placed Reaganites as an architect of 1920s prosperity.

But the appeal of the decade went beyond economics. Other Republican thinkers found cultural reasons. *National Review* editor Jeffrey Hart, a sometime Reagan speechwriter and chairman of the English department at Dartmouth, painted a picture as early as 1979 of the 1920s as a heady, vital era worth replicating.[7] Then, according to Hart, sports like baseball, football and boxing, rigid and slow-moving before World War I, came alive. So did music and dance, painting and sculpture, and literature: within the space of about a year, in 1925–26, Fitzgerald published *Gatsby*, Hemingway brought out *The Sun Also Rises*, and Dreiser *An American Tragedy*. Other critics, of course, have pictured the decade as one of frivolity and excess. The underlying point is simple: among key conservative elites, the 1920s revisionism, hailing the era of flappers, bathtub gin, low taxes, glittering estates, unregulated stock issues and run-amok speculation leading to the Depression, was implicit in Reagan's 1980 campaign, quietly espoused by determined GOP supply-side innovators (who blamed the Great Depression on *tariffs*, not irresponsible excess capacity). Yet to the electorate, such considerations went unnoticed or were considered irrelevant. Was the economic policy making of the 1920s an election issue of 1980? Of course not.

Nevertheless, the parallel between the Coolidge era and the opening impetus of the Reagan Administration is uncanny. Consider how Coolidge is characterized by a famous chronicler of the period, Frederick Lewis Allen, in his book *Only Yesterday:*

> Calvin Coolidge still believed in the old American copy-book maxims when almost everybody else had half forgotten them or was beginning to doubt them. "The success which is made in any walk of life is measured almost exactly by the amount of hard work that is put into it . . . There is only one form of political strategy in which I have any confidence and that is to try to do the right thing and sometimes be able to succeed . . . if society lacks learning and virtue it will perish . . . The nation with the greatest moral power will win . . ." This philosophy of hard work and frugal living and piety crowned with success might have been brought down from some Vermont attic where McGuffey's Reader gathered dust. But it was so old that it looked new; it was so exactly what uncounted Americans had been taught at their mother's knee that it touched what remained of the pioneer spirit in their hearts.[8]

And the Coolidge political record, as seen by Allen, also turns out to be a Gatsbyesque preview of the credo that would take power in Washington in 1981:

> He maintained the status quo for the benefit of business. Twice he vetoed farm relief legislation—to the immense satisfaction of the industrial and banking community which constituted his strongest support—on the grounds that the McNary-Haugen bills were economically unsound. He vetoed the soldier bonus, too, on the ground of its expense, though in this case his veto was overruled. His proudest boast was that he cut down the cost of running the government by systematic cheeseparing, reduced the public debt, and brought about four reductions in federal taxes, aiding not only those with small incomes but even more conspicuously those with large. Meanwhile, his Secretary of Commerce, Herbert Hoover, ingeniously helped business to help itself; on the various governmental commissions, critics of contemporary commercial practices were replaced, as far as possible, by those who would look upon business with a lenient eye . . .[9]

Coolidge-parallel theorists also like to note that Ronald Reagan and his principal advisers came to the White House from precisely that region of the country most amenable to white-picket-fence restoration. In the 1920s and 1930s many Southern Californians longingly recalled the Midwest, from which so many of them—like Ronald Reagan in 1935—had recently emigrated. As Carey McWilliams later wrote: "Here the 'alien patrimony' is not European, but America. The nostalgia is for an America that no longer exists, for an America that former Kansans, Missourians and Iowans literally gaze back upon, looking backward over their shoulders."[10] Hollywood, as Reagan first knew it, was very much involved in re-creating that America. Nor has any of that changed much. Ronald Reagan's generation of emigrants is still mythologizing, as are later arrivals, and the huge demographic strength of the Sun Belt now makes conservatism-cum-restoration an awesomely powerful force.

The politics of the 1980s also seems to be trying to restore the role of religion sixty years ago—not just in the evangelist's tent but in the country clubs and chambers of commerce. From time to time, theology has been a powerful ally of conservative economics. At the height of the ballyhoo era in 1925, publicist Bruce Barton linked business and religion by saying that Jesus Christ was the world's greatest salesman. Religion was yoked to capitalism as of yore. In

1981, author George Gilder proclaimed the interrelationship of capitalism and faith, and Michael Novak, a scholar in residence at the American Enterprise Institute, called for a move to define "a theology of the corporation" because "the corporation mirrors God's presence also in its liberty, by which I mean independence from the state." One liberal pundit scoffed at "Heaven, Inc." and suggested that "the most determined effort in 50 years is underway by doctrinaire, determined men to restore the old order, to restore to corporate America the sanctity it lost on October 29, 1929."[11] In a sense, the effort invokes and involves *two* Calvins: President Calvin Coolidge and the sixteenth-century reformer John Calvin, through whose Protestantism historians link religion and the rise of capitalism.[12]

The difference, of course, is that Ronald Reagan and his supporters, on coming to power, and unlike Coolidge Republicans, were not really trying to maintain the status quo. On the contrary, in some important ways they sought to restore the *status quo ante* of fifteen, twenty-five or even sixty years earlier. This is why the Shadow Empire notion—far-fetched as it may seem to use such terminology —has some legitimacy. Given the confusion, bureaucracy and complexity of American government in the 1980s, the Reagan Administration's firmly pronounced goals—to return massive program responsibility to the states with the New Federalism, to follow up by also repatriating revenue sources, to cut back the public sector, to relegitimize business, to "reprivatize" various federal functions, and in some cases to turn federal regulatory agencies into spokesmen for the industries they supervise—represent a revolutionary blueprint more akin to other attempts at national restoration than to conservatism's usual efforts to maintain threatened existing institutions and relationships. Toynbee, one must note, suggests that such efforts invariably disrupt, fail or degenerate into Caesarism.[13]

The revolutionary explicitness of the Reagan blueprint has varied. As late as 1979, Ronald Reagan the presidential candidate couched much of his political rhetoric in quasi-revolutionary terms that condemned the established Washington governmental order. In 1976, the Bicentennial year, he likened Washington to the oppressive London of George III. The closer he drew to the White House, however, the less of that there seemed to be. The general election campaign rhetoric of 1980 was distinctly muted. But, in part, that was because the task of defining Reagan philosophy for the true believers had shifted to young brain trusters—such as New York Congressman Kemp, former Reagan aide and New Jersey 1978 Republican Senate candidate Jeffrey Bell, and authors Jude Wanniski and George Gilder. Throughout the late 1970s and the first years of the new decade, these men showed no reticence whatever as they described the Republican vision as "radical," "populist" and "revolutionary," as opposed to the failed institutionalism of Democratic liberalism and Keynesian economics. Not only did the brain trusters believe in the essential radicalism of their vision, they also believed that the American electorate would respond positively to such populism and radicalism.

On another front, leaders of the overtly populist New Right— Richard Viguerie, Paul Weyrich and Howard Phillips, among others —also waved the banner of radical conservatism, invoking the tactics of Andrew Jackson, inveighing against the *Fortune* 500, mobilizing single-issue movements, criticizing the institutionalized elites of both parties, and occasionally even acknowledging their roles as radicals, not as traditional conservatives.*

Yet despite these radical forces, the new President himself is perhaps the only Chief Executive of the twentieth century to have had some knowledge of and fidelity to such relatively obscure but important conservative traditionalists as Ludwig von Mises, Richard Weaver and Leo Strauss. Their ideas constitute a very different framework and set of influences. As one gleeful conservative noted on Inauguration Day: "It's uncertain whether Mr. Reagan ever read Von Mises, Weaver or Strauss. Rather, their ideas came to him via cultural osmosis, from conservative publicists and pamphleteering over the last forty years."[15] In fact, only two months later the new President told cheering attendees at the 1981 Conservative Political Action Conference: "There are so many people and institutions who come to mind for their role in the success we celebrate tonight. Intellectual leaders like Russell Kirk, Friedrich A. Hayek, Henry Hazlitt, Milton Friedman, James Burnham, and Ludwig von Mises shaped so much of our thought."[16] Nothing radical there in *theory*. Implementing yesteryear's conservatism, however, would prove considerably more disruptive in practice.

*In 1975 Viguerie indicated that if the New Right organized a new party, they would avoid the word "conservative," and he later proclaimed: "We are no longer working to preserve the status quo. We are radicals working to overthrow the power structure of this country."[14]

At the same conference, moreover, Reagan voiced an extraordinary affirmation: "Who can forget that July night in San Francisco when Barry Goldwater told us that we must set the tides running again in the cause of freedom 'until our cause has won the day, inspired the world and shown the way to a tomorrow worthy of all our yesteryears'? Had there not been a Barry Goldwater willing to make that lonely walk, we would not be talking of a celebration tonight." The acceptance of that continuity by the newly elected President was important. Seventeen years earlier, Goldwater had been the first U.S. presidential nominee to embody a new force: the interaction of conservatism and *radicalism.*

An extraordinary synthesis seems to have developed. In retrospect, conservatism had undergone a fundamental change in form and style in 1964, and Goldwater's defeat at the polls was not the utter rout contemporary chroniclers supposed. Nevertheless, it's worth pointing out that although Ronald Reagan improved Barry Goldwater's showing by 12 points (from 39 percent in 1964 to 50.4 percent in 1980), Reagan's increment over Gerald Ford's 1976 total was quite small—a bit more than 2 percentage points, by no means the surge one would imagine from 1980 press accounts. As for constituency support, Reagan actually ran *behind* Ford among business and professional people, according to the Gallup poll, while chalking up most of his largest gains among voters with cultural and religious issues on their minds—Northern Catholics, Orthodox Jews, Western Mormons and white Southern fundamentalist Protestants. Great Plains wheat farmers, historically radical, were another massive trend group. The rhetoric and impression of landslide have overshadowed these constituency rearrangements. Even many Republicans seem disposed to ignore them.

Demography is destiny, the saying goes, and the grass-roots trends of the 1980 elections provide good reason not to portray the Reagan electorate in traditional conservative terms. To some extent, correlations showing Reagan with heavy support from upper-income groups, while accurate, are also misleading. His coalition's regional base—Sun Belt, Farm Belt and Western—coincides with the traditional populist and antielite component of U.S. political geography, so proven in support for Andrew Jackson, William Jennings Bryan, Franklin D. Roosevelt and George C. Wallace. Moreover, the coalition's critical new religious adherents—Northern Catholic right-to-life and Southern fundamentalist Protestant—represent constituencies whose traditionalist morality, over the last fifty years, has been complemented by support for the New Deal and economic activism. Finally, the tax-revolt element in the Reagan coalition has a populist genealogy reaching from Shays' Rebellion of 1786 to Howard Jarvis' Proposition 13 insurgency of 1978.

If conservatism is no longer traditional, and if traditional conservatism is no longer adequate, that is in some considerable measure a failure of historical timing. In the late 1960s or early 1970s, a substantial infusion of traditional conservative ideas—fiscal restraint, industrial incentive, strong defense-mindedness, support for religion and traditional morality, all widely accepted *general* correctives as the early 1980s arrived—would have had a great restorative effect on the nation as a polity and economy. However, that infusion never really took place, and as a partial result the 1960s and 1970s witnessed a crippling prolongation of domestic spending and inflation, social fragmentation and American global military erosion. These conditions, in turn, set the scene for a far more sweeping political reaction. One could reasonably call the two decades in question a period of national breakdown. So already leaning (witness 1964) toward an antiestablishment brand of politics, conservatism fattened further on outsiderism, antielitism and populism, emerging in the crucible of the late 1970s partially metamorphosed into radicalism.

I underscore *partially*. The extent of the radical shift can be overstated. As Hofstadter and other historians have made clear, progressive and radical American political movements have possessed significant conservative tendencies, restraints or constituencies. The right-tilting politics of the early 1980s, for its part, clearly contains such tendencies, restraints and constituencies. Although the idea of restoring Coolidge-era free enterprise may smack of populist revolution in one sense, the idea simultaneously involves big business. That is the uniqueness of Shadow Empire politics, which can and does link constituencies that otherwise might be incompatible: cultural restorationist and nationalist themes bond the lower-middle-class populists with economic conservatives. In any event, the traditionally conservative mass of the Republican Party and business community remains a major force in the equation.

But the assorted radicalisms contained within Reagan's coalition, not its traditional conservative components, support the possibility of a major 1980s watershed. If we look at American electoral precedents, all of the political movements that triggered acknowledged party-system upheavals—in 1800, 1828, 1860, 1896 and 1932—had substantial populist or radical dynamics. And only one of them failed to triumph electorally—the populist William Jennings Bryan lost to conservative Republican William McKinley in 1896. Even so, Bryan's defeated populism influenced the Washington legislative agenda for the next twenty years. Harvard's James Q. Wilson, among the most trenchant of observers, feels that the current genteel, antipopulist statement of conservatism "is enchanting, but alas, from the point of view of the fundamental forces at work in American politics today, it is [as usual] largely irrelevant. Fundamental political change has not, since the Philadelphia convention of 1787, been the result of deliberation or moderation, but rather of the accumulation of elemental passions that seek to redefine the principles of a good society and that arise out of widely shared dissatisfactions rather than carefully tempered reflections."[17] In short, the radical cutting edge is the essential denominator.

Yet in this case it is also the stuff of ambiguity. By many criteria —regionalism, populism, provision of an alternative to the intellectual atrophy of the party previously in power—the forces responsible for Ronald Reagan's 1980 success *should* represent the makings of a watershed election and a new political era. The chance that we will probably not see a lasting new era rests on the extent to which these very same traumas and dislocations of the past twenty years have helped to create an unprecedented nostalgia-based "shadow" coalition. Movements aimed at recapturing an idealized past are notoriously unstable, changing shape in success as well as failure.

2

THE
TWO-DECADE
BREAKDOWN

I think it would be difficult to find a single decade in the history of
Western culture when so much barbarism—so much calculated on-
slaught against culture and convention in any form, and so much sheer
degradation of both culture and the individual—passed into print, into
music, into art and onto the American stage as the decade of the
Nineteen Sixties.

—Robert Nisbet, *The Twilight of Authority* (1976)

EXAGGERATION, TOO, HAS ITS CYCLES. AND NISBET
perhaps exaggerates here. But what he says remains a powerful
statement of a potent conservative thesis, and other scholars have
voiced similar analyses of the erosion of American economic productivity, civic commitment and global determination. At the very least,
the economic, social, moral, political, institutional, military and diplomatic burdens accumulated by the United States during the 1960s
and 1970s add up to an awesome weight. Establishing both the magnitude and character of the breakdown is important. No physical law
of politics says that for every action there must be a comparable
reaction, yet a reading of history suggests just such a relationship.

Things would be easier if there were a Richter scale for sociopoliti-
cal earthquakes and if we had seismic graphs—or even Gallup polls
—of the past major American tremors. My own inclination is that
the 1960s and 1970s are second only to the Civil War and the decade
preceding it as a time of national breakdown. That estimate, correct

or not, undergirds my assumptions of political volatility and our system's vulnerability.

Some historical context is needed. The United States, one can argue, has had *five* major and minor periods of breakdown: (1) the years preceding and including the Civil War; (2) the era of defeat in Vietnam, urban riots, Watergate and soaring inflation (its chronology as yet less than fully defined); (3) the Great Depression of the 1930s; (4) the decade of the War of 1812, the threatened secession of New England and the break-up of the Federalist Party; and (5) the twenty-year agricultural slump of 1873–96, the dramatic growth of U.S. industry, and the rise of the Populist Party in response. The last two are obviously the minor breakdowns, mostly regional in their impact. The first three genuinely tested the country.

Not surprisingly, such breakdowns have also occasioned upheavals in the party system and institutions of government. Out of each trauma has come a new party system and a new party supremacy. But all of this happened in sunnier historical times. The question is, Can the same mode of democratic resolution of crises occur if the United States is over the hill, historically speaking, and if the very process of national breakdown is at least partially linked to that deterioration and disillusionment? No one knows. For one thing, the United States has never before experienced a real downcycle, and for another, the intensity of the breakdown is still being measured. Even the chronology of what happened is still unclear—at both ends. Did it begin, as sentimentalists argue, with the assassination of John F. Kennedy on November 22, 1963, or do the roots really go further back, to the Kennedy "New Economics," the Bay of Pigs, the McNamara Pentagon, the build-up of advisers in Vietnam, and the escalation of racial confrontation from Little Rock, Arkansas, to Philadelphia, Mississippi? Likewise, did the breakdown end in 1980 with the election of Reagan or does it go on in our economy and society?

So much for the uncertainties of calendar. Reviewing the twenty-year period of breakdown, one is struck by the relentless deepening of the crisis as politicians chose the wrong options, as elites pursued various self-interests, and as historical forces played themselves out. Lyndon Johnson did not have to exceed the mandate of 1964 so egregiously, or did he? The political economics of the Great Society —guns *and* butter *and* fiscal sleight of hand—were not inevitable, or were they? Richard Nixon did not have to continue the war in Vietnam and the expansion of domestic transfer payments, or did he? As for Watergate, no one can maintain that it was inevitable, or would his antagonists have seized some other pretext to unravel the conservative counterrevolution of 1972 even if the burglary of the Democratic National Committee had not occurred? The failures in many ways constitute a seamless web. Watergate was rooted in a breakdown of national security itself attendant the failing war in Indochina. Then the election of Jimmy Carter in 1976—an obscure Southern Democratic moderate and Baptist Sunday school teacher who campaigned on morality themes (from "Trust me . . ." to "a government of love")—manifestly depended on Watergate, the 1973–76 suspension of pro-Republican realignment in the South, and the public's demand for moral reassurance. By the time the Carter Administration, too, had played itself out, achieving little success on any front, the United States was in a quiet but deep crisis. No soldiers were dying in foreign wars; there were no bread lines, and prosperity continued across much of the land; nevertheless, public opinion surveys showed 80 percent of Americans believing that the United States was "on the wrong track," and all too much evidence supported their pessimism.

The twenty-year period of breakdown, and the frustrations and countermovements set in motion, can best be calibrated in four ways: (a) social and moral, (b) economic, (c) patriotic and nationalistic, and (d) institutional. I have put the social and moral first, because the "politics of cultural despair" thereby unleashed is probably the most powerful grass-roots component in the revolutionary conservatism of the early 1980s.

A. SOCIAL AND MORAL UPHEAVAL

The notion of "moral decay"—apprehension about changing cultural, religious and sexual behavior—antedates Sodom and Gomorrah. So does the rebellion of youth and the discontent of the urban poor. But in the United States at least, the 1960s saw it all on an unprecedented scale, with the scale abetted by three other, related phenomena. First, and most important, one must cite the huge number of teen-agers and young adults, born in the first (1940–50) wave of the World War II baby boom and, by 1960, just beginning to enter college in massive numbers, thereby greatly increasing the importance of universities, "reform" and youth cultism. Second, we must pay special attention to the legal consummation of the civil rights revolution, to the urban riots of the 1960s and to Washington's decision to use federal power and dollars to improve the lot of the poor in general and blacks in particular. Notions of the perfectibility and equality of man reached levels reminiscent of Rousseau and the French Revolution. The resultant attempts to blueprint new sociological relationships went far *beyond* the implementation of civil rights. And third, the war in Vietnam disrupted—as wars always do —pre-existing moral and social norms.

With some understanding of world history, we can see that the results were more predictable than unprecedented. As Will and Ariel Durant have noted, after the violence and social disruption of the Peloponnesian War, Alcibiades felt free to flout the moral code of his ancestors. And after the wars of Marius and Sulla, Caesar and Pompey, Antony and Octavius, "Rome was full of men who had lost their economic footing and their moral stability; soldiers who had tasted adventure and had learned to kill; citizens who had seen their savings consumed in the taxes and inflation caused by war; . . . women dizzy with freedom, multiplying divorces, abortions and adulteries . . . A shallow sophistication prided itself upon its cynicism and pessimism."[1] There are many other comparable periods in human history. But in the United States, as old cultural and sexual standards were cast aside, much of the population had a sense of unprecedented upheaval; given our relatively short history as a nation, perhaps it *was* unprecedented. Traditionalists fumed about federal courts that imposed restrictions on school prayer and municipal Christmas displays while striking down restraints on abortion and nude dancing. And on the racial and urban front, the Great Society's innovative new social schemes—from the so-called War on Poverty to school busing, rent subsidies, suburban dispersal of public housing, metropolitan-wide planning, and the like—went against the national grain by ignoring established conceptions of human nature and human motivation, and also against the established lessons of the New Deal: that government succeeds best with direct subsidies and minimal sociological manipulation.

By the early 1970s, perception of the excesses of the prior decade began to take hold as the innovative trend itself began to ease. Federal sociological experimentation ebbed. Even the universities quieted down, soothed by the peace agreement in Vietnam, the passing of the great "baby boom" wave, and the disgrace of Richard Nixon. Nevertheless, the moral and sexual barriers lowered during the 1960s more or less stayed down, confirming a basic shift and stimulating what by the end of the 1970s would become a massive reaction of traditionalism, (white) ethnicity, pro-family sentiment and religious fundamentalism—a Counter Reformation on the heels of the Reformation.

Programs purporting to achieve racial balance and other forms of social engineering also persisted long enough—and with little enough success—to fan the fires of white middle-class resentment. As late as 1980, the Justice Department found itself considering proposals that would require urban and suburban school busing for metropolitan-wide racial balance, and the federal Department of Housing and Urban Development periodically entertained ideas of forced suburban dispersal of (nonwhite) public housing. Federal insistence on sexual and racial balance had even spread to employment with "affirmative action" requirements that barely circumvented the opprobrium of hiring and promotion quotas. Some of the ultimate regulatory directives on equality—especially sexual directives—were ludicrous on their face. One is tempted to cite Department of Health, Education and Welfare attacks on the discriminatory aspects of boys' choirs and girls' basketball teams. The conservative counterattack, meanwhile, was fueled by reluctant acknowledgment of error by a number of Great Society architects. One of them, Daniel Patrick Moynihan, has characterized its underlying fallibility: "A program was launched that was not understood, and not explained, and this brought about social losses that need not have occurred . . . The government did not know what it was doing. It had a theory. Or, rather, a set of theories. Nothing more."[2]

Liberals listened to too many naïve theorists and too few "old hands" during the years of the Great Society—a mistake conservatives repeated in the first Reagan months—and the results, I think, fell well short of balance. On the positive side, blacks, or at least the black middle class, were brought into the national mainstream. Official segregation was pretty well eliminated. Poverty was substantially reduced. Victorian social and sexual restraints were eased. But on the negative side, social engineering and judicial permissiveness drove the middle class, whites and blacks alike, from the old Northern cities, making residential integration impossible and worsening the municipal revenue crisis. Racial prescriptions—from busing to job preferences—provoked three- or four-to-one negative majorities in national opinion polls, and voter indignation followed suit.

Indeed, I would go so far as to say that racial issues were probably among the two or three principal factors in the 1948–72 upheaval in U.S. presidential voting patterns. A cynic might want to suggest that it began in 1948 with South Carolina's Governor Strom Thurmond running for President—as an independent States' Rights candidate —and peaked in 1972 with (Republican) Senator Strom Thurmond as a close ally of the White House, and with a Thurmond ally (Harry S. Dent) as the chief White House political operative. During that quarter of a century the white South marched out of its historical alignment with the Democrats into a new alignment with the Republicans in presidential politics, and the race issue was probably the central reason. Watergate suspended but did not reverse these shifts. Without Civil War–based loyalty to the Democratic Party, white Southerners found themselves drawn to the greater ideological attractions of presidential Republican conservatism. Racial issues were also a major factor in the conservative drift of "peripheral urban ethnic" voters from South Boston and Queens, in New York, to Detroit and San Francisco. Here the importance of the 1960s revolution in moral and social norms—or, more accurately, of the backlash and reaction against them—can hardly be overstated.

In the late 1960s and early 1970s, race-linked issues had generated the principal social-issue electoral backlash. By 1980, however, a second social-issue wave, pivoting on religious, moral and sexual controversies, had moved to the fore. In retrospect, by championing permissiveness, homosexuality and abortion while implicitly derogating the family, prayer and Biblical teachings, the morals revolution ultimately served to energize an increasing militant neo-puritan counterforce that encompasses 20 to 30 percent of the American people. Ultimately *Oh! Calcutta!* begat not more of the same, but the rise of Reverend Jerry Falwell and Senator Jeremiah Denton. Except on general issues like school prayer and pornography, neo-puritans are by no means a moral majority. Still, they do constitute a large minority, and their less controversial efforts to restore traditional mores probably command the support of the middle third of the public. The Reformation has given way to the Counter Reformation with a vengeance.

That may change. The Counter Reformation itself may cause a

reaction. Zealousness makes most Americans uncomfortable, and the right-to-life movement, the most dedicated of the current moral-cause groups, goes so far as to proclaim abortion the greatest human rights issue since slavery. If so, it may generate one of the greatest —and most divisive—debates of the 1980s. What seems less debatable is that the various issues generated during the turmoil of the last two decades have infused national politics with a social and moral fervor not seen since the 1850s and the Volstead Act of the 1920s.

B. PRODUCTIVITY, TAXES AND PRICES

In economics as well as in sociology, the progressives of the 1960s believed that old standards and old restraints could easily be ignored. Enthusiasts of the New Economics ceased to worry about budget deficits, disdained currency linkage to precious metals (silver coins being scrapped in early Great Society legislation), and boldly introduced a whole new array of off-budget revenue devices and gimmicks. Meanwhile, public-policy expectations soared. In a go-go society and a go-go economy, all kinds of expenses and liabilities could safely be assumed and imposed on the future: enormous pension obligations, wasteful grant and loan programs, extravagant spending obligations, the inordinate costs of ensuring almost-zero air and water pollution, and the like. From 1965 through the mid-1970s that philosophy prevailed—and not just in the public sector. The expansion of private credit was also vast. Savings and investment were subverted by consumption as the American public sold its seed corn for entitlement programs and Caribbean vacations.

As a source of national disappointment and frustration, then, liberal economics yielded nothing to liberal sociology. The principal difference is that the public burden is far easier to quantify. Chart 1 shows the 1961–80 ebb and then absolute decline of productivity in U.S. industry; Chart 2 shows the enormous 1940–80 explosion of federal personal income tax receipts (and burdens); and Chart 3 profiles the dramatic climb of a family's weekly living costs as measured each year by the Gallup poll. The numbers almost leap off the page. The unprecedented extent of all three shifts goes a long way to explain the unpredecented extent to which liberal and Democratic politicians found the economic issue an albatross by 1980.

At various times during the 1970s, and then again during the 1980

Productivity, Taxes and Prices: Yardsticks of 1961–80 Change

Chart 1 *Declining Annual Increases in Productivity, 1961–80*

Year	% Increase in	Year	% Increase In
1961	3.3	1971	3.6
1962	3.8	1972	3.5
1963	3.7	1973	2.7
1964	4.3	1974	−2.3
1965	3.5	1975	2.3
1966	3.1	1976	3.3
1967	2.2	1977	2.1
1968	3.3	1978	−0.2
1969	0.2	1979	−0.3
1970	0.9	1980	−0.2

Source: U.S. Labor Department

Chart 2 *Exploding Annual Federal Personal Income Tax Collections, 1940–80*

Year	Receipts ($ billions)	Year	Receipts ($ billions)
1940	$ 1	1965	$ 54
1945	19	1970	104
1950	17	1975	156
1955	32	1980	288
1960	45		

Source: The Statistical History of the United States, U.S. Treasury Department

presidential campaign, a number of economic analysts and politicians charged that although nominal wages and incomes have been rising because of inflation, *real* wages and living standards have generally fallen. The official data are mixed: inflation-adjusted figures compiled by the federal government showed a rise from 1970 to 1978, but in 1979–80 the average family's real disposable income fell—even by Washington's data.

The matter is not worth belaboring. I have seen published numbers proving anything and everything. Whatever the precise statistical truth, though, the extent of national pain is less debatable. The productivity, tax-burden and price trends laid out in these three charts weighed heavily. Scores of essays on the threat to the middle

Chart 3 *Soaring Gallup Poll Annual "Cost of Living Audit"*
(Smallest amount of money on which public perceives
a family of four can get along for one week)

Year	Amount	Year	Amount	Year	Amount
1937	$30	1967	$101	1977	$199
1947	43	1969	120	1978	201
1951	50	1971	127	1979	223
1954	60	1973	149	1980	250
1957	72	1974	152	1981	277
1959	79	1975	161		
1964	81	1976	177		

Source: Gallup Poll (March 1981)

class have profiled John Q. Citizen's inability to maintain yesteryear's living standards in the face of rising tax brackets and of
escalating food, fuel, housing and transportation costs. Public fear
was almost tangible in the 1980 election; for the first time since the
Great Depression a Gallup poll found the electorate substantially
more trusting of the Republicans in economic matters than of the
Democrats. Whether or not that turns out to be justified, by 1980 the
U.S. economy had developed disarray and weakness of a magnitude
not seen since the 1930s.

C. THE UNITED STATES AS AN EMPIRE IN RETREAT

Given the opportunity to examine a large map of United States
global military facilities in 1962 put next to a similar map for 1982,
a visitor to the E-Ring inner sanctum of the Pentagon would be
surprised. It is impossible to look at the arc from Libya to Morocco
and Spain, where half a dozen U.S. Air Force bases once stood guard,
or at Southeast Asia, or at the Panama Canal, without sensing a
gnawing parallel to Rome's fatal withdrawal of its legions in the fifth
century. Some scholars argue that advanced missile technology
moots any parallel, but others have amplified the U.S.-Roman comparison.*

*Two books stand out: Michael Grant's *The Fall of the Roman Empire: A Reap-
praisal* (Philadelphia, Annenberg School Press, 1976) and Edward Luttwak's *The
Grand Strategy of the Roman Empire* (Baltimore, Johns Hopkins Press, 1976).

Debate has been relatively muted, though. Not being a professed empire, the United States has been able to disengage quietly, and the liberal-to-centrist foreign policy establishment that presided over that withdrawal has spun off all sorts of rationalizations, not the least of which is their argument that multinational organizations can maintain a kindred but less overt and provocative hegemony. However, the extent to which the American global pullback offended national pride became clear in 1977–78 over the issue of giving up that schoolboy textbook triumph of American engineering, fortitude and republican imperialism—the Panama Canal. Few developments took policy makers so much by surprise.

My own sense is to once again cite William Appleton Williams' instruction: America can only be understood as an empire in retreat. The same power elite that had underestimated the consequences of an American defeat in Vietnam usually failed to anticipate, when President Carter proposed the Panama Canal treaties in 1977, that the public would become greatly upset over the issue. Yet roughly two thirds of Americans *were* concerned, a small minority even outraged, because the Canal quickly became—as populist conservatives had sensed it would—a popular symbol of the quasi-imperial debacle that had accelerated so embarrassingly during the Vietnam war. In 1977–78, so soon after the collapse in Southeast Asia, the American people were not prepared to refight the rights and wrongs of the war in Vietnam. However, unwillingness to abandon the Panama Canal became a kind of simplistic surrogate for frustrated nationalism. In the party primaries and general elections of 1978 and 1980, from Maine to Alaska, eighteen liberal-to-moderate U.S. senators who supported the treaties were identified and defeated, frequently with the Canal issue right up front.*

I believe that the "easy" patriotism of the anti–Panama Canal treaty position provides an important measurement of the public mood. End-of-empire frustration seems like a reasonable description of the feeling: hostile to leaders who promote (or even acknowledge) U.S. withdrawal, supportive of resolute rhetoric, but leery of actual military risk taking in any but the most essential circumstances. Clearly, it would be wrong to suggest that Americans have become warlike in the 1980s. Public sentiment is too ambivalent. Even as

*In a postelection discussion, defeated President Carter also cited the costly fight over ratification of the Panama Canal treaties as one of the single largest factors in the undoing of his Administration.

support for increased defense expenditures is strong and vastly increased over 1975, polls also show abiding fear of any overseas military venture—in Central America, the Middle East, or anywhere else —likely to trap the United States in "another Vietnam." What *can* be safely said is that the public *is* painfully aware of the forced retreat of U.S. global power over the last two decades, and the pathology of national response to that embarrassment is still taking shape.

⁓ D. LOSS OF FAITH IN INSTITUTIONS

Naturally enough, turn-of-the-decade surveys illustrated a massive public loss of faith in the political and government institutions responsible for multiple American policy failures. The cumulative impact of the country's longest political assassination wave, of its first defeat in war, and of the first President to be forced from office, all added up to a broad profile in national disillusionment.

A statistical picture is probably worth a thousand words. If one looks at the public opinion polls, a major institutional-confidence fall-off is obvious by 1970–71, and by 1974–76, in the wake of Watergate and Richard Nixon's resignation, civic faith was at a recent (and perhaps all-time) low. Chart 4 shows the ebb. The realignment of our politics, historically due every 28–36 years (and thus due in 1968 or thereabouts), failed to occur in 1972, despite a plausible opportunity, at least partially because Watergate caused faith in the new majority-seeking Republican Party to plummet. Historians began to talk about the "twilight of authority," and about the loss in the United States of *civitas*—the old Roman concept of shared community and civic obligation.

Nor did the problem end with Watergate. During the Carter Administration—itself a political, institutional and moral extension of the era of Vietnam-Watergate—the national trends continued. Chart 4 does not show month-to-month variations, but after a brief early 1977 flurry of hope and expectation, public skepticism resumed. Confidence in the institutions of politics and government sank so low that in mid-1979 the President delivered a controversial speech postulating a "national malaise." Opinion polls found that the public to some extent endorsed this analysis, yet many Americans also felt that Carter's style and ineffective leadership were a major part of the problem and a factor in the prolongation of the extended crisis. By

Chart 4   *Percent of Poll Expressing a Great Deal of Confidence in Nine American Institutions, 1966–81*

Question: As far as people in charge of running [each institution on the list below] are concerned, would you say you have a great deal of confidence, only some confidence, or hardly any confidence at all in them?

	1966	1971	1973	1974	1975	1976	1977	1978	1979	1981
Average of Nine Major Institutions	43%	27%	33%	28%	24%	20%	24%	25%	23%	22%
TV News	25	—	41	31	35	28	28	35	37	24
Medical Establishment	73	61	57	50	43	42	43	42	30	37
Military	62	27	40	33	24	23	27	29	29	28
Press	29	18	30	25	26	20	18	23	28	16
Organized Religion	41	27	36	32	32	24	29	34	20	22
Major Companies	55	27	29	21	19	16	20	22	18	16
Congress	42	19	29	18	13	9	17	10	18	16
Executive Branch	41	23	19	28	13	11	23	14	17	24
Organized Labor	22	14	20	18	14	10	14	15	10	12

Source: Compiled from surveys by Louis Harris and Associates, reported in *Public Opinion* (October/November 1979):30.

1980 the public was ripe for inspiration, for charisma, for a reason to believe—all psychologies to which Ronald Reagan catered. His election thereupon renewed confidence, but the inauguration of new Presidents has done that before—in 1974 and in 1977—only to see those hopes eventually dissipate, as the new Administration bogged down in Washington inertia and minutiae. (Subsequent 1981 data have begun to limn the outlines of yet another recurrence of disappointment.)

By 1980, however, the country's breakdown had indisputably brought the public to a point of deep concern and smoldering political reaction. Tangible measurements—of inflation, unemployment, interest rates, productivity, drug addiction, illegitimate births, crime, educational test scores, military enlistment, comparative U.S.-Soviet military strength—bespoke national difficulties with few national precedents. Slumping *intangible* measurements were perhaps even more discouraging—surveys showing that at least 30–40 percent of Americans nurtured pervasive doubts about the efficacy of the U.S. political system, that 60–80 percent had begun to worry that their children would not enjoy living standards comparable to their own.

The stage was set for a massive political shift, which began with the major move to the right in the 1980 election. The big question is whether our most recent national trauma is a prelude to even greater political upheaval ahead.

3

TO THE NASHVILLE STATION: THE (PARTIAL) TRANSFORMATION OF U.S. CONSERVATISM

> We want to change the existing power structure. We are not conservatives in the sense that conservative means accepting the status quo. Today isn't the same as the 1950s, when conservatives were trying to protect what was, constitutionally, economically and morally, in the control of more or less conservative people.
>
> —New Right leader Paul Weyrich, quoted in *Conservative Digest* (July 1981)

FEW CONSERVATIVES ARE AS BLUNT AS WEYRICH, BUT during the 1960s and 1970s the nature of "conservatism" underwent a transformation—not complete, by any means, but substantial. Indeed, the whole ideological framework underwent dramatic change. As the mid-1970s fashion in everything from government and foreign policy to culture and morality became "liberal"—as understood by establishment progressives—many opponents of that status quo found themselves cast as conservatives. Or at least they embraced that term, some more than a bit wryly aware of the irony involved. And the irony was considerable. By 1980, most of the *plausible* radical forces in the country were arrayed under the conservative banner, however impermanent any such arrangement must be.

The metamorphosis of both ideological "sides" took a fair time to sink in. Liberalism, for better or worse, became associated less and less with blue-collar politics and more and more with middle-class reformism and permissivism of various economic, diplomatic, sociological and sexual hues. Of the latter, relatively affluent areas were the common seedbeds—correlation between liberalism and high in-come and high education surged.* Conservatism, meanwhile, in-creasingly took on the coloration of popular, even populist, animosity toward taxes, bureaucracies, regulations, judicial rulings and sociology by administrative fiat, all phenomena linked to liberal-ism. The two ideological transitions were reverse sides of the same political and cultural evolutionary coin.

It is important to underscore the point that both transitions in-volved are only *partial*. Thus, on the one hand, "liberal politics" continues to command the allegiance of large numbers of factory workers and morally traditionalist minority group members; on the other, conservatism still musters huge numbers of suburban and rural defenders of the status quo. Yet we are beyond the point where changes are just taking place on the peripheries of political ideologies and constituencies. They are too pervasive for that; the shift involved is beginning to reshape core values and modes of operation. The extent of that transformation is the subject of this chapter.

In some measure the transformation—some critics allege a perver-sion—of liberalism during the 1960s was an inevitable consequence of liberal success. So little of the broad-based progressive agenda remained to be realized by the late years of the decade that en-thusiasts pursued tangents almost unthinkable eight or ten years earlier, when civil rights, federal aid to education and Medicare were only on the drawing board and not yet achievements. In another sense, though, the ideological mutation of American liberalism was also a consequence of the profound status shift, from outsiderism to cosmopolitan elitism, an evolution that began during the New Deal, escalated in the Adlai Stevenson years and achieved a zenith under the New Frontier and the Great Society. By the late 1960s the socio-institutional die was cast: increasingly an establishmentarian credo, liberalism had pretty much forsaken the values of red-brick factory towns for those of gentrified urban brownstones.

From another perspective my essential point involves the ebb and flow of American populism. Britain's Margaret Canovan, the histo-rian who has most recently tried to script a broad, worldwide frame-work of what populism is and isn't, defines populism as "a family of related ideas" that usually features agrarian radicalism, antielitism

*For the best data on the liberal socioeconomic transformation, see Everett Carll Ladd, Jr., *Transformations of the American Party System* (New York, Norton, 1977).

or both, and that invariably puts great emphasis on idealizing or mobilizing "the people." The very term "populism" is American in its coinage, and Canovan—rightly, I think—describes the United States as "the most stridently populistic of nations."[1] Through most of American history, certainly until just after World War I, populism was a force of the economic left. During the 1920s and 1930s there were signs of change, and by the 1950s and 1960s, *mass* populism (as opposed to the narrow-based campus/Ralph Nader variety) shifted rightward and came to embrace cultural themes—Wisconsin senator Joseph McCarthy and Alabama Governor George Wallace being two such populists. I think the case can be made—and I will make it later in various ways—that much of the political upheaval of our recent past has been a movement of populist electorates and voting streams from "left" to "right" in their operational politics.

Genealogists of transformed liberalism and declassé conservatism, lacking neat parish records, must necessarily be somewhat imprecise. Right-wing populism can find some ancestry in the Anti-Saloon League, nationalist and Ku Klux Klan politicking of the 1920s; chic liberalism, in turn, can trace antecedents back to the Greenwich Village circles of World War I, and certainly to the Washington salons of the New Deal. But in the larger sense—if major electorates and mushrooming demographics are to be considered—the metamorphoses in question attained real mass only in the 1950s with (1) the beginnings of the so-called Post-Industrial Revolution and the explosion in the ranks of the college-educated white-collar class and the communications/knowledge industry professionals; and (2) the emergence of the political-cultural poles epitomized by Senator McCarthy, a right-wing populist of sorts, and two-time Democratic presidential candidate Adlai Stevenson, a reformer whose intellectualism evoked the putdown "egghead." First-wave elements of the electoral-ideological transformation can be found in 1952–56 voting patterns, not least those around New York City: Stevenson made inroads in fashionable suburban and downtown sections, while conservative populism in the form of Republican pro-McCarthy Eisenhower support scored advances in the lower-middle-class Irish, German and Italian strongholds. It was a forecast of bigger shifts to come.

The elite metamorphosis took power first. Populist conservatism, poorly organized, held no office in the Administration of Dwight Eisenhower, who generally spurned Senator McCarthy and his allies.

But campus-and-brownstone liberalism began to put its stamp on the country under John Kennedy's New Frontier and then under Lyndon Johnson's Great Society. As this happened, more and more of liberalism's goals and methodologies became theoretical, technological and sociological—blueprinting a war in Vietnam with computers, rearranging schools and neighborhoods to promote racial balance, philosophizing about the irrelevance of budget deficits and gold. Slowly but surely, liberalism lost much of its Jacksonian and Trumanesque moorings in rural Missouri and steelmaking East Baltimore, and led by the ascendant professors, urban planners, social-welfare workers, minority causists and international economists, managed to become increasingly the political vehicle and banner of *those* interests, not of blue-collar Americans. As the Republican Party flirted with Goldwater nationalism, multinational corporate leaders became more closely allied with liberal internationalists. I grant that one-paragraph descriptions of this sort inevitably generalize too much. As capsules go, however, this one is hardly unfair. Not a few of those involved have said much the same thing in doleful retrospect.

Conservatism, meanwhile, was out of power as the New Frontier and Great Society gathered force, and for good reason. The conservative standard in the 1958–62 elections had been principally carried by stereotyped old guardsmen—senators like William Knowland, Homer Capehart and William Jenner are good examples—whose election defeats served notice that America did indeed favor much of the remaining *serious* portion of the liberal agenda: federal aid to education, Medicaid, civil rights, expanded housing assistance, and so forth. Only after 1964–65, when that agenda had been largely enacted and when progressive strategists turned to a blueprint the country would ultimately reject, did the right regroup.

The process was slow, and little noticed. Yet by almost any measure, the conservative transition-cum-political comeback began in 1963–64 with the nomination of Barry Goldwater, even though his selection was sloughed off as a fatal dalliance with extremism. Whatever else Goldwater was, he represented both a new wave of citizen activism—his was the campaign, remember, that launched ex-Democrat Ronald Reagan into a new career as a GOP conservative spokesman—and a new geopolitics in which a "conservative" West and South took up the antiestablishment gauntlet against the "liberal establishment" Northeast, a region that Goldwater at one point suggested he would like to set adrift into the cold waters of the North Atlantic. Barry Goldwater was no Homer Capehart of 1950s Indiana. The Goldwater campaign represented an insurgency, not an attempt at traditional Republican preservationism. The senator from Arizona would mellow and later oppose the New Right, but conservatism had begun to develop the base of outsidership that would emerge in the elections four, eight and sixteen years hence.

In the wake of the sea change of 1964, conservative politics became serious. Its reactive and combative opportunities soon mushroomed, its intellectual creativity accelerated, its popular appeal began to swell, and its nature began to shift and even to radicalize. The best way to highlight the phenonemon is to break it down into what can pass for sequence: first, the shift in conservative political and cultural geography; then the internal upheaval in the Republican Party; next, the rise of the "conservative movement"; the emergence of neoconservatism; the rise of the New Right; the appearance of a radical new economics; and finally, the election of Ronald Reagan.

A. THE SHIFT IN CONSERVATIVE POLITICAL GEOGRAPHY

When conservatism, in the unlucky person of Herbert Hoover, left the White House in disrepute after the election of 1932, its political geography was Eastern—the only states Hoover carried were four in New England, DuPont's Delaware and the heavy-industry–dominated state of Pennsylvania. During the 1920s the Northeast had been the stronghold of conservative politics. That remained pretty much the case in the 1930s—Massachusetts was the only state to elect a new Republican senator in 1936 (Henry Cabot Lodge)—and even in the 1940s. Radicalism, populism and economic liberalism had strength in Northern industrial areas, to be sure, but these ideologies were strongest in the *poorest* regions of the country. As late as 1948, Harry Truman won most of the South and West (while losing most of the Northeast) with campaign rhetoric proclaiming that the Northeast treated the South and West like colonies and that the Republicans "had stuck a pitchfork" in the farmer's back.

In short, the postwar era began with liberalism still principally an economic credo of socioeconomic outsiders, and in that respect its major electoral lines still followed the old familiar patterns apparent in the triumphs of Thomas Jefferson, Andrew Jackson and Franklin D. Roosevelt: support among the urban working classes of the North and among the populations of the poorer regions, the South and the West (be it the trans-Appalachian "New West" of the early nineteenth century or the angry Rocky Mountain and Plains states of 1932). Conservatism had its areas of maximum strength in the Northeastern and Midwestern locales so well chronicled by John P. Marquand, John O'Hara and Sinclair Lewis—from the residential strongholds of the New England gentry to Pennsylvania country clubs and Zenith (Minnesota) Rotary Clubs.

Losing shape in the East, and to a lesser extent in the Midwest, this political geography was out of date by 1960. Democratic liberalism was establishing itself and finding a regional home in the Northeast, while Republican conservatism was going the other way— following the sun (and the population) south and west. That year John Kennedy became the first Democratic presidential candidate to achieve his highest regional percentage in New England, while Richard Nixon became the first GOP candidate to lose despite sweeping the West and winning three Southern states. Experts wrongly wrote off the result to pro- and anti-Catholic voting. In retrospect, underlying socioeconomics was more compelling. Then, four years later, the Barry Goldwater–Lyndon Johnson presidential race carved the new political geography in stone: Texas Democrat Johnson scored his best regional percentage in once bedrock Republican New England, while Goldwater ran best in the South and next-best in the West (especially the long-populist Rocky Mountains)!

Come 1968, Democratic nominee Hubert Humphrey scored his highest ratios in New England, and his two opponents—Nixon and George Wallace—pulled their best percentages in the South and West. Four years later, with Wallace off the ballot, Nixon swept the Wallace constituency and won huge vote percentages in the South and West. Democrat George McGovern drew his strongest support in New England, winning only one state—Massachusetts—plus the District of Columbia. The post-Watergate aberration of the Democrats' nomination of Jimmy Carter suspended the pattern in 1976, but the trend established itself in 1980, with conservative Ronald Reagan drawing his heaviest support ratios in the Sun Belt and West.

No one need search for the meaning. From the Civil War through the 1950s, Republicanism and conservatism tended to be based in the parts of the country that were the most prosperous, bourgeois and instinctively conservative in the traditional, institutional sense. By the 1960s and certainly by the 1970s, "conservatism" was embracing a new cultural and political geography—in "outsider" America.

B. THE INTERNAL UPHEAVAL IN THE REPUBLICAN PARTY

Robert La Follette, Smith Brookhart, Gerald P. Nye, William Borah, George Norris, Hiram Johnson. Americans may recall some of their names but not much of their political geography.

Most of us don't know that in the 1920s, the Progressives of the Republican Party were Midwesterners and Westerners—agrarians, populists of a sort, "Sons of the Wild Jackass," in the words of one New Hampshire party regular. By contrast, establishment conservatives dominated the Grand Old Party in the Northeast and Great Lakes industrial states. By the late 1930s, however, foreign policy issues, notably isolationism, made the Farm Belt and Rocky Mountains react against both Roosevelt's New Deal and the Eastern internationalist wing of the Republican Party. The result, by the 1940s, was that the Midwest and much of the West had moved to the right and assumed a kind of antiestablishment conservative role in the GOP.

These conservatives had no real success, at least at the level of the presidential nomination. Just as the Eastern–Great Lakes Republican establishment had always managed to beat back the presidential attempts of the progressive West in the first third of the century, blocking the La Follettes and the Borahs, so they managed to put down the challenge of the conservative hinterland in the second third of the century. Alfred Landon, Wendell Willkie, Thomas E. Dewey and Dwight Eisenhower were all nominated by what could reasonably be called the Eastern-establishment wing of the party. Richard Nixon, in 1960, represented a kind of transition, although the long-dominant party elites retained enough leverage to oblige Nixon to meet with New York Governor Nelson Rockefeller and agree to the "Treaty of Fifth Avenue." The occasion rankled Southern and Western conservative insurgents, and four years later they took revenge when Senator Barry Goldwater of Arizona defeated Governor William Scranton of Pennsylvania in the first insurrectionist capture of a Republican presidential convention and nomination.

Victory proved fleeting. In the general election, elements of the Northeastern Republican establishment helped the Democrats administer a drubbing to Goldwater. Scores of corporate chief executive officers transferred their allegiance to Democratic nominee Lyndon Johnson. From Maine and Cape Cod to the Pacific Northwest, scores of traditional Republican counties wheeled out of line and gave Goldwater 30–35 percent of the vote in contrast to the 60–80 percent they had delivered to Dwight Eisenhower and even Richard Nixon. Even so, the *status quo ante* was beyond recall. Basic economic, cultural and demographic forces were changing the lines of American politics and rendering obsolete the century-old Republican-Democratic lines forged in the Civil War. Sociologist Daniel Bell's Post-Industrial Revolution, the institutionalization of white-collar liberalism and the rise of the Sun Belt as a new national force all spelled an end to the *ancien régime* alignment.

Simply put, the insurgent Sun Belt capture of the Republican Party and operational "conservatism," foreshadowed in the nomination of Southern Californian Richard Nixon in 1960 and confirmed in the years that followed, could not be thwarted. Nixon won in 1968 against the opposition of Nelson Rockefeller and the Northeast–Great Lakes GOP establishment, and by 1972, when he won a landslide re-election, Nixon was already contemplating a reshaped Republican Party—or even a new party—institutionalizing the new nonestablishment ascendancy.

Watergate, of course, gave the old Northeast-Midwest forces a period of minor renaissance within the GOP. Even some New Left observers interpreted the Watergate affair as a kind of Northeastern "Yankee" countercoup against the Sun Belt interlopers. Certainly, the whole Key Biscayne–Texas–Southern California wheeler-dealer political image—of Richard Nixon, John Connally, White House aides Haldeman and Ehrlichman and their cadres of California advancemen, wiretaps, espionage, eavesdropping and massive corporate election fund raising—was impugned, reversing the tide of Sun Belt fortune. The new Republican President, elevated by Nixon's resignation, was Gerald Ford of Michigan, a Yale graduate and party establishmentarian. He promptly picked New York Governor Nelson Rockefeller as his Vice President.

For a brief time, the Republicanism portrayed by John P. Marquand, John O'Hara and Sinclair Lewis appeared to have made a comeback. But it couldn't last. Both Goldwaterite and New Right conservatives balked at Ford and Rockefeller. Former California Governor Ronald Reagan raised the Sun Belt standard in a bid to deny Ford the 1976 nomination, and almost succeeded. Even before Reagan's move, conservative pressure created a climate in which Ford had to announce that Vice President Nelson Rockefeller would step down and not seek election in 1976. Despite this, a large number of insurgent conservatives sat on their hands, preferring to see Ford replaced by a Democrat as they looked toward 1980.

The race for the 1980 nomination was itself confirmation of the magnitude of the intraparty upheaval. All four leading Republican contenders were from the Sun Belt, even the moderate conservatives —George Bush of Texas and Howard Baker of Tennessee. Reagan, of course, won in a walk after a decisive New Hampshire primary, in which Bush, New England–born and the candidate of the old party establishment, was savaged (in an effort at the time encouraged by Reagan lieutenants) for his connections with banker David Rockefeller's Trilateral Commission.

The extraordinary size of Reagan's November majority, scarcely anticipated, underscored how much had changed since 1964. Public attitudes were different, of course. Liberalism had had its chance and floundered. Images of right-wing bogeymen were no longer salable. But party attitudes were also different. Once Reagan, with some reluctance, chose moderate GOP favorite George Bush as his running mate, virtually all moderate Republican officials and legislators endorsed the ticket. The contrast to 1964 was especially vivid because this time moderate Republicanism had a splinter candidate of its own —Congressman John Anderson of Illinois, whose proclaimed "Lincoln strategy" failed to win a single electoral vote, but who drew 7 percent of the total presidential vote in a pattern heavily based on New England, the Great Lakes, the Pacific Northwest and other areas of rural, Civil War GOP tradition.* Institutionalization of an Anderson Center Party, should it occur, would continue the exodus,

*Party officials held fast, but the common wisdom that Reagan did not stumble among moderate Republicans as Goldwater did is exaggerated. According to George Gallup, Reagan's share of the Republican vote was just 86 percent, the lowest since Goldwater's 80 percent. And if you look at the ultimate in Maine, Vermont and Cape Cod Yankee Republican counties, ones where Eisenhower drew 80–85 percent in 1956 and even Alfred Landon had won 2:1 in 1936, you will find a surprising Goldwater-Reagan parallelism. Goldwater dropped to just 35–45 percent in these counties in 1964, and Reagan won only 40–55 percent sixteen years later.

cementing the Sun Belt hold on the Republican Party (or any new coalition that might form around it). Even in the Northeast, what with the ebb of local GOP fortunes and the vacation of power by the old party establishment, yesteryear's conservative insurgents and even right-wing populists were, by the late 1970s and early 1980s, winning state party chairmanships in New York, New Hampshire, Massachusetts and elsewhere. The essential shift of party power onto the old insurgent base seems irreversible, and the larger question is the ultimate consequence to the Republican party as an institution.

C. THE RISE OF THE CONSERVATIVE MOVEMENT

As of the late 1950s, the conservative movement in the United States was of little significance, politically or intellectually. Since then, the conservative resurgence—on both dimensions—has been so striking that chronicles have become numerous. Most have been written by movement intellectuals who take the whole *risorgimento* at face value. I think they are mistaken to do so.

A number of historians, of whom Louis Hartz, with his *Liberal Tradition in America,* is probably the best-known, have made the point that liberalism, at least in the eighteenth- and nineteenth-century sense, has been so pervasive in the United States that conservative tradition has been minimal and conservative thinkers few and far between.[2] Lacking a landed aristocracy and an established church of the European variety, the United States has accordingly lacked the basis of a "conservative class" in the European style. In the limited sense that I have stated it, the argument seems irrefutable. Sympathetic historians of U.S. conservatism over the last few years acknowledge the partial truth of Hartz's observations but tiptoe around their implications: *that conservatism in the United States is not always very conservative.*

My own view on the matter takes a leaf from nineteenth-century historian Frederick Jackson Turner and his famous theory of the frontier. For starters, to the extent that conservatism was a doctrine or a sociology, obliged to come to the United States on the *Mayflower,* on the *Susan Constant* or in the steerage quarters of a hundred later ships, we got little of it. The political and ideological traditions brought to this country fell more on the other side of history's great, ongoing debate, being Lockean, liberal, revolutionary or—in later years—anarchic or socialist. However, the larger definition of American politics and culture has been derived from the frontier and melting pot, be it Appalachian or urban, Oregon Trail or New York City tenement trail. That impress has been empirical, not theoretical. The theories and hierarchical legacies of Europe have been sloughed. And over two centuries, the new stamp has been one of egalitarianism, populism, middle-class economics, self-help and personalized religion. Aristocratic or doctrinal conservatism, having little in common with such phenomena, rarely succeeded; a nondoctrinal, seat-of-the-pants, mood-of-the-middle-class conservatism, by contrast, has often done very well.

Conservative ideology's ongoing American failure is instructive. Until the broad-based metamorphosis of economics and politics in the 1960s, the make-up of the conservative intellectual movement here served principally to underscore its limited relevance. If one looks at the two dozen portraits on the front cover of George Nash's postwar history of the U.S. conservative movement, a full half are either (1) repentant former Communists or fellow travelers or (2) émigrés from Austria, Germany or some other portion of Central Europe. If one adds yet a third category to the list—a category of archtraditionalist upper-middle-class Catholics entranced by tradition, age-old ritual and the nineteenth-century English Catholic gentility of G. K. Chesterton, Cardinal Newman, et al.—the bulk of the stalwarts of the "conservative intellectual movement" are encompassed. Doctrinalists dominate, people only partially shaped by the American experience. On the fringes, elements of the movement went so far as to derogate the modern age, espousing the "remnant" theory of Albert Jay Nock, a minor theorist of the early twentieth-century, or deploring "gnosticism," the divinization of society and government. A band of thinkers less likely to command mass loyalties or organize a mass popular movement in the United States could hardly be imagined.

By the late 1960s, though, as liberalism stepped into the prescriptive shoes of yesteryear's elites and began seeking to impose its view of morality, neighborhood, fraternity and society on a dubious Middle America, the community of interest between the conservative movement and the oft-despised majority took a great leap forward. The electoral availability of the George Wallace constituency was an important factor. Conservative theoreticians stopped complaining about the evils of majorities and started invoking, variously, the Emerging Republican Majority, the Silent Majority, the New Majority and Middle America. In 1970, as the children of the elite demonstrated on a hundred quadrangles, *National Review* editor Frank Meyer proclaimed that "Middle America is the last heir of Western Civilization."[3] Traditional conservative theorists also found themselves linked to Levittown and the New Majority by a shared animosity for the "New Class" of wordsmiths, Knowledge Industry professionals, bureaucrats, run-amok academicians and federal program entrepreneurs. New bonds were being forged—and a new relevance.

Of course, the traditional conservative turnabout was by no means total. Several of the leading lights at *National Review*—publisher William Rusher, senior editor Jeffrey Hart—espoused the populist-conservative alliance in 1973–76, others held back. In retrospect, I believe that traditional conservative support for a populist antielite alliance probably peaked during the period from 1974–78 when anger at the elite or New Class "countercoup" of Watergate still lingered, when the Republican Party was flattest on its back (and alternatives were being weighed), and before the separate, populist conservative New Right achieved the size it would attain by the end of the decade. Thereafter, increasing prospects of success worked divisively. As rightists got back on their feet in the late 1970s, and as the chances of electing Ronald Reagan on the Republican ticket in 1980 grew, a number of traditional conservatives became deeply troubled over the philosophical, institutional and ideological pitfalls of an alliance with what they deemed to be the radicalism and populism of the New Right. Honoring the credo "No enemies to the right," most of the disenchanted kept their criticism to themselves, but at least two went public: Chilton Williamson, Jr., literary editor of *National Review,* penned an analysis entitled "Country & Western Marxism: To the Nashville Station," which suggested that as populism gained influence, "the last gossamer threads that connect conservative politics to the conservative mind" were being snapped.[4] And Alan Crawford, a publicist for the traditionalist faction in the American Conservative Union, wrote in *Thunder on the Right* that the New Right ought to be shunned as a group whose methods and goals were inimicable to those of true conservatives.[5]

In a nutshell, as "conservatism" found itself poised on the brink of power in 1979–80, much of the media coverage and no small part of the serious political attention was focused on two new component groups of dubious ideological lineage. The old conservative-core movement of Burkean scholars, Austrian émigrés, Catholic traditionalists and converts, and recusant Communists occupied too narrow a cultural and political band to be a major force. The press continued to ignore them, with one or two exceptions. But it could not similarly dismiss the neoconservatives and the New Right. They were vital forces by *liberal* as well as conservative standards. Postulate, if you will, Louis Hartz's theory of America (the pre-1960s America, at least) as a country of liberal tradition. By that hypothesis the neoconservatives, most of them liberals and Democrats until the 1970s, amount to a new elite in the Hartz tradition dedicated to preserving *pre*-1960s liberal ideals and interests. The New Right, by contrast, exemplifies a new mass politics in the ongoing U.S. tradition—more populist than conservative, compelled to strike down what it considers the handiwork of the aberrant elites empowered in the 1960s. The vital new forces under the conservative label have roots in a politics more potent and closer to the mainstream of U.S. history.

To talk about the rise of conservatism, then, is to misrepresent some of the forces at work. The movement goes far beyond conservatism.

D. THE EMERGENCE OF THE
NEOCONSERVATIVES

Overt, self-professed neoconservatism is a product of the mid-1970s. William Safire's 1972 *Political Dictionary* moved from "neanderthal" to "nepotism" without so much as a bow to the group since marshaled under the banner of Irving Kristol, Norman Podhoretz, Daniel Patrick Moynihan and company. But when Watergate destroyed the political framework erected by Richard Nixon and sent the national debate slipping leftward, a number of the increasingly conservative Democratic intellectuals who had rejected George McGovern in 1972 found themselves even more troubled by the new state of affairs. Publications like *Commentary* and the *Public Interest,* already hostile to the left, drew national attention in the mid-to-late 1970s by the incessant attacks they mounted on everything from racial quotas to the strategic arms limitation talks. Even hostile liberals had to admit that many of the critiques penned by the neoconservatives were telling indictments. And in 1979, journalist Peter Steinfels brought the movement front-and-center with his book *The Neoconservatives: The Men Who Are Changing America's Politics,* in which he proclaimed that "neoconservatism is the serious and intelligent conservatism America has lacked and whose absence has been roundly lamented by the American Left."[6]

In part because of the Steinfels volume, the year 1979 was one when considerable attention was devoted to neoconservatism. Quite a few of the neoconservatives were New Yorkers, most of them certified members of the Eastern intelligentsia, and they enjoyed access to the opinion-molding community from the *Wall Street Journal* to the Washington *Post.* Their prominence also reflected the substantial veracity of what they were writing. But no small part of the attention came from neoconservatism's essential political and philosophical dynamic. Like many other Americans, not least in the knowledge professions, the bulk of the neoconservatives were former liberals who had reformed their politics in response to what they regarded as the incursions of the left on traditional liberal policies and values. Most were still Democrats. Their unease with both the conservatism of the country club and the religious fundamentalists was transparent. What they really wanted was not a new conservatism but the old pre-Vietnam, pre-McGovern liberalism—or so they claimed. "The definition of a neoconservative is someone who wasn't a conservative," says neoconservative Harvard professor Nathan Glazer.[7]

Perhaps the best way to understand neoconservatism is to think in terms of *Commentary* editor Norman Podhoretz's political autobiography, *Making It.* Neoconservatism, in many ways, represents the process by which a number of liberals were indeed "making it" —becoming *personally* establishmentarian much as liberalism itself had become *institutionally* establishmentarian.

This distinction is central. In contrast to the other post–World War II conservative intellectual elites, few of whom were ever taken very seriously, the neoconservatives were and are a Hartzian elite, a product of American *liberal* traditions. This is true, although several of the movement's leading figures have since imbibed a fair amount of theoretical conservatism. The logic is that many conservative tenets now operate to preserve the intellectual and institutional structure liberalism built. Thus the irony that, for *liberal* reasons, neoconservatism is the first respectable intellectual American conservatism in recent memory.

Nevertheless, to the extent that politics is a function of ideas, neoconservatism has been a powerful force. Its leading journals and intellectuals have been stalwarts on the polemical firing line, as they helped to batter down the credibility of yesteryear's left-liberal consensus. Not surprisingly, intellectuals, who make their living by ideas, tend to believe in literary and verbal suasion, to rate such influences highly.

In some limited sense, that analysis is justified. Without the intellectual gridwork built by neoconservatives, Ronald Reagan might have been mocked and scoffed at like Barry Goldwater in 1964. Electorally, however, the impact of neoconservatism was probably minimal. As I wrote in 1979, neoconservatives were long on magazine editors and short on hod carriers, long on chiefs and short on Indians.[8] The truth is that the American public had intuited by 1968 or 1972 most of what the neoconservatives began to write in 1975 or 1979. Just one or two professors linked to neoconservatism were early articulators of pointed critiques—Robert Nisbet's *Twilight of Authority* comes to mind, as does Edward Banfield's *The Unheavenly City.* For the most part, neoconservatives were Johnnies-come-lately to the ranks of those telling us just how the United States had gone wrong in the 1960s, in part because not a few of them had been involved in the policy mistakes made.

With the exception of one or two issues, the neoconservatives tend to be reviewers and reconstructors, not activists. Author George Gilder, himself a refugee from liberal Republicanism, has summed up the mechanics:

> The neoconservative believes not chiefly in principles but in empirical techniques . . . This approach means that the neoconservative usually cannot tell you what is wrong with social programs until they have already been entrenched and done their damage. Then the neoconservative will tell you that these programs are part of the very fabric of our political culture and cannot be repealed. What use is that? . . . I have no doubt that at some future date when these [liberal social] trends have reached some climax sufficiently foul and overwhelming, the neoconservatives will provide elegant scholarly analyses of the problem. They will cogently shows its roots in the very movements which only the New Right and old conservatives dare to denounce.[9]

In political terms, Gilder's criticism is probably correct. The views of several others seem to misstate the issue. One, from the New Left, suggests that neoconservatism is a response of the major elements of the Jewish intelligentsia to the domestic threat of ethnic/racial quotas and the international (Soviet, leftist Arab) threat to Israel. In somewhat related fashion, Harvard sociologist David Riesman, a collaborator and friend of several prominent neoconservatives, sees weakness in the movement's basic parochialism:

> New York provincialism is so important in the outlooks of these people. It is a question of being encapsulated. Their knowledge of American history is slim. They fear the wrong enemies and do not see where their friends are. The ideological construct of the neoconservatives is dated, in space and time. It is hard to learn the country, but many of the neoconservatives see only each other.[10]

For all that such arguments understate the 1978 neoconservative role and the importance of their infusion of reformed liberalism into reshaped "conservatism," these same doubts may be on target in forecasting a lesser neoconservative influence and prominence in the 1980s. For the future, both what Gilder and Riesman say would seem to apply: the neoconservatives may be too cautious, too parochial to play a major role in electoral politics. They may be more concerned with "making it" as centrists and with discrediting whatever remains of the mutant liberalism of the 1960s than with building a new ideological framework for a new decade. In that respect, coupled with the skeptical view taken toward right-wing populism, the neoconservatives would seem to be ambivalent participants in right-of-center coalitions for the 1980s.

E. THE NEW RIGHT

Surprising as it may seem, the neoconservatives and the New Right actually have a lot in common. Both have Democratic constituency antecedents. Both, in many respects, have their origins in the liberal-to-populist traditions cited by Louis Hartz rather than in traditional conservative doctrine. And both movements really came into being at more or·less the same time in 1974–75, spurred by Watergate and the apparent triumph of "New Politics" liberalism over Richard

Nixon's New Majority. The first was an anti-left reaction of upper-middle-class intellectuals, the second a mass movement of lower-middle-class fundamentalists. My reading of U.S. history leads me to believe that the latter is more important.

At first, back in the mid-1970s, established conservative groups argued that there was no New Right, or that, at most, it involved only minor nuances of difference from the Old Right of Goldwater conservatives and their organizations. Time was to make a mockery of such assertions. By the elections of 1978 and 1980 the New Right, its social-issue focus, its guerrilla politics and its plebiscitary methodology were established political realities. Traditionalists had reason to be nervous: conservatism had a new, not very conservative ideological component.

Let us begin with a few definitions. The term "New Right," like the two words "New Left" of the 1960s, is used with more frequency than precision. I pushed the term into the political idiom in 1974, and I meant to describe specifically the populist-conservative groups in the orbit of fund raiser Richard Viguerie, the focus being the newness of these rightist elements emphasizing social issues, religious and cultural alienation, antielite rhetoric, lower-middle-class constituencies, populist fund raising and plebiscitary opinion-mobilization. Despite some overlapping Old Right–New Right positions on taxes, military preparedness and federal social programs, the "New" Right did then and still does represent a *major* cultural and tactical departure for a "conservative" politics. In conversations with the chief architects of the New Right I never heard a single citation of Adam Smith or Edmund Burke. George Wallace and Andrew Jackson were mentioned frequently. In fact, it is fair to say that the New Right is a partial heir of the Wallace movement.

In any case, the key leaders of the New Right—Richard Viguerie, Paul Weyrich, Howard Phillips, Rev. Jerry Falwell, among others—are far more upset with the *moral* and *cultural* tone of 1970s liberalism than with its effect on free-market economics. Parenthetically, neoconservatism finds itself in somewhat the same position, as it reacted principally against the social engineer or a weak foreign policy, though both movements do want to roll back the burden of taxation and government spending. Paul Weyrich, who may have done more than anyone else to merge the secular New Right political machines with the growing religious fundamentalist organizations, not only admits to a basic radicalism of methodology but links the conservative part of his politics to religion: "The very essence of the New Right is a morally based conservatism. As a matter of fact, our view is not based in economics but in a religious view."[11] His further views are also worth note.*

The populist, noneconomic conservatism of the New Right is epitomized by the background of the four leaders cited above: a Louisiana French Catholic, a Wisconsin German Catholic, a Boston Jew and a Southside Virginia fundamentalist Baptist.[12] Not bred in the genteel tradition, the men here frequently criticize the Republican Party for its "big business" sympathy and "country club" mentality. In like vein, the constituencies on which the Conservative Caucus, the Moral Majority, the Religious Roundtable and their allies draw are predominantly lower-middle-class and Democratic by registration or cultural tradition. Only rarely would they be drawn to Republican or conservative candidates by free-market or business economics. What *does* draw them are issues like busing, the Panama Canal, abortion and excessive power of federal judges, or the tax-revolt crusades of feisty political outsiders like California's Howard

*Weyrich, head of the Washington-based Committee for the Survival of a Free Congress, is the circa-1982 chief coordinator and strategist of the capital's network of New Right organizations and strategy groups. He is also the most outspoken, enunciating populist perceptions muted by most of his colleagues. In an interview with Richard Neuhaus in the October 9, 1981, issue of *Commonweal,* Weyrich sounds an unmistakably populist trumpet. *On traditional conservatism:* "The Old Right is as elitist as the liberal intellectuals. I'm not an intellectual, but they don't know a thing about precincts and neighborhoods and they don't want to know." *On participatory and plebiscitary democracy:* "Direct democracy is not just an expedient until we get into power. It's a necessary part of the political process; it's the only way to make the government responsive, to make sure that people keep promises after they're elected." *On the two-party system:* "The Republican Party is not built on principles, it's a tradition maintained by effete gentlemen of the Northeastern Establishment who play games with other effete gentlemen who call themselves Democrats." *On big business:* "Big corporations are as bad as big government. They're in bed together." *On social programs:* "Of course I care about the people who are treated unfairly. In that sense, I feel a lot closer to William Jennings Bryan than to the Tories of whatever stripe. The liberals' compassion is really condescending, it's patronizing." *On free-market economics:* "Laissez-faire is not enough, there has to be some higher value in a society. There can be no such thing as an entirely free market. The market has to be responsive to social responsibility. Here I even agree with some liberals, but we disagree on what those social responsibilities are and how you translate them into policy." On the evidence, it is ludicrous to place Weyrich—the son of a Racine, Wisconsin, blue-collar worker—in the conservative tradition of Hamilton, Burke, et al. On the contrary, his roots could hardly be more obvious—foursquare in the populist and Middle American radical tradition of Andrew Jackson, William Jennings Bryan and George C. Wallace.

Jarvis and Michigan's Robert Tisch (the Shiawassee County drains commissioner, no less).

I submit that the New Right combines three powerful trend patterns that recur in American history and politics. First, to some measure it is an extension of the Wallace movement, and as such represents a current expression of the ongoing populism of the white lower middle classes, principally in the South and West.* All the right symbols are present: antimetropolitanism, antielitism, cultural fundamentalism. Second, the New Right is closely allied with the sometimes potent right-to-life or antiabortion movement, the current version, perhaps, of the great one-issue moral crusades of the American past—the pre–Civil War abolitionists and the early-twentieth-century prohibitionists. And this one-issue element, in turn, folds into the third phenomenon—the possible fourth occurrence of the religious revivals or "Great Awakenings" that have swept across the land since the middle of the eighteenth century. If so, the *religious* wing of the New Right may be the *political* wing of a major national "awakening."

So the New Right is an electoral force to be taken seriously. Back in the mid-1970s, pollster Daniel Yankelovich, who has sometimes felt we face the possibility of a populist upheaval, suggested that 40–45 percent of American conservatives were populists, not traditionalists. A few days after the 1980 presidential election, after Moral Majority preachers spurred 1 to 2 million in new voter registration by white Southern fundamentalists, pollster Louis Harris suggested that Moral Majority–influenced voters were responsible for some two thirds of Ronald Reagan's 10-point majority.[13] These are serious numbers. Viguerie, taking a somewhat different perspective, has suggested that social-issue voters represent the difference between conservatives getting 43–44 percent nationally and climbing to 51–52 percent.[14]

In the 1980 election, probably so. The increment of social- and religious-issue voters may well have provided 5–6 percentage points of Reagan's 10-point edge. But for the politics of the rest of the 1980s, the radical aspects of the New Right movement and constituency may coexist badly with traditional conservatism.† Low-church fun-

*New Right leader Richard Viguerie, in fact, handled George Wallace's 1976 direct-mail fund raising.
†Consider the extraordinary attack on the New Right made by Senator Barry Goldwater on September 15, 1981: "In the past couple years, I have seen many news

damentalism will perhaps continue to displace high-church cosmopolitanisms as the stuff of which conservative politics is shaped, which would be compatible with the other transformations described in this chapter. But any such politics would put great stress on any majority coalition or aspiring majority coalition.

F. THE RADICAL TRANSFORMATION OF CONSERVATIVE ECONOMICS

When the first histories of the 1980s are written, the place of the radical transformation of conservative economics will be as important as that of any other transformation—geographical, cultural or institutional. As the 1970s opened, conservative economic theories were outsider credos barely taken seriously by either the Republican Administration of Richard Nixon or the business community; in 1981, monetarism, supply-side economics and gold currency convertibility were recognized as the official economic theology of a new revolutionary conservative government.

The nomination of Barry Goldwater in 1964 provided an early signal. Economist Milton Friedman, hero of the monetarist school, played a role in party councils he had never had before. But the election of Nixon in 1968 and then again in 1972 curbed any rightward radicalization of GOP economics. One has only to remember the 1971 imposition of wage and price controls and Nixon's stunning statement that "We're all Keynesians now." By most other yardsticks—regional, party factional, cultural and populist—Nixon was a transitional figure, fueling the transformation from establishment to antiestablishment conservatism. But his economics were conformist—by some critiques even statist.*

The four major components of radical conservative economics—supply-side theory, monetarism, gold convertibility and far-reaching

items that referred to the Moral Majority, pro-life and other religious groups as 'the new right' and the 'new conservatism.' Well, I have spent quite a number of years carrying the flag of the 'old conservatism.' And I can say with conviction that the religious issues of these groups have little or nothing to do with conservative or liberal politics." Ironically, Goldwater's own 1964 presidential bid, in which he courted fundamentalist assistance, is generally regarded as the religious right's first major move into presidential politics since the 1920s (see Chapter 14).
*However, the possibility that Nixon's corporatist and statist tendencies also predict the populist-conservative direction on *this* dimension is entertained in Chapter 11.

economic deregulation—all began to gather real force in the mid-1970s. *None* got its impetus from the executive suites of the Business Roundtable. *All* came from the conservative periphery, and all, at least to some extent, made the corporate and traditional GOP economic policy elites initially quite uncomfortable. More about these ideas later, but I will say here that politically they are revolutionary. So clear was this by 1980 that the principal agitators for supply-side (deep tax cut) theory and restoration of the gold standard—Congressman Jack Kemp, Professor Arthur Laffer, author Jude Wanniski, et al.—were collectively labeled by Wanniski as "The Wild Men." Their goal was to take the economic policy back to the 1920s, back to the gold standard, and back to concepts that obtained before the New Deal, and they knew that was radicalism writ large. From time to time, several described themselves as members of the New Right, although Kemp expressed preference for the neoconservative label. Throughout the 1980 campaign, the old and new guard fought a battle for Ronald Reagan's mind. In the end, when the Administration proposed its 1981 program, radical economics carried the day.

G. THE REAGAN SYNTHESIS

All of these trends came together in 1980 for Ronald Reagan as they could have for no other U.S. politician, and he rode them to a huge victory. By my analysis, Reagan's own Sun Belt politics, party insurgency, anti-Washington outsidership, religious- and social-issue sympathies and supply-side/gold standard economics simultaneously mirrored and encompassed all the radical transformations. Yet by his easygoing manner and relaxed persona, Reagan muted their harsher implications and contradictions, and the public took comfort and relaxed. At the same time, and this is perhaps more important, his generalized call for an American renaissance-cum-restoration provided a psychological tent for a great deal of hope and nostalgia. There was room for everyone and everything. For foreign policy hawks, the country would return to the era of Pax Americana; for supply-siders, the Treasury would take a stab at Coolidge economics; for business, a return to the days before Ralph Nader; for the New Right, a return to the days before the Supreme Court rejected God and embraced abortion; and for the neoconservatives, a chance to dance on the political grave of the New Class and recall the days when City College of New York students respected their professors, and people like Scoop Jackson could be elected chairman of the Democratic National Committee.

And therein lies the volatility. So eager were Americans to turn away from Jimmy Carter and the failures of the late 1970s that the contradictions of the various Reagan constituencies made little difference. With various radical transformations little perceived, the terms of the Reagan synthesis were never debated. But as the 1980s unfold, that is no longer true. The question is, Can radical "conservatism" work?

4

THE EMERGING
REPUBLICAN MAJORITY:
A RETROSPECTIVE

Just recently, and for the first time in almost twenty years of GOP-gazing, I have seen an analysis which rises above wishful thinking. Kevin Phillips, currently a young assistant to the incumbent Attorney General, believes our country now possesses an "emerging Republican majority."

—Andrew Hacker, "Is There a New Republican Majority?" *Commentary* (November 1969)

BACK IN LATE 1968, I COULDN'T DECIDE WHETHER TO call my book *The Emerging Republican Majority* or *The Emerging Conservative Majority.* A case could be made for either then; surprisingly enough on the day after the 1980 election, the same was true. The ideological and institutional currents involved have never quite washed up on the same shore.

Since being advanced, the thesis of the emerging Republican majority has pivoted on two complementary but quite different arguments: first, the break-up of the old New Deal Democratic coalition in the face of a conservative trend; and second, the emergence of the *Republican* Party as the majority political vehicle of a new cycle. A decade ago the artificial benefits of Watergate allowed many nervous Democrats to relax. Since the election of Ronald Reagan and a Republican Senate, they have become nervous again—for good reason.

The electoral alliance Franklin D. Roosevelt built is shattered. That coalition's break-up—outlined in 1966–68, confirmed in prelim-

53

inary fashion in 1972, thrown into limbo from 1973 to 1978, and fully confirmed in 1980—now no longer seems in question. Even most academicians now seem to admit as much. The crux of the matter, as things now stand, rests on the *second* question: Is the Republican Party the vehicle of a new political majority? Arguably, a new Republican majority of a traditional variety might conceivably have emerged in the wake of the 1972 election but for Watergate, despite Richard Nixon's less-than-inspirational characteristics of leadership. A look at American history and its cyclical chronology supported the case for such an emergence. Indeed, our history dispenses an extraordinary cyclical regularity: watershed presidential elections have occurred, and new party supremacies have been launched, at recurring 28–36 year political intervals in 1800, 1828, 1860, 1896 and 1932. Political scientists have generally come to accept these dates, and accordingly, another watershed and party supremacy was due in 1968–72. Without Watergate, an emerging Republican majority could conceivably have come into place. More on that shortly, and on the subsequent implications of a "bottled up" realignment.

A brief note on the 28–36 year cyclical of watershed presidential elections. Among analysts, the chronology has been accepted since the 1940s and 1950s. The dynamics of just why are harder to pin down, but the cyclical "waves" of American political history, standing in such sharp contrast to the political evolutionary processes in Europe, seem closely linked to the movement of population west and then into the cities. At some risk of generalizing too much, it is still fair to say that our parties and ideologies, once successful, have tended to entrench themselves in the Northeast—in the stronghold of the business-financial establishment and of the political power structure.* Conversely, the periodic upheavals that challenge or change the structure tend to be launched in the South and West, be it the trans-Appalachian West of 1828, the Great Plains of 1896, or the dust bowl of 1932. All such insurgencies were in some measure populist and antiestablishmentarian, which helps to give American politics its special character and quality: periodic, popular, antielite renewal. *No other nation has had comparable cycles. We have our revolutions at the ballot box, not in the Tuileries.*

Thus the reason for the expectations for 1968–72, another such

---

*All of these dynamics and regional patterns are analyzed and described at much greater length in Chapter 3 of my previous book *Mediacracy: American Parties and Politics in the Communications Age* (1975).

historical convulsion was overdue. In retrospect, however, the theory was neat and the realities of the time confused. The four cycles of 1800 through 1932 occurred during a prolonged period of American agrandizement and continuity—the physical occupation of the continent, the rise and zenith of the *industrial* (as opposed to agricultural or post-industrial) era, and the emergence of a mass electorate and the first mass-based political parties. That part of our history possessed a cohesion we may have since lost. The 1960s, as everyone now knows all too well, saw the United States move into a post-industrial, communications-based era, one in which the institutional logic and deep loyalty roots of political parties eroded. Moreover, inflation became an increasingly disruptive peacetime phenomenon for the first time in American history. And our parties began to decay and *de-align,* not realign.

Enough of cyclical theory. Even conservative partisans of one sort or another must acknowledge the Republican Party of 1968 to 1972 as something less than the powerful stuff of which history was usually made. The elections of 1966 had pretty much shown the way— surprisingly large gains had been chalked up in the Southern, Western and Midwestern states where social, cultural and anti-Washington themes seemed most pervasive. The Democrats, in turn, had maintained many of their 1964 inroads in the Northeast, where social liberalism and opposition to the war in Vietnam were strongest. A new geopolitics was in the works. Yet Republican strategists had proved ambivalent in their interpretations of 1966, tending to credit antiwar reaction for party gains. They would be again less than confident after the 1968 election. Confusion was heightened by the closeness of the outcome, and underscored as Hubert Humphrey rallied from 29 percent in September to 43 percent on Election Day 1968 when he moved in an antiwar direction. Was liberalism still the future? Given hindsight, the Southern-Western metamorphosis of the GOP was totally obvious, but was camouflaged in 1968–69, both by the October Humphrey rally and the division of the 1968's 57 percent electoral majority shared by Republican Nixon *and* third-party conservative populist George Wallace.

The Emerging Republican Majority, published in the summer of 1969, was quickly characterized by *Newsweek* as "the political bible of the Nixon Era," and other publications followed suit. The reality was something less. Administration officials hoped for the fulfillment of the book's title, but had much less interest in understanding the social and economic dynamics at work. Confronting perceived pressure, the new GOP Administration temporized in ways that surprised realignment advocates and theorists. Moderates like domestic adviser Daniel Patrick Moynihan, Housing Secretary George Romney and Health, Education and Welfare Secretary Robert Finch helped secure full funding of controversial, realignment-provoking Great Society programs on the basis of "continuity" and liberal secular trends. Continuing to accept underlying liberal sociological premises, from busing to rent subsidies, Nixon Administration tacticians faced the 1970 elections—during a mushrooming recession—with little sociocultural weaponry save for a shallow law-and-order campaign theme based on the issues identified in a *counter*strategy by Democrats Richard Scammon and Ben Wattenberg. These two men—quite logically—were urging elected Democratic officials to ride around in police cars and to duck identification with permissivism and welfarism. The Nixon Administration people, who could and should have mounted a critique going to the roots of liberal-policy miscalculation, did not do so. The GOP disappointment in 1970—a gain of two Senate seats but a loss of a dozen in the House —cast a long midterm shadow on the thesis of an emerging Republican majority.

Yet because the underlying electoral trends involved were fundamental, the trends themselves did not dissipate easily. If the Republicans were not going to grab an opportunity, the Democrats were nevertheless being pulled apart by the breakdown of their constituency, a disintegration that burst into public view early in 1972 in the Democratic presidential primaries. Edmund Muskie, candidate of the not very vital Democratic center, was destroyed in the opening contests as the party split between the candidacies of its two wings: populist George Wallace and George McGovern, the liberal hero of the campus/causist "New Class." The split was deep—and fatal. Wallace's hospitalization after the attempt on his life in May and the nomination of McGovern in July assured the Republicans of a November victory that followed region for region, constituency for constituency, the outline presented in *The Emerging Republican Majority*.

For the Nixon White House, that proof came only with the eating, too late. Until the spring of 1972, the Nixon people did not think a watershed Republican opportunity would materialize. Few fully understood how the Wallace and McGovern phenomena were flip sides of the same pattern of Democratic decomposition. Would anybody who saw the massive electoral opportunity coming have given G. Gordon Liddy a go-ahead on an inane political attempt at espionage?

Not a few Republican leaders were busy anticipating the strategy of 1972 by denying that its electoral premises could ever be sustained. Northeastern and Midwestern moderates and liberals simply did not fancy the geopolitical opportunity implicit in the Sun Belt and Southern strategies. A constant stream of vitriol was poured on the idea of an emerging Republican majority by Northeastern moderate and liberal GOP leaders and by activists ranging from Senate Minority Leader Hugh Scott of Pennsylvania to the Massachusetts-based Ripon Society. They correctly saw a century of geopolitical history on the verge of being undone. By their calculations of self-interest, a Republican Anschluss with the conservative Democratic South was a consummation to be *avoided,* not one to be *achieved.*

Dixie, of course, was the necessary linchpin of any political rearrangement or realignment. As of 1972, the Republicans lagged in party identification by 45 to 30 percent, in the Senate by 56 to 44, in the House by 255 to 180. *More than just an election would be necessary to create a new majority; a basic transfer of allegiance by much of the conservative South would also be required.* The mechanics of that was, in a word, sticky. And so a number of alternative vehicles were discussed in mid-1972.

As the November 1972 election results poured in, the Democratic breakdown in the South pretty much fulfilled the quarter-century trend line beginning in the 1940s: Richard Nixon swept each and every state of the Old Confederacy. On the presidential level, the targets of the Southern Strategy had fallen into place like the movements of a Swiss watch; on the congressional level, however, the results were less solid: Dixie elected two additional Republican senators and three more Republican representatives. The larger regional opportunity had slipped away.

I have a bone to pick with history here. Watergate was *a* principal reason, if not *the* principal reason, for the electoral miscarriage. Given the other, more sinister, ramifications to contemplate, too little attention has been paid to the impact of Watergate on the 1972 election. It was, in fact, considerable. As of late August and early September, when Richard Nixon had just been renominated triumphantly and the already doomed Democratic ticket was fresh from replacing vice-presidential nominee Thomas Eagleton, new voter-registration statistics from around the country showed a major Republican surge. The Republicans also narrowed the party-identification gap and took a solid lead in voter key-issue–handling preference.* (Because the phenomenon lasted only a few weeks, minimal research has been done on the trends involved, but it would make some Ph.D. candidate an interesting and useful dissertation.) By October, however, the GOP advance faltered in the face of the growing publicity, largely generated by the Washington *Post,* over apparent White House involvement in the Watergate break-in in June. Oval Office transcripts suggest that top Nixon aides and the President himself had been edgy and nervous almost from the day of the break-in, undercutting the creativity and élan of their campaign and contributing to its mechanical, uninspired quality. Things deteriorated still further in October as the Watergate scandal grew more encompassing, and the Nixon reelection campaign turned manifestly defensive. Gone was any prospect of a grand offensive to harness the imagination of an amenable electorate around a new Republican vision for the 1970s. The possibility of a top-to-bottom Republican trend began to evaporate.

The public are not fools. As press coverage of Watergate intensified in late October, so did the cynicism of the electorate. Something was obviously rotten in Richard Nixon's Denmark. November voting intentions began to slip. Pennsylvania pollster Albert Sindlinger told his clients that some 5 to 7 million potential voters dropped out in the last two weeks before the election. And in contrast to the disproportionately uneducated, low-income persons who had never planned to vote, these late-hour dropouts were predominantly Republicans and Independents from Northern locales where GOP tradition has its roots in morality and righteousness, especially in middle-class suburbs, rural Yankee counties and states like Maine and Iowa. The election outcome—a stillborn realignment—was shaped accordingly, to the detriment of the GOP. There was little joy on election night for the President or anyone associated with him.

No one will ever know, but absent the debilitating circumstances the November results could well have been substantially different. My own hypothesis is that without the strategic, moral and turnout

*Pollster Albert Sindlinger found the Democratic lead over the GOP dropping from 38–23 percent in July to just 36–32 percent in September. Gallup has not released week-by-week figures. But as to which party voters preferred in 1972 to handle the country's top problem, Gallup agreed—the Republicans.

depressant of Watergate, Richard Nixon would have beaten George McGovern with a record majority of 63–65 percent of the total vote instead of just under 61 percent. And the better side of Nixon might well have emerged in such a campaign. We now have a firmer appreciation of how ready the public was for an articulate, populist-tinged conservatism. Likewise, instead of losing two Senate seats net, the GOP could well have added one to four (climbing to a total of 45–48). And in the House of Representatives, the gain might have been twenty to thirty seats instead of just twelve, to near-controlling levels that could have fueled at least a dozen party switches in 1973, mostly by Southerners. Organization of Congress might well have passed to the GOP or a conservative coalition. Some of the groundwork for that was actually laid before the election, but the disappointing results and the escalation of Watergate soon scotched any preliminary arrangements. Let no one doubt: the two Southern democrats who *did* switch to the Republican Party in 1973, Watergate notwithstanding—former governors John Connally of Texas and Mills Godwin of Virginia—were only the tip of a regional iceberg. Absent Watergate, political control of the South could also have passed into the hands of a new coalition. Connally was to be Nixon's heir in 1976, and one of his prime tasks from 1973 to 1976 would have been to orchestrate the congressional, state and local transformation of Dixie loyalties. White House strategists were aware that the Republican Party might have to give way to some new vehicle, and Nixon himself recalls in his memoirs that after the election "we even deliberated for several days about starting a new party."[1] After the election, of course, the larger opportunity was gone, even though the full enormity of Watergate remained to be disclosed.

Could such a new majority have held up through the oil shock of 1973–74, the further strengthening of OPEC, the severe recession of 1974–75 and the collapse of the Indochinese war in 1975? Those who say "no" can state a fair case. But then again, so can those who argue that the U.S. policy debacles of 1973–75 were closely linked to the disruptions of Watergate, and might not have occurred—or would have occurred in very different form—without the scandal and its consequences. (Those arguments, made by White House chief of staff H. R. Haldeman and others, are recapitulated in Chapter 5.)

Moreover, I contend that the repression of the emerging Republican majority in 1973 and 1974 greatly dislocated American politics. Instead of *normal* Democratic strength reasserting itself, we now

know that an *abnormal* Democratic resurgence occurred, camou-
flaging the fundamental erosion of its constituency and artifically
shifting political currents into new channels. Underlying Southern
political trends were suspended, producing the anomaly of Jimmy
Carter, with the liberals taking false heart. Meanwhile the New
Right, mobilizing populist-conservatives from Nixon's New Majority, began to move away from the Republican Party after the acces-
sion of Gerald Ford and Ford's selection of Nelson Rockefeller as
Vice President. As Kansas Senator and 1972 Republican National
Chairman Robert Dole said in an interview, "Nixon believed he
could build a new national majority, including Democrats and independents as well as Republicans, based on the so-called sunbelt
strategy [Kevin Phillips' theory that a majority party could be
formed around conservative populists in the South and West]. Ford's
objective was more simple. He aimed to be a good Republican President, moving within the traditional Republican philosophy."[2]

Fair enough. Gerald Ford mooted realignment and the new majority. Geographically and temperamentally, he represented the old
Northern middle class, high-church Republicanism uncomfortable
with Southern preachers and Polish ethnic leaders.

Nevertheless, by the late 1970s not a few observers began to postulate a second Republican opportunity, and speculative hopes soared
after the Republican victories of 1980. But my own doubts about
another traditional realignment in the 1980s—the majority and minority parties simply swapping places and roles—remain. If the election of 1972 was an *aborted* realignment, the 1980 election was
transparently *not* a realignment in itself.

Negative indices abound. First of all, realignment elections—like
those of 1828, 1860 and 1932—have almost always occurred in periods
of rising turnout and voter interest. The realignment of 1896, the one
exception, occurred just after the all-time peak of U.S. voter participation. By contrast, the 53 percent turnout of 1980 marked the fifth
downturn in a row and the lowest rate of voter participation since
1948. Second, no realignment election ever produced a split Congress.
Third, there is no precedent for a sequence composed of an *aborted*
realignment followed a decade or so later by an *actual* realignment
moving in the same basic direction. Fourth, the public may well have
lost essential faith in the party system during the 1970s. And fifth,
when new Presidents have won office in watershed elections, they
have always done so by capturing a substantially increased share of

the total vote when compared to the prior candidate of their party: Jackson in 1828 (up to 55 percent from 41 percent in 1824); Lincoln in 1860 (up to 39.8 percent from John C. Fremont's 33 percent in 1856); McKinley in 1896 (up to 51 percent from Benjamin Harrison's 43 percent in 1892); and Franklin D. Roosevelt in 1932 (up to 57 percent from Alfred E. Smith's 41 percent in 1928). Reagan's percentage gain over Gerald Ford was small—just 2 percent. To be sure, many 1981 public opinion polls showed the Republicans making substantial party-identification gains, overtaking the Democrats enough for Reagan pollster Richard Wirthlin to suggest that a "creeping realignment" had begun. The trouble is, there's never been any such animal before.

The question of what really happened (or was about to happen) to the emerging Republican majority may well have a little understood significance for the 1980s. In 1980 and 1981, many Republican officials involved in the national committee's effort to rebuild the party during the years 1977 to 1980, along with people in the Reagan presidential campaign and Administration, held forth at some length on the notion of a new GOP momentum and opportunity far greater than those presented in the Nixon era. Postulating a very different dynamics, they tended to down-play the strategies of 1968–72, stressing economic, not social issues. They see the former shaping the new party opportunity of the 1980s. Unfortunately, however, if the aborted 1968–72 political regrouping did indeed constitute *the* failed opportunity, and if what we saw in 1980 was a kind of decade-delayed nostalgia and frustration-driven "shadow" election following the electoral pattern of 1972, the electoral tide here bears only superficial resemblance to realignment. A much more volatile process may be under way. Thus, one can argue that the political scientists who failed to see significance in the pro-conservative 1968–72 electoral surge—call it aborted realignment, conservative de-alignment, or whatever—have neglected a phenomenon almost certain to have enormous implications for the party system during this decade.

With various independent candidacies and new parties in sight for 1984 and 1988, I'm tempted to suggest that the system may be about to undergo a convulsion bigger and more intense than one involving just Republicans and Democrats. That, by the way, would be entirely in keeping with historical precedent. Three of our five realignment elections—those of 1800, 1828 and 1860—produced the emergence of new parties *and* major changes in the mechanics of presidential selection or a constitutional crisis. By contrast, the realignment of 1932 is the *only one* in which a prior majority and a prior minority party simply swapped eminences and roles. Whether that can happen again is one of the great questions of the 1980s. Republicans believe that it can. My own feeling, less sanguine, is that the legacy of Watergate—lost Republican opportunities, national fragmentation and the subsequent accumulation of national problems—will probably demand a more complicated restructuring of American politics.

5

THE
WATERGATE
WARP

Seen in historical and strategic perspective, Watergate was the climax
of the domestic political civil war fought to determine who would
explain America's defeat in Vietnam and who would be blamed for it.

—Richard J. Whalen, 1980[1]

THAT THE UNITED STATES WILL COMMEMORATE THE
tenth anniversary of Richard Nixon's resignation from office in 1984
is nicely Orwellian. Yet in what sense? Was Nixon the foiled authoritarian architect, or was he himself the victim of an unprecedented
communications-era cabal, and pushed toward the trap door of history by a Kafkaesque process, as one columnist observed, in which
"the media has reviled and degraded Nixon with everything from
accusations of cheating on his income tax, to sexual impotence, to
broad hints that he's gay."[2] Most Americans who care think they
know how they feel about Nixon, but do they really?

In the late 1970s, Watergate slipped from the national mind as the
stream of books and movies came to an end, and as the ineptitude
of the Carter Administration, elected as a "government of love" that
repudiated Nixonism, helped restore a more balanced assessment of
the former regime. Although scandal ceased to be a factor in the 1978
and 1980 elections, one must still wonder whether the exit is permanent, whether such a politically bloody affair—arguably the Ameri-

can equivalent of regicide—can be completely eliminated from the national psyche, or whether we are simply experiencing a lull, marking a transition from Watergate-as-liberal issue to Watergate-as-conservative remonstrance. With the Republicans busy attempting to revise the national economic understanding of 1929, the peculiar political circumstances of 1972 may prove even more compelling. No re-examination of how the United States went wrong in Southeast Asia, or in foreign policy, or even in our society as a polity from 1963 to 1972, can be achieved without getting to the root of Watergate and the warp it caused: Who really did what to whom, why, and with what results?

Several scholars, mind you, have seen such revision implicit from the beginning. Robert Nisbet, Albert Schweitzer Professor of Humanities at Columbia University, theorized in his book *Twilight of Authority:*

> Once the seamier details have been forgotten, which will not take very long, the number of those in this country for whom Watergate will become a veritable Golgotha will surely grow. Whether we like it or not, the potential for martyrdom in Watergate is a significant one. And, as is always the case in martyrdom in history, ordinary conventional criteria of wickedness and guilt do not apply. It is too early to be certain, but on balance, I think Watergate will prove to be the American Dreyfus case. If so, there are dangerous implications to the political process.[3]

A. L. Goodhart, emeritus professor of jurisprudence at Oxford University, told a reporter that he had begun to work on an opus comparing Richard Nixon with Captain Alfred Dreyfus. "I met Dreyfus in Paris in 1920," Goodhart said, "and I met him when he came to Oxford. It's quite amazing how many points of comparison there are. The cases against both were very poor, and they both had very weak judges. Had they tried Nixon, I am sure he would have got off."[4]

The lingering dimensions of Watergate—what it was, what it aborted, what it ultimately meant—are as convoluted as they are multiple. I propose to entertain and analyze four questions: First, what was Watergate as espionage—a plot, a counterplot, or both? Second, what was Watergate as a political event—an opportunity seized and maximized, or a coup of sorts? Third, what was Watergate as a matter of economic, energy, bureaucratic reform and foreign policy—a massive dislocation of American planning and ability and policy, or more a result of national breakdown than a cause? And fourth, what are the prospects that Watergate, in 1985 or 1990, will come to mean a somewhat different plot and politics, and thus embody a somewhat different form of evil, than it did in 1973–76?

Question One is technical but essential. What are the mechanical underpinnings of the famous break-in and burglary? Are they the stuff of future revisionism? Quite possibly. On its face, Watergate was a break-in and attempted burglary at the Democratic National Committee, one of a series of attempts at political espionage mounted by the Committee to Re-elect the President—CREEP, as the acronym went. The real objective of the break-in is more open to debate. Was it information the Democrats had on Nixon? Material linking the John F. Kennedy assassination to Cuba and the CIA-Mafia plot to kill Fidel Castro? Evidence of Cuban funds flowing into the Democratic presidential campaign of George McGovern? Opinions vary. But the pivotal question, central to any attempt at historical revisionism, is this: Was there just one Watergate operation, run by CREEP, or were there two, the second involving a *parallel* operation by the Central Intelligence Agency to infiltrate, "set up," sabotage and then slowly expose and unravel CREEP operations to undercut the Nixon White House? The Administration, by almost everyone's analysis, was at loggerheads with the agency and maneuvering to gain control of CIA secret files and operations.

The evidence here, while circumstantial, is more abundant. Since the mid-1970s, various the-CIA-was-up-to-something theses have been put forward by former Nixon officials, the Watergate burglars themselves, journalists and investigators. One of the most recent is also among the most compelling: a January 1980 *Harper's* article, "The McCord File," by James Hougan, one of the magazine's Washington editors. Hougan's thesis, in a nutshell, is that James McCord, who led the Watergate burglar team, was not simply a *retired* CIA agent (chief of their technical security division as late as 1970) but *an active double agent*—a man who had earlier directed the agency's "infiltration" of the White House, and who in 1972 would insist on carrying out the June 16–17 break-in, sabotage that entry, and ultimately, the following March, send an explosive letter to Judge John Sirica alleging perjury, political pressure and White House involvement. In an exhaustive study, complete with new information, Hougan also suggests that it "seems likely" that "the [Washington] *Post*" —and therefore Watergate—"was manipulated for political reasons."[5] His suspected manipulator: CIA Counterintelligence.

This being an inquiry into political circumstances, it is not the place to review the minutiae of the revisionist approaches taken by Hougan and others. But the conspiracy-as-literature outpourings of the last decade have called up an extraordinary array of linked plots, with Norman Mailer even suggesting that the CIA killed Marilyn Monroe to frame the Kennedy brothers with whom the actress was entangled. A full fat volume would be necessary to catalogue the various schemes and their alleged linkage. In historical terms, however, suffice it to say that not only is the more recently assembled evidence in the Watergate affair modestly revisionist, but the more important thing is that CIA plot charges have been made by reputable and well-placed journalists, and they have been taken up with various degrees of anger, belated comprehension and agreement by a number of the Watergate burglars and former senior Nixon White House officials. For purposes of politically charged revisionism, and considering that the CIA burned its relevant files almost immediately after Watergate (sending an agent to McCord's house to burn his, too), this is an adequate basis. The actual fact is another matter. The exact truth will obviously never be known.

The various allegations can be summed up by two of the Watergate burglars, Howard Hunt and Frank Sturgis, who think they were set up. Hunt maintains that James McCord deliberately fouled up the burglary and had the police waiting. Sturgis says that Watergate was hatched by the CIA because Nixon was becoming too powerful: "I believe Nixon would have uncovered the true facts in the assassination of President Kennedy, and that would have taken off the heat in Watergate. Because Nixon wanted files, the CIA felt they had to get rid of him."[6]

The retrospective accounts of senior White House aides are even more extraordinary. Nixon's longtime chief of staff, H. R. Haldeman, has suggested that Alexander Butterfield, the presidential aide who disclosed the Oval Office taping system, might have been a CIA agent. "In retrospect," Haldeman observed, "I'm ambivalent about whether the agency was out to get Nixon. I don't dismiss it as an impossibility. I do believe there are a lot of unanswered questions about the break-in at Watergate."[7] Haldeman discusses the various possibilities at some length in his book *The Ends of Power,* saying that as of 1974, both Charles Colson *and* Richard Nixon himself appear to have been convinced of a CIA plot.[8] Chief Nixon White House speechwriter Raymond Price, a moderate at odds with Nixon's Sun Belt tactical leanings, also embraces the CIA counter-plot thesis in his book, *With Nixon.*[9] White House counsel John Dean, in *Blind Ambition,* recounts prison discussions with fellow aide Colson in which they, too, compared notes on how those with CIA connections seemed to come through Watergate unscathed.[10] And Nixon White House counselor John Ehrlichman created a multi-scandal in his fascinating Watergate *roman à clef* in which a President seeks a CIA document explaining the murder of a previous President but is frustrated when the CIA stakes out an expected burglary site and photographs White House dirty-tricksters at work.[11]

If one goes back over the record, there seem to be two ways in which Nixon aides perceived CIA involvement. In late June 1972 the White House was not sure just what had happened at Watergate—remember that Watergate prosecutor James Neal affirms that Nixon himself did not know of the break-in before the fact, nor, presumably, did his senior aides. There was a White House assumption, given the CIA background of the burglars, that the agency had been involved in some (benign for the White House) collateral fashion, and that if the episode could be laid at the doorstep of the CIA, that would solve the law-enforcement problem. Only in later years, as new documentation and evidence began accumulating and gaining publication, did aides' perception of the CIA role shift to a possible anti-Nixon counterplot.

A number of writers and political analysts, while not necessarily sharing any theory of a counterplot, agree that once the Watergate opportunity did materialize, Nixon's transgressions were grossly trumped up by an Eastern establishment—including the CIA, which very much wanted to tie Nixon's hands so that he could not proceed as expected during his second term. In *The Yankee and Cowboy War* —a book about the rivalry between the "old money of the Eastern Seaboard" and the new cowboy millionaires of the West—New Left activist and writer Carl Oglesby argued that "the arrest of the Water-gate burglars was the result of a set up, that it was no more an accident that the Plumbers were caught than that they were in the offices of the Democratic National Committee to begin with, that there were actually two secret operations at Watergate, colliding invisibly as hunter and prey . . . Watergate, like Dallas, was a coup d'état, culminating in the installation of a new president and a new governing elite."[12]

Others on the New Left point in a similar direction. Marcus Raskin, head of the Institute for Policy Studies, offered this embellishment:

> To forestall a politically revolutionary consciousness, it was necessary to develop a theory that Nixon and his activities were distinguishable from the System's usual operations . . . Nixon had to be perceived by a majority in Congress and the media, as well as by the American audience, as a pathological occupant of the presidency . . . If people decided that Nixon as a President was no different from others, it could result in greater instability and a possible internal upheaval against the elites who exercised broad control over the society . . .[13]

Raskin's analysis leads to the obvious, related issue: Did Nixon really do anything new, and did he even really do all that much? At the time, in 1973 and 1974, while Nixon was being portrayed as the American presidency's unique ugly frog, a minority of commentators said, Hey, wait a minute, this sort of stuff has gone on before: Remember Lyndon Johnson and Bobby Baker? Remember the Kennedys wiretapping Martin Luther King? But such parallels were ignored. The press, or at least the influential press, did not want any precedents to get in the way of the biggest story imaginable (or for those who are more Machiavellian, to get in the way of the firestorm consuming the Nixon presidency). Only in 1975 and 1976, and even later, did the history of pre-Nixon Nixonism come to light thanks to Senator Frank Church's committee's investigation of intelligence activities. A staff committee report showed that from Franklin D. Roosevelt on, every President used the FBI for quasi-political surveillance. Wiretaps were common stuff. And the committee proceedings make it quite evident that the Kennedy White House knew of the CIA's arrangement with the Mafia to kill Fidel Castro.

With Nixon back in San Clemente, evidence that his predecessors had used similar methods elicited scarcely a peep from the Washington political and journalistic establishment. Indeed, some academicians began to hint that Nixon's tactics had been a lot less effective than those of his predecessors. Consider an analysis by Seymour Martin Lipset and Earl Raab:

The White House antics were nasty, but relatively ineffectual as an administrative game plan. A. Mitchell Palmer, attorney general after World War I, set up an extralegal intelligence agency, and promptly swept thousands of people into jail. Nixon's first attempt to set up an extralegal intelligence agency got shot down by one cross word from Hoover. The modified plumbers operation was neither massive nor very efficient. Second-story men all over the nation must still be chuckling over the Mack Sennett nature of the Watergate break-in itself.

The White House staff prepared lists of enemies, but for the most part they ended up in John Dean's files without being acted on. To harass people through their income tax, the White House staff sometimes had to resort to sending anonymous citizens letters to the IRS. And the results were scarcely impressive. They bugged the wrong phones. They tried to get something on Daniel Schorr of CBS, but only succeeded in annoying him. They produced little of the chilling effect that Senator McCarthy achieved in an essentially one-man operation. They found out nothing about Ellsberg, and indeed, managed only to guarantee his acquittal.[14]

For all that Nixon helped create his own problems, few Presidents were so surrounded by hostile capital elites, bureaucrats and journalists. Partly for that reason, his aides were simultaneously much less effective abusing civil liberties than other Administrations and much more likely to be brought to the bar for what they *did* attempt. Nicholas Von Hoffman, an iconoclastic columnist, has contended that Nixon was targeted by the establishment, impeached and destroyed because he was too much of a threat to the power structure. Conservatives are less inclined to voice that thesis so bluntly, but many share the suspicion.

The stakes were certainly high enough. Without Watergate, the 1972 election might (as argued in Chapter 4) have become a watershed election in American politics. Vested liberal interests and bureaucracies would have been challenged in much the way they were by Ronald Reagan, but eight years earlier. And the de-escalation and resolution of conflict in Southeast Asia would have been carried out in such a way as to put the blame for the embarrassment on the left or even the "liberal establishment."

Whether a second Nixon Administration would have been successful (the third of the questions posed a few pages back) is purely conjectural. Even without Watergate, the forces hostile to Nixon might well have been able to frustrate him politically within a year or two because of the 1973 oil shock and the 1973–75 recession. In his 1978 *Memoirs,* the former President himself does not dwell on the dynamics of what might have been. However, in an assessment published in 1976, Haldeman alleged that history had been most grievously frustrated:

It is interesting in looking back now, to think of what might have been, and what would not have been if Watergate had not swamped Nixon at the outset of his second term:

South Viet Nam would not have fallen. The final outcome in Viet Nam would have taken a far different turn than the tragic ending that did occur had Nixon not been weakened and instead had been able to deal with it firmly rather than in the wake of a collapse of U.S. credibility.

America's position in world diplomacy would be one of towering strength and leadership. Nixon, whom Bill Rogers [Secretary of State 1969–1973] referred to as the world's youngest elder statesman, had acquired enormous stature in world affairs, overseeing a thrust which would have placed this nation in the role less of a bullying policeman, and more in the terms of an innovative persuader.

Henry Kissinger would not be Secretary of State. There was never any thought of this appointment as a possibility—although there were going to be substantial changes at the State Department, from the top down.

The clumsy and regressive federal bureaucracy would have been totally restructured, despite stubborn resistance from bitter, anti-Nixon elitists entrenched in the woodwork. My firm view is that many bureaucrats, who knew that they would be fired or relocated by executive order (Congress simply would not provide the legislation), played a gleeful and decisive role in undoing the Nixon administration. In 1973 and 1974 the federal government became a massive sieve in an orgy of self-preservation.

The Republican Party would be entering Campaign '76 with the enormous strength of the New American Majority coalition Nixon had put together in winning the 1972 election. And there was every reason to believe that new gains would have been achieved in the congressional campaigns of 1974, and again this year.

The 1976 Republican presidential candidate would not have been either Jerry Ford or Ronald Reagan—but John Connally. Following Agnew's resignation, Connally would have been Nixon's selection for Vice President. But the President's weakened position dictated against fighting the Connally nomination through Senate confirmation hearings. The candidate this year would not have been Agnew even if his fall from grace had not occurred. The President would have decisively resolved that long before the convention.[15]

Haldeman makes for something less than a disinterested analyst, and his portrait of what might have been badly neglects energy problems and troubles with the economy. Vietnam, I think, would *not* have fallen with Nixon in the White House—former South Vietnamese Premier and, later, Vice President Nguyen Cao Ky has argued as much, and so have others.[16] But the oil shock of 1973 and the ensuing stagflation are something else again. Former Treasury Secretary John Connally, very much involved on this front, has suggested that his dealings with Saudi Arabia could have averted the problem by aborting OPEC's leverage before the 1973 oil price rise. The argument, however, that an energy price explosion was inevitable by 1972 seems far more compelling.

The institutional weaknesses of the American governmental system constitute another reason to be skeptical.

No one will ever know; but I, for one, am inclined to think that for the New Republican Majority to have successfully entrenched itself during the years 1973 to 1976 would have required a substantial, semiauthoritarian escalation of the Imperial Presidency. Without a concentration of political power—and we may yet see such escalation in the 1980s—national fragmentation and Balkanization probably would have gone on apace, Watergate or not. Former *Saturday Review* editor Norman Cousins characterized Watergate "a massive bill of particulars against the idea that history pays no attention to happenstance." Yes and no. We are still not sure what kind of event the burglary was, or whether a Nixon unburdened by Watergate could have surmounted the powerful forces working against him and Republican ascendance.

Which brings us to Question Four: Is Watergate the American Dreyfus case, a double-edged knife that will ultimately cut in a very different political direction? Professors Nisbet and Goodhart have by no means been the only ones to discuss the possibility. In *Harper's*, Jim Hougan quoted Howard Simons, managing editor of the Washington *Post*, as saying, "I had this nagging feeling that the Watergate might turn out like the Reichstag fire. You know, forty years from now will people still be asking did the guy set it and was he a German or was he just a crazy Dutchman?"[17]

Perhaps so. People may then still be asking. Although the controversy has done a thorough job of besmirching Richard Nixon's character, we live in an iconoclastic time. A history lecturer named Vincent Lindner has devoted himself to the rehabilitation of Revolutionary War archtraitor Benedict Arnold, and even the Roman Emperor Nero has his admirers—scholars who claim that Nero owes his disrepute to the biased chronicles of the early Christians. Besides, there are substantial, if not compelling, political and historical reasons to expect the Watergate issue to resurface. The resurgence of populist conservativism in the late 1970s and early 1980s has demonstrated the extent to which Watergate interrupted a long-term political trend. Arguably, the liberal interregnum that followed Nixon's overthrow was the aberration, not the tenure of Nixon himself. If that interpretation starts to attract adherents, interest should grow in the events of 1972–74. This is especially true with regard to foreign affairs, where the legacy of Watergate and Vietnam has been extremely crippling. If Watergate temporarily resolved the issue of whom to blame for Vietnam by undermining the presidency and rejecting conservative precepts of national security, then at some point conservatives may feel that maintenance of a conservative posture on defense issues requires a re-evaluation of what happened in Vietnam, which in turn could also lead to Watergate revisionism. As Chapter 13 points out, American political history has, without exception, seen past wars refought at the polls. Because of Watergate, the war in Vietnam may—or may not—be the exception.

The Reagan Administration, with its notion of an American renaissance linked to free enterprise, has shown little inclination to rake these coals. Ronald Reagan, unlike his rivals for the 1980 Republican nomination, had no connection, no involvement with Watergate. Unanswered questions about the break-in haunt him not at all. But if the economic hopes of the Reaganites go a-glimmering, if social tensions and fragmentation redevelop, if the country resumes its post-1974 historical slippage, then the Watergate issue is likely to fester and grow, because as the cynical Nicholas Von Hoffman put it back in 1975:

> In 15 or 20 years what will the revisionist historians make of all the moralistic onanism prompted by the Nixon fantasy figure? For sure, the future historians will make short work of the idea of a diabolic Nixon and will, instead, interest themselves in how and why virtually a whole society lost the remnants of balanced judgment and fell on the man like a compacted mob.[18]

6

THE
BALKANIZATION
OF AMERICA*

BY NO MEANS ALL OF THE DISILLUSIONMENT AND DIS-
solution visited on the United States since the 1960s can be encompassed in simple categories: morality, economics, military preparedness and the public's perception of its institutions. And it is not
enough to calibrate the alleged decline of the nation by the disruptions fostered by Vietnam and Watergate, the inflationary increase
in the money supply, or the second-place number of ship miles
logged by our Navy in the Indian Ocean. Would that our national
problem were a simple statistical matter. Unhappily for us all, the
larger crisis of spirit engaging the nation has relatively little to do
with vagaries of M-1B versus M-1C or the too old and too few heavy
bombers able or unable to reach Novosibirsk in a Maximum Alert.
One can argue—and I will—that the Union of the United States
(both as an idea and as a matter of domestic political geography) has
been unraveling in more fundamental ways. It is no small irony that

*Adapted from my article with the same title, in *Harper's* (May 1978).

even as modern American technology has learned to package instant steel-bonding cyanoacrylate in a dime-store tube, the bonds of the society itself should be weakening or dissolving.

All too many examples suggest themselves: the congealing of the melting pot and the re-emergence of ethnicity; the proliferation of sexual preference and religious cults; the new political geography of localism and neighborhoods; the substitution of causes for political parties; the fragmentation of government; the narrowing of personal loyalties in general; the twilight of authority. In 1976 James Schlesinger, who had not yet ascended to the dismal Cabinet eminence of Energy Secretary, suggested that the energy crisis might bring about the "Balkanization" of America. Fair enough. The parochial politics of energy do smack enough of Bulgarian or Serbian bickering circa 1911 to make the term "Balkanization" reasonably appropriate. In a larger perspective, however, the trend that Schlesinger feared had already established itself as a fact of national life. As the politics of natural-gas pipelines resembles the plots and counterplots of Sofia and Zagreb, so also one can find just as much social Balkanization in the rise of feminism or "gay rights," or in the "Red Power" demands of American Indians—for tribal sovereignty and the return of Indian lands—from Maine to California. Throughout the 1970s the symptoms of decomposition appeared throughout the body politic—in the economic, geographic, ethnic, religious, cultural, biological components of our society. Small loyalties have been replacing larger ones. Small views have been replacing larger ones.

Some would offer "tribalism" as a better descriptive word. But "Balkanization," though in some ways conceptually inadequate to a new teletronic age, has a unique historical-imperial relevance. For most of us, the Balkans are vague enough geographically. (Is Greece Balkan? Is Hungary?) Balkan history, in turn, is no more than a blue haze of Turkish cigarette smoke in an Eric Ambler movie. But the Balkans were once part of the Turkish and Austro-Hungarian empires. In the eighteenth century, when those imperial realms were relatively stable, the Balkans had yet to become a symbol for the cultural and political crumbling of empire. Collapsed imperialism is among the richest and most fertile of soil for the growth of separatism and parochialism.

By historical analogy, then, the Balkanization of America is closely related to what Andrew Hacker has called "the end of the American era." Can it be coincidental that U.S. political and social decomposition accelerated with our exit from Vietnam and the end of Pax Americana, the concurrent failure of the Great Society, the end of energy abundance, the downfall of cultural optimism, and—of course—Watergate and public loss of confidence in the political system? On the contrary, the breakdown of these unities, hopes and glories has been enough to send Americans, too, scrambling after less exalting forms of self-identification: ethnicity, regionalism, selfish economic interests, sects and neighborhoods.

At this point, let me admit that regionalism, separatism, fragmentation and rampant ethnicity are hardly new in the United States. On the contrary, they are as old as Jamestown, New Amsterdam and Plymouth. But the critical historical distinction must lie in tidal flow and ebb: from George Washington's day through the Trajan-like imperial high-water mark of the early 1960s, Americans saw ethnicity, regionalism and states' rights yield before concepts of global optimism, the melting pot, equality, homogeneity and centralization of (benign federal) power. Since the early 1960s, however, the re-emergence of localism has occurred in a very different psychological climate—amidst the *end* of optimism, the *collapse* of Manifest Destiny, the *failure* of the Great Society, the *failure* of the melting pot, and of all the other hopes and slogans of America's national rise. Accept the distinction, and the force of the current Balkanization takes on a significance little rebutted by invocations of ethnicity circa 1880, regionalism circa 1896, feminism circa 1912, or states' rights circa 1948. Only the time before the Civil War offers some parallel.

Let's begin with the most frequently discussed example of the phenomenon, which in many ways is also the pivot: Sun Belt versus Frost Belt. To be sure, regional conflict has been a staple of American history—as late as 1948, Harry Truman declaimed that the Northeast treated the South and the West like colonies. What *is* new is the first regional attempt in over a century to remove national leadership from the Northeast. Thirteen years ago, when I coined the term "Sun Belt," it seemed like a good phrase for a boom region owing its ascendance to the shining of the sun: tourism, retirement, irrigated agribusiness, year-round military facilities. But over the past decade the term has come to represent a phenomenon of much greater importance.

So competition for natural and energy resources is one major factor in the increasingly high-voltage regional rivalries. By and large the Sun Belt states, which contain most of the country's oil and natural gas, favor energy deregulation. Support for allocation and conservation, meanwhile, is centered in the North. Mutual suspicion characterizes the attitudes of both factions. The Washington lobbyist for the state of Louisiana told an interviewer in 1977 that "the attitudes today are the same as those preceding the Civil War. The North wants everything its own way. This time it won't get it." Louisiana's governor threatened to withhold natural gas from interstate markets, claiming that while the U.S. Constitution may prohibit the restraint of interstate trade, "it doesn't prohibit the conservation of natural resources." True enough.

The point hardly need be dwelt upon for anyone who has seen Texas bumper stickers ("Drive fast, freeze a Yankee") or who has noticed hostile alignments of Sun Belt and Frost Belt political organizations and lobby groups. Less well known is the extent of squabbles over water and energy at the state level. Virginia and North Carolina have been fighting over water from the Roanoke and Chowan rivers; Arizona and California over the Colorado River. Dixy Lee Ray, as governor of Washington, told Congress that "the Northwest is poised for a regional civil war—an interstate battle over the allocation of low-cost federal power." Washington has even quarreled with Idaho over rain clouds. When the state of Washington in 1977 proposed cloud seeding that might divert potential Idaho rainfall to Washington, Wayne Kidwell, Idaho's attorney general, threatened to go to the U.S. Supreme Court.

The state of Michigan has tried—and failed—to recruit neighboring Ohio, Indiana, Illinois, Wisconsin and Minnesota for a "Great Lakes Common Market." Oregon, Hawaii and other states plot to stem the flow of new immigrants, taking a leaf from cities like Boca Raton, Florida; Boulder, Colorado; Petaluma, California; and Ramapo, New York. But Hawaiians have thought more boldly: Governor George R. Ariyoshi has urged amending the Constitution to permit a state to limit the number of new residents it accepts.

Such demographic protectionism could be dismissed if it didn't square so fully, or so disturbingly, with other aspects of economic Balkanization. In Congress, for example, an unprecedented number of special-interest caucuses have grown up alongside the regular party and committee structures. Some of these caucuses are *geographic*—New England, Sun Belt, suburban—but others are *economic* in nature, namely steel, tobacco and ports (maritime). They reflect the domestic aspect of the trade wars taking place in the international arena. Industry after industry, meanwhile, puts more emphasis on mobilizing influence, establishing or beefing up industry-wide political-action committees, and moving its trade association to Washington, where the critical political-economic wars are being fought.

Economic and geographic Balkanization is at once confirmed and, if anything, surpassed by the biological fragmentation rampant in the country. Five biological denominators currently lend themselves to civil rights campaigns and the assertion of group identities: sex, sexual preference, age, race and ethnic origin.

Fragmentation of American society by sex and sexual-preference groups need not be elaborated on here, given the massive extent to which it has been dwelt upon elsewhere. Escalating definitions of "rights" produce at least two unfortunate results: group categorization and militancy. Feminism, of course, has gone far beyond the precepts of Susan B. Anthony. And certainly the organization, cohesion and civil rights militancy of homosexuals is a new phenomenon in American society—"Gay Power" has as much political weight in San Francisco, and perhaps Manhattan, as does the steel caucus in Ohio's Mahoning Valley.

Age is yet another denominator. The group awareness of senior citizens—"gray power"—is a considerable phenomenon in Florida, Arizona and California. At the other end of the age chart, more and more legal rights are being defined for children. Even second- and third-trimester fetuses have had their own biopolitical Balkan army marshaled for them in the right-to-life movement.

Racial Balkanization can be seen in two ways. On the one hand, pre-1960s segregation resulted in what was in effect two nations—one white, one black. Against *that* historical reality, desegregation has increased racial unity. On the other hand, the last few years have seen a definite resegregation in many cities, coupled with a growth of black sentiment to go it alone. Today's trend toward predominantly non-white central cities raises critical questions, as does the racial-quota notion. Indeed, the use of either quotas or "affirmative action" programs verging on quotas is tantamount to an official recognition of Balkanization—acceptance of the notion that equality can be pursued only by racial and ethnic group categorization.

Therein lies the problem. The consequence of the attempt to *proscribe* discrimination may be to *prescribe* opportunity by various biological categories. Officially mandated quotas and preference for nonwhites have already produced a variety of unfortunate practices. In Queens County, New York, parents claiming a certain racial background in order to get their children assigned to a local school have been obliged to present themselves at a Board of Education racial-inspection office. Under the signature of the Honorable Bert Lance, the federal Office of Management and Budget in May 1977 promulgated guidelines for collecting uniform racial and ethnic data. Central or South American antecedents put you in a minority group; Middle East antecedents did not. Senator Daniel P. Moynihan invoked the specter of Germany's Nuremberg race laws.

There will be those who say, quite correctly, that such criteria are nothing new to America, that through the 1960s many state statutes included definitions of Negroes as persons of one-eighth or even one-thirty-second Negro ancestry. Such classifications were indisputably the stuff of cultural apartheid. The point is that we had seemed to be getting away from such racial measurements for a decade or so, but in the 1970s they re-emerged, along with official prescriptions for housing, education and employment eligibility. For public authorities to allocate jobs, school positions or apartments to blacks or Jamaicans rather than whites or Dutchmen is to put renewed emphasis on group consciousness, organization and politicking. No system can allocate benefits by race and ethnic group without making racial and ethnic group competition an overt component of politics.*

Meanwhile, ethnic consciousness is resurgent. Rev. Jesse Jackson, currently a black favorite of the white media, preaches a gospel of self-determination—"for us, by us, of us." In Joliet, Illinois, black parents have set up their own school rather than let their children be bused to predominantly white schools. Meanwhile, from Eastport and Nantucket to Palm Springs, Indians are asserting Red Power and seeking tribal sovereignty. What's more, the melting pot has become less attractive for Northwestern Europeans—even for the basic "Anglo-Saxon America" H. L. Mencken loathed so much. Dozens of Midwestern German towns have begun celebrating the *Oktoberfest* again, and Pan American World Airways has run commercials reminding white Anglo-Saxons of their British-American

*For example, the Italian-American caucus of the New York State legislature has talked about holding up funding of the CUNY (City University of New York) system because, whereas 25 percent of the students are Italo-Americans, few student advisers and only 6.4 percent of the faculty are.

heritage to get them to fly back to *their* "old country" the way the Italians and Norwegians do.

All in all, there's virtually no facet of human biology—sex, color, age, ethnic heritage—that did not become a denominator of social fragmentation during the 1970s. That phenomenon may have a precedent, but I don't know of one.

Predictably enough, the various geo-, eco- and bio-fragmentations are reflected in American cultural life. Despite the trend for local newspapers to be bought out by national chains, the trend with much more import is toward specialized publications. Our economic, geographic and biological Balkans all have their Baedekers and Michelins. More and more states and cities now claim their own magazines. Parochializing communications also rests on the growing Balkanization of language and knowledge. To an increasing extent, Americans speak different, and specialized, languages.

Several recent studies conclude that the effective life span of technical and vocational knowledge has been dramatically abbreviated. Scientists and engineers now find half of their technical expertise becoming obsolete every six years. Dentists and doctors suffer from kindred problems, at least in some specialized fields. So do lawyers and accountants. In George Washington's day, a man of intellect had relatively little printed matter to engage him—some Greek and Roman tracts, the writings of Locke and Blackstone, and a few local newspapers. The larger, more useful sum of knowledge came from the actual experience—in farming, say, and in commanding troops and participating in government. The expansion of knowledge has changed all that. Specialized expertise is necessary to be effective in more and more endeavors.

If biological and cultural Balkanization illustrates the breadth of our impetus for national fragmentation, potentially more important symptoms are visible in the decomposition of the American polity. Only ten to fifteen years ago, it seemed that states' rights would succumb to a benign centralism, that the flow of public opinion favored federal authority, with less and less of a role for local government, education and customs. The presidency became increasingly potent, its imperial promise accredited by no less a prophet than Professor Arthur Schlesinger, Jr. If anything, we expected further growth in universal norms—for the onset of metropolitan government in our cities, for racial integration, for the disappearance of state lines, and even for the possible loss of national identity to a new world order.

Instead, over the past few years, the tide has begun running strongly in the other direction. Far from becoming an effective world federation, the United Nations is being made less and less useful by the admission of dozens of small states and mini-states. The collapse of colonial empires has created nearly a hundred new nations, many of them barely credible. In Europe, Belgium and Luxembourg have *not* been incorporated into a new United States of Europe. Belgium itself is dissolving into Flemings and Walloons. Resurgent parochialism is the theme. Scotland flies its Red Lion once again, and Wales its Dragon. Brittany and Corsica would like to detach themselves from France. Nearer home, Quebec threatens to secede from Canada.

Too few Americans realize the extent to which we have similar problems. As former Congressman Lloyd Meeds put it, the growing demand of American Indian tribes for "sovereignty" over their reservation lands presents the prospect of *two hundred and sixty* Quebecs! In Washington State, the Tacoma Indians bought up lots in Tacoma (which used to be Indian land), opened package stores and claimed immunity from local liquor-sales ordinances. Some of Arizona's Navajos would like to secede and join their fellow tribesmen in New Mexico. And so on.

Demographers also have begun to draw attention to the huge and fast-growing American Hispanic minority, with Hispanics outnumbering blacks in a generation. Each year the Southwestern states increase their percentage of Spanish-speaking residents—many of them legal, many not. In Texas and California the concentration of huge Hispanic populations (and the prospect that Mexico's poverty and birth rate can only spur more emigration) has prompted talk of a *reconquista*—a literal Spanish reconquest of the once Spanish Southwest.

Nor is the splintering impulse confined to nonwhites. If the Indians of Mashpee, Massachusetts, have been trying to reclaim lost land, only a few miles away on Nantucket and Martha's Vineyard white Massachusetts citizens have raised their own banner of separatism, threatening to secede from the Bay State and attach themselves to another New England state. Even the landlocked town of Salisbury on the Massachusetts–New Hampshire line considered trying to join low-tax New Hampshire. The phenomenon is national. The rumors and possibilities extend from southern New Jersey and the Outer Banks of North Carolina to Michigan's Upper Peninsula, Northern California and the panhandles of Idaho and Nebraska.

Moreover, similar moods and movements exist on an *intrastate* level. In California, for example, residents of eastern San Bernardino and Riverside counties have urged formation of a new desert county, while some northwest Los Angeles County residents continued their campaign for a new "Canyon County." Just across Lake Tahoe in Nevada, residents of one stretch of lakefront would like to secede from Washoe County (Reno) and establish a new Lake County. Parallels abound.

Then there is Washington, D.C. Over the past fifteen years the executive and legislative branches of the federal government have beefed themselves up in a new kind of staff war rivalry. Congressional staffs have multiplied to enable representatives and senators to entrench themselves institutionally as well as electorally. If the White House has a Budget Office (or a National Security Council or a Science/Technology Office), well, then, so must the Congress. For years, much of this intellectual-political arms race was attributed to the 1969–76 desire of a Democratic Congress to match the resources of the GOP White House. But during the presidency of Democrat Jimmy Carter, the institutional Balkanization of Washington took on a life of its own.

The phenomenon is a long way from being quaint or harmless. Richard Nixon was infuriated by his inability to control the government from the White House, and his frustration brought him much of the way to Watergate. In his book *The Ends of Power,* Haldeman explains how, as of 1972 and 1973, the "four major power blocs in Washington"—the press, the bureaucracy, the Congress, the intelligence community—were "under threat" by a President who hoped to use various reorganization techniques to break the independent, unresponsive authority of the bureaucracy and the Central Intelligence Agency. As noted, Haldeman saw the critical Watergate events of the spring of 1973 not as the grinding of the wheels of justice but as a coup d'état by the threatened interests. To be sure, most Americans will not accept Haldeman's effort to make Watergate into a power play engendered by the Washington elite. It's an interesting analysis, however, and worth pondering with a larger question: How can any President curb these power blocs for any length of time? The experience of the last twenty years suggests that it will be difficult within the existing framework of government. The U.S. Constitution's notion of "separation of powers," borrowed by the Founding Fathers from the eighteenth-century French philosopher Montesquieu, has become a trap. The "separate" powers are now *too* separate. Government in Washington all too often resembles a series of bunkers held by mutually suspicious troops, and nothing in the Constitution provides for issuing orders to demobilize.

Elsewhere along the Potomac, the judicial branch has also usurped an independent role for itself—virtually legislative—unmatched by the judiciary of any other major Western nation. In the country at large, federal judges are even taking over administration of state prisons and urban school systems, and scholars are seriously arguing whether our judiciary may now be running amok.

Further evidence of Balkanization can be found *within* the several branches of government. If the executive has rival bureaucracies, Congress, for its part, has been divided by new subgroups and special-interest mechanisms. An article several years ago in *Roll Call,* the weekly newspaper of Capitol Hill, brought to light new feudal arrangement of things: "Subcommittee staffs have grown which no longer feel responsible to the committee chairman, central authority and discipline have eroded, and lobbyists have learned how to take advantage of this situation by playing one committee against another, or as one veteran put it, 'playing one Balkan prince against another Balkan prince.' " From yet another perspective, the early ideological subgroupings that took shape in Congress during the 1960s paralleled and respected party divisions—the Democratic Study Group for party liberals, the Republican Study Group for GOP conservatives, the Wednesday Club for GOP liberals. Over the past decade, a new set of caucuses has grown up to promote special interests across party lines. And Sun Belt and Frost Belt forces are already marching up and down the aisles of Congress, turning debate after debate into a display of comparative and combative economic geography.

Arguably, these nonparty mechanisms have come into being in part because the 125-year-old Republican-Democratic party system is no longer an effective arbiter of regional, cultural and economic differences (just as its predecessor system during the 1850s wasn't). Indeed, talk of a breakdown in the two-party system or the need for new parties is a periodic but recurrent item of political discussion. There is nothing unusual about this; we have had splinter movements before, usually absorbed by one of the major parties in periodic realignments. What *is* unusual is the way the party mechanisms, at least prior to 1980, have been unwilling to respond to public desires. Many Americans have either loosened their affiliation, begun to put ideology ahead of party or simply decided not to vote. From time to time, issues like abortion, gun control, the right to work, taxes, busing, feminism and "gay" liberation appear to be superseding parties as the basis of political mobilization. The obvious description: *ideological* Balkanization.

Under the circumstances, with Washington divided against itself and the expansion of federal power increasingly forsworn or discredited, small wonder that the individual states are now trying to reassert their roles. Vitality is now local, not federal, and the trend of the 1960s has been reversed. Thirty-some years ago, the late Hubert Humphrey urged the Democratic Party to leave the shadow of states' rights and step into the sunlight of human rights. Now, sad to say, "human rights" has become a cliché, while states' rights—everything from water policy to urban development—is a battle cry heard with increased frequency and attention. Colorado's Democratic governor, Richard Lamm, has said: "The day of the state has come and gone —and come back again." Similarly, state and local governments with employees in the tens of thousands have been opting out of the federal Social Security system, with termination notices delivered to Washington by units ranging from the Sewerage and Water Board of New Orleans to the entire state of Alaska.

Our nation has been divided and fragmented before, but (save for the Civil War) the underlying trend pointed toward unity, fraternity and increasing federal authority. Major elements of American society now seem determined to pursue smaller loyalties: regional, economic, political, ethnic and even sexual. Unless the trend reverses itself in the next few years—and no such prospect is apparent—it may bespeak a fundamental reversal in the American experience. The heterogeneity of America could become a burden, the constitutional separation of powers an albatross, and the cohesion of society further diminished. Which brings us to the unhappy question: Is American Balkanization a sign of national decline?

I think it is such a sign, despite the optimism and relevance of counterarguments perceiving strength, not weakness, in the renewed closeness of Americans to neighborhood, ethnic and regional roots. The overall hypothesis of decline is too well supported by the great theories of biological, psychological and historical-cultural evolution. Progress and growth has always come from a movement away from the limited, the parochial, to the more general and universal. This is true whether one cites Charles Darwin on the evolution of species, Sigmund Freud's analyses of personality, or Arnold Toynbee's theories of history. A species, a personality or an empire—all grow or rise from the parochial to the general and then, as their hour or role passes, become parochial once again. When the impetus toward the universal expires, particularisms—of function, personality, culture or politics—reassert themselves. "Parochial" and "clannish" are negative concepts, even though terms like "grass roots," "homeland," "kinfolk" and "bedrock" sound fine.

Given the imperial, political and social aspects of the Balkanization of America, Toynbee's analysis is perhaps the most useful here, linking as it does the rise of a great nation to its *élan vital* and the leadership of a creative minority able to define national values and goals. But that period of growth does not last forever. Sooner or later there comes a failure of creativity and an end to mass inspiration. At this point, in Toynbee's words,

> the loss of harmony between elements which had formerly coexisted in a society as an integral whole leads inevitably to an outbreak of social discord. The broken-down society is rent in two different dimensions simultaneously by the social schisms in which this discord is expressed. There are "vertical" schisms between geographically segregated communities and "horizontal" schisms between geographically intermingled but socially segregated classes.

Too much schema, perhaps, but insightful nonetheless. The "articulation of society into a number of parochial states" that Toynbee posited describes all too well the process at work in contemporary America. Various kinds of vertical and horizontal schisms are apparent all around us. Less apparent to most upper-middle-income Americans, however, is the deepening socioeconomic disillusionment of the poorer third of the American population, with consumer-confidence surveys illustrating a marked attitudinal disparity. Upper-middle-income professionals may be buying imported cheese at $4.50 a pound, but low-income and lower-middle-income Americans are losing economic hope. The American Dream is slipping away. A few pollsters such as Louis Harris play down such attitudes, saying that people are developing a new nonmaterialist outlook. Perhaps. If Harris isn't correct, though, economically and socially disillusioned "Middle America" may represent the "internal proletariat" that Toynbee found characteristic of every disintegrating major civilization.

For another of Toynbee's measurements—unproductive leadership by a "dominant minority" that has lost its earlier creativity—we have only to look at our current national leadership elites. The "Eastern establishment" that imposed Pax Americana on the post–World War II world has now given way to a "Parody establishment" wearing the same tailored suits and bench-made shoes but lacking the élan of their predecessors in the 1940s, 1950s and even in the 1960s. The national media elite is no better. Indeed, today's American Balkanization in large measure represents the failure of these leadership elites to understand the simple facts of race, ethnicity, territory, greed and inequality.

Approached from yet another direction, the failures of the 1960s and 1970s have helped bring on what conservative sociologist Robert Nisbet has called "the twilight of authority." His thesis: the United States has lost its sense of authority and common purpose—more or less Toynbee's *élan vital* and the Romans' *civitas*. The crumbling of authority is certainly clear enough, not just in polls measuring popular attitudes toward leading institutions but in the events of the past decade and a half. Yesterday's "Eastern establishment" has been partially displaced by provincial centers of power—regional, cultural and institutional—but none of these has had the energy to assume effective national command. Ronald Reagan's three elected predecessors, Johnson, Nixon and Carter, all from the aspirant Sun Belt, epitomize the process of disintegration. The old establishment can no longer elect a President, but its influence, combined with the simultaneous institutional and political confusion of Balkanization, can make it almost impossible for an arriviste to govern. The verdict is still out on Ronald Reagan. But Jimmy Carter couldn't. Lyndon Johnson couldn't. And Richard Nixon was impeached. Choke on the thought as many will, it's even possible that the former President may become a rallying point of sorts. As noted in the prior chapter, both conservatives and New Left critics feel that Nixon was, in essence, driven from office by the machinations of Washington's

established power blocs after the election of 1972 suggested that a
new elite was, finally, on the verge of taking command.

Finally, the sexual and religious Balkanization of America offers
another glum thought. In an interview Will and Ariel Durant expressed concern that

> we're in the stage in which Greece was when the gods ceased to be gods
> and became mere poetry, and therefore exercised no element of order or
> command upon human behavior. There was the development of city life,
> of science and philosophy, and the result was a period of pagan license
> —say around 200 B.C. to 100 A.D.—in which morals floundered in an
> ocean of competing religions, just as you have a flotsam and jetsam of
> religions today. By the time of Caesar, you had a permissive society and
> a pagan society in the sense of sexual enjoyment with a minimal moral
> restraint. Now . . . we shall have to wait for a new religion, the way the
> Greeks and Romans did, because . . . what happened was the old civiliza-
> tion decayed to a point where it cried out for a new religion, for some-
> thing to worship and obey.

Of course, Balkanization is not all bad. No doubt cheerful things
can be said about the new commitment to localism, to neighborhood,
to the near and dear, to family and church. But much of this now
seems romantic and sentimental—the obverse of the last decade's
romantic universalism. Too many of the same naïve people who were
for global unity a decade or two ago are now saying "Small is
beautiful" and waxing poetic over self-governing Vermont com-
munes and renovated central-city blocks of brownstones. The trouble
is that these regional, ethnic and local forces are now taking place
within a general movement of social fragmentation and decomposition, and do not show as they did in our past evidence of grass-roots
cultural vigor and a functioning political federalism. *Decomposition
is not revitalized diversity.* Moreover, our country as it is today and
its role in the world means that small-is-beautiful is likely to be
subverted by small-is-divisive or even small-is-dangerous. An ineffective American political system during the 1980s cannot be compared
to the loose, immature political system of the 1880s. Under current
circumstances, a Balkanized America is likely to lose its way, in the
external word of nuclear missiles and global oil supplies, and in the
internal world—the mind of the American people.

And the future? Just as nature abhors a vacuum, history abhors fragmentation. Some sort of new, sweeping force—a charismatic politics or a religious revival—could come out of America's contemporary muddle. A new universalism may yet unite our political, geographic, religious, biological and economic factions. In the meantime, policies that do not recognize our Balkanization are probably doomed to promote it.

7

AFTER THE SUN BELT, WHAT NEW FORCES?

> Kevin Phillips, constructing charts on the new shape of the elector-
> ate, lays special emphasis on what he calls "the Sunbelt"—a new
> geographic and demographic phenomenon of great importance: it
> stretches from Florida across Texas and Arizona to Southern Califor-
> nia, a particularly bilious compound of the new and old, of space
> programs and retirement villas, honky-tonks and superconservatism.
> This may be the face of America tomorrow, technological and affluent,
> disillusioned and reactionary, wanting all the comforts of science and
> of simplicity, a world of cushy gerontology . . .
>
> —Garry Wills, "God So Loves Spiro Agnew," *Esquire* (February
> 1969)

THE BALKANIZATION OF THE COUNTRY DURING THE
1970s helped to define and therefore fuel the emergence of the Sun
Belt, the victor in a geopolitical struggle. And as of the early 1980s,
a new regional supremacy had been established. But now the forces
that elevated the constituencies of J. R. Ewing and Jerry Falwell to
such a pivotal political importance are well-entrenched, middle-aged
at the very least. By the late 1980s, new trends, and various new
cutting edges, will demand attention. So the future of the hype
machine producing the "new" and "better" in data and electoral
surmises is safe.

But in politics very little is as fresh as it first appears. In 1965 the
shape of our politics to come in the 1970s could be predicted: it would
feature a competition between three sets of demographics. Migration
to the Sun Belt comprised one set, but the other two buttressed very
different political forecasts—first, the tremendous "war baby" bulge,
then just beginning to work its way into the adult population and
moral ethos, and second, the already well established migration

north of millions of Southern-born blacks, a shift that was to ensure the success of the civil rights revolution. Forecasters noted that the youth bulge, the largest of its sort in American history, would peak in the mid-to-late 1960s, vastly enlarging the university community, nurturing semi-intellectual conurbations from Back Bay and SoHo to Haight-Ashbury, commissioning a new fervor in music, fueling and upheaval in sexual and moral behavior, and unleashing a general cult of youth in culture and commerce alike. That much was generally predictable. The war in Vietnam, soon to be the catalyst for an unforeseen impact, could *not* be predicted. Neither could the scope of the moral and sexual revolution—or the backlash it would produce. As for the black migration to the urban North, analysts could and did anticipate new social pressures on the South. Civil rights progress would accelerate. Racial issues would come even more to the fore. But few observers, even black militants, predicted the riots that would break out.

From the late 1950s through the early 1970s, attention was focused on the two more newsworthy and visible trends with liberal consequences. The third demographic force—older, quieter and with profound conservative implications—drew less attention. But if blacks had been coming North in large numbers since World War II, leaving South Carolina for Newark and Tennessee for Chicago, white Americans—most of them middle-class and many of them retirees —had been flocking to what seemed to me appropriate in 1968 to characterize as the "Sun Belt."* The attractions were aerospace and high technology, military installations and employment, sunny vacations or retirement, and a sociology very different from that of the urban North. Even by 1960, the regional and geopolitical implications of postwar population trends were unmistakable.

At first, as the various convulsions of the 1960s widened and deepened, initial advantage accrued to the *liberal* political-demographic streams. In the 1964 presidential election the Sun Belt lost,

*Not realizing that my term would gain such wide embrace, I used it in 1968 in *The Emerging Republican Majority* without any definition more precise than "from the Charleston-Savannah-Jacksonville coastal strip to California's urban South." By 1972 I found myself citing the 37th parallel, a line a bit north of the North Carolina–Tennessee border, to the west following the Oklahoma, New Mexico and Arizona boundaries, and then cutting through Nevada and California. That seems to be the present-day consensus, but the term was in use for some years before it gained wide currency in 1973–74, so the definition has always been a bit vague—and no boundary is entirely satisfactory.

and the civil rights and youth movements won. Then, by 1968, the two liberal trends-cum-demographic streams had begun to generate a large backlash, enabling Richard Nixon to put the Sun Belt in the White House. Four years later, with George Wallace—voice of the 1968 backlash—out of the race, the regional dynamics crushed the liberals. The Sun Belt was the dominant feature of the Nixon landslide, while blacks and youth causists were pillars of George McGovern's losing candidacy. Even the U.S. constitutional amendment extending the franchise to eighteen-year-olds made no real difference. Sun Belt and Southern trend groups dominated the upcoming decade.

Ironically, though, a fierce and political-demographic interpretative battle continued to rage through the Nixon years. Moderates argued that the future lay with a coalition capable of winning young and pro-change voters, along with the blacks, who they thought would play an increasingly pivotal role in Southern elections. The liberal Republican Ripon Society played this trumpet lovingly. Conservatives, by contrast, plunked for going after Sun Belt votes, along with three other demographic groups identifiable and emergent since the sixties: (1) the new suburbanites and peripheral urban ethnics of the Northern cities, many of them chased out of the cities by crime, riots, social engineering and high taxes; (2) the rapidly mushrooming evangelical/fundamentalist segment of the religious electorate; and (3) the elderly. Of the new conservative targets, the first two were reactive groups—religious and sociological refugees—while the third, the elderly, were perhaps psychological refugees. Meanwhile, as the population began to age, the political importance of those born from 1945 to 1955 started to wane as that of the escalating ranks of persons over 65 came to the fore. The 1970s was a decade in which the concerns of the old would begin to overmatch those of the young, which could have been predicted even as the last antiwar demonstration raged on the last angry campus.

The new power balance was writ large in 1972 returns. But Watergate enveloped the election, crushing awareness of its significance— the triumph of the new conservative demographics. No matter what the election demonstrated, analysts assumed they had no meaning for the future, a conclusion partially confirmed by the results of the 1976 election. Trading on Watergate, winner Jimmy Carter flukishly cut into two GOP trend groups: the South/Sun Belt and evangelical Protestants. No changing demographics were involved. Without the institutional devastation of Watergate and election law reform to the party structures and nominating processes, the Democrats would never have nominated a middle-of-the-road Georgia Baptist Sunday school teacher, and the electoral aberrations would not have occurred. However, Carter's very geopolitical flukishness, to say nothing of his own personal style, made Carter not only a Washington outsider but also a preordained failure. His Administration thereby spurred Balkanization and fragmentation. The Watergate warp thus coming to an end, the various constituencies on the demographic board of presidential politics in 1980 became free to arrange themselves in more logical alliances—to resurrect many of the trends of 1972.

And that is what happened. "New Majority" demographics returned with a vengeance. Although Ronald Reagan's share of the total popular vote was just slightly over 2 percentage points above Gerald Ford's, the 1980 Republican vote was much more Sun Belt–tilted and much more strongly infused by white Southern evangelical Protestants. Chart 5 shows the massive Reagan edge in five archetypal Sun Belt counties. To an extent hardly anyone would have believed possible in 1960, these counties and others like them are now massively outvoting the Bostons, Newarks, Baltimores, St. Louises and Milwaukees. The geopolitical balance of power is now firmly in the hands of the Sun Belters. As for the fundamentalist Protestants, several national polls gave us pointed confirmation of *their* 1976–80 shift. In a little-noted post-election analysis, pollster Louis Harris said the key to the election rested in the hands of the 28 percent of the voters who are "followers of the so-called Moral Majority TV preachers." "Most specifically," Harris said, "it was their efforts which largely turned around the Baptist vote in the South. Jimmy Carter won the white Baptist vote in 1976 by 56–43% against Gerald Ford. This time, he *lost* the white Baptists by a 56–34% margin. The white followers of TV evangelical preachers gave Reagan two thirds of his 10-point margin in the election."[1]

Other polls confirm the basic trend: CBS/New York Times Election Day surveys found the white born-again Christian vote going to Reagan over Carter by 64–32 percent; ABC News exit polls found white Southern Protestants picking Reagan over Carter by 66–30 percent. A Southern Regional Council analysis found Dixie blacks going 90 percent for Carter, while Southern whites went 70 percent for Reagan. Meanwhile, the youth vote splintered; the black elector-

Chart 5   *The Sun Belt–Frost Belt Metropolitan Power Shift*

Sun Belt County	1960		1972		1980	
	%R	GOP Majority	%R	GOP Majority	%R	GOP Majority
Orange (Fla.)						
—Orlando	71%	29,000	80%	71,000	61%	39,000
Dallas (Texas)	62	60,000	70	176,000	59	116,000
Maricopa (Ariz.)						
—Phoenix	59	40,000	69	149,000	65	196,000
Orange (Calif.)						
—Anaheim	61	63,000	68	271,000	68	347,000
San Diego (Calif.)	56	52,000	62	165,000	61	233,000

Frost Belt County	1960		1972		1980	
	%R	Dem. Majority	%R	Dem. Majority	%R	Dem. Majority
Suffolk (Mass.)						
—Boston	25%	167,000	34%	81,000	34%	40,000
Essex (N.J.)						
—Newark	43	50,000	50	(GOP majority)	41	28,000
Baltimore City (Md.)	36	88,000	45	22,000	22	134,000
St. Louis City (Mo.)	33	101,000	38	47,000	29	62,000
Milwaukee (Wis.)	42	71,000	46	19,000	40	57,000

ate demonstrated relatively weak participation (7 percent of the total) and no pivotal leverage.

In short, between 1960 and 1980 the demographic balance had tipped to right-leaning national constituencies. Of the three contending demographic forces apparent in 1960, the potential of the youth and black vote dissipated, but only after first generating a backlash among what Richard Nixon called "the Silent Majority." And so the Sun Belt came into dominance, with the Reagan election cementing fashionable understanding. Journalists to whom the Sun Belt forecasts of 1969 had seemed an arcane implausibility came to use the term "Sun Belt power" as a cliché by 1981. In 1982, for the first time in history, the South and West received more than half the seats in the U.S. House of Representatives. The population center of the United States had crossed the Mississippi River, to De Soto, Missouri, en route to the Ozarks and possibly Oklahoma. And someone figured out that (such was the extent of the population and electoral vote migration) a presidential candidate could now *win* by carrying the same states loser Richard Nixon took in 1960.* Six of the ten biggest cities—Los Angeles, Houston, Dallas, San Antonio, San Diego and Phoenix—now lie in the Sun Belt. And as Map 1 shows, population forecasts predict more of the same through at least the year 2000. In the face of such data, even former Lyndon Johnson Great Society drumbeaters found themselves saying that the Reagan Administration marked the beginning of a new Sun Belt conservative era.

Which is why one should begin to entertain doubts. American politics works like the stock market: when all the experts agree it's time to buy, it's usually time to sell. Too often analysts assess the past and project from that into the future rather than trying to look at the future itself. For many of the commentators embracing the political demographic revolution of the 1980 election, it really was new— or at least new as an *accepted* trend. A few years earlier they had been buying notions of a "brownstone" revolution of young progressives pouring back into the cities. Or Louis Harris' notion of a neo-McGovernite "change coalition." Or the periodic incantation of a liberal, biracial "New South." All of these concepts-cum-hopes became fashionable during the post-Watergate interregnum, then

*Under the new electoral calculus, William Jennings Bryan would also have been an easy winner in 1896.

withered on the electoral vine in 1980, as naïve demography yielded to statistical self-flagellation. Liberal America, shattered, came to accept "Dallas" not just as a television program but as a new political and social era.

Far be it from me to denigrate the Sun Belt and associated trends. I knew them as pups, and that's the point. They're not pups anymore. It's been over twenty years since the United States elected a non–Sun Belt President. The age of the average American voter started climbing in the 1970s, and "gray power" came into the political lexicon a decade ago. The shift right of the evangelical vote has been apparent since 1968, paralleling the growth of fundamentalist churches and country music. All of these electorates have been largely conservative since the 1960s, a decade in which—if I may be bluntly perjorative —American liberalism allowed itself to become tagged as the politics of drugs, dudes, deficits and disarmament. Adverse reaction in the Sun Belt and the mushrooming evangelical constituency was inevitable.

The upcoming decade may tell a different story. The Sun Belt, the fundamentalist Protestant electorate and the elderly will be powerful, high-profile constituencies, bathing in national attention. But the larger question is whether they can maintain conservative headway as the terms of political debate change. If they can't, the analysis predicated on the institutionalization of electoral patterns of 1980 must go by the boards. Republican free-market, Coolidge-restoration economics in particular may raise regional fears.

Consider Sun Belt political and economic history. Two generations ago, no major region of the United States provided less support for Calvin Coolidge or more for Franklin D. Roosevelt. Which is another way of saying that the Sun Belt possesses little local Republican tradition, though it does have a long record of affection for government help—from cotton, peanut and tobacco subsidies to the oil-depletion allowance, military installations, aerospace development, waterways and irrigation projects. The free market has historically meant less to the Sun Belt than friendly chairmen of key congressional committees. Given a regional tradition of economic activism and pork-barrel politics, substantial ongoing poverty, plus a lingering rural and small-town delight in populist, anti–Wall Street rhetoric, the South has changed less than its new portraitists may imagine. Even affluent suburban Houston is by no means one big Galleria. My point is this: in 1980, local conservatism enjoyed the

Map I **Continuing Sun Belt/Western Growth Projections, 1980-2000**

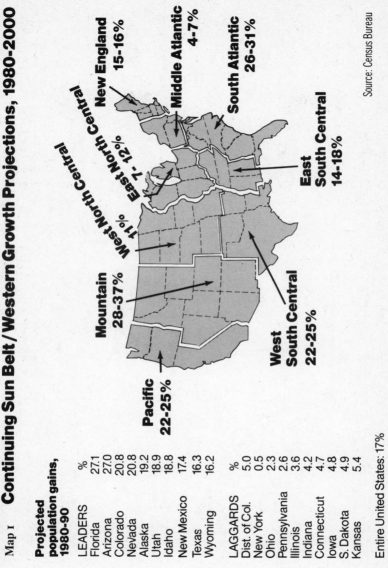

New England
15-16%

Middle Atlantic
4-7%

South Atlantic
26-31%

East North Central
7-12%

East South Central
14-18%

West North Central
11%

Mountain
28-37%

West South Central
22-25%

Pacific
22-25%

Source: Census Bureau

Projected population gains, 1980-90

LEADERS	%
Florida	27.1
Arizona	27.0
Colorado	20.8
Nevada	20.8
Alaska	19.2
Utah	18.9
Idaho	18.8
New Mexico	17.4
Texas	16.3
Wyoming	16.2

LAGGARDS	%
Dist. of Col.	5.0
New York	0.5
Ohio	2.3
Pennsylvania	2.6
Illinois	3.6
Indiana	4.2
Connecticut	4.7
Iowa	4.8
S. Dakota	4.9
Kansas	5.4

Entire United States: 17%

Map 2

The 10 fastest growing U.S. cities for the next 10 years

Average annual job growth in percent and growth industries, 1979-90*

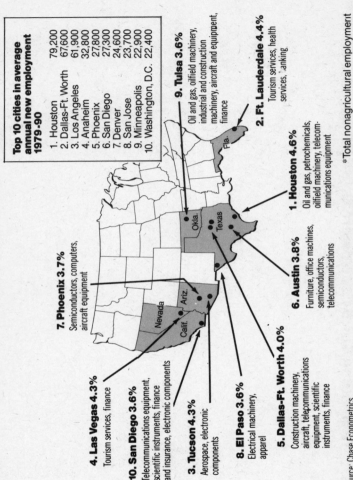

Top 10 cities in average annual new employment 1979-90

1. Houston — 79,200
2. Dallas-Ft. Worth — 67,600
3. Los Angeles — 61,900
4. Anaheim — 32,800
5. Phoenix — 27,800
6. San Diego — 27,300
7. Denver — 24,600
8. San Jose — 23,700
9. Minneapolis — 22,900
10. Washington, D.C. — 22,400

9. Tulsa 3.6%
Oil and gas, oilfield machinery, industrial and construction machinery, aircraft and equipment, finance

2. Ft. Lauderdale 4.4%
Tourism services, health services, banking

1. Houston 4.6%
Oil and gas, petrochemicals, oilfield machinery, telecommunications equipment

6. Austin 3.8%
Furniture, office machines, semiconductors, telecommunications

7. Phoenix 3.7%
Semiconductors, computers, aircraft equipment

4. Las Vegas 4.3%
Tourism services, finance

10. San Diego 3.6%
Telecommunications equipment, scientific instruments, finance and insurance, electronic components

3. Tucson 4.3%
Aerospace, electronic components

8. El Paso 3.6%
Electrical machinery, apparel

5. Dallas-Ft. Worth 4.0%
Construction machinery, aircraft, telecommunications equipment, scientific instruments, finance

Source: Chase Econometrics

*Total nonagricultural employment

benefit of practically every issue from patriotism and religion to economic growth and support for traditional cultural values, a context almost sure to change.

Consider two scenarios. For one, the Sun Belt is unlikely to vote for a Northern liberal presidential nominee, but a "conservative" government resting on a Sun Belt base stands a better chance of moving toward the views of John Connally than of Adam Smith—toward pork barreling, crop subsidies, agribusiness, high technology and aerospace mercantilism rather than fidelity to free-market principles. For another scenario, harder times could push the Sun Belt away from a free-market conservatism, provided the economic interventionist alternative was acceptable patriotically and culturally. Polls in 1980 showed Sun Belt support for conservatism and Ronald Reagan strongly correlating with individual optimism, not least in matters of economic opportunity. Clouding optimism would increase demands for federal economic action.

Somewhat similar caution applies to the Southern fundamentalist vote, along with its ecumenical cousin, the Northern Catholic right-to-life constituency. Without religious and moral issues front and center, many of these voters tend toward the more liberal or populist side of economics. To maintain their adherence, conservatives could conceivably be obliged to give religious and moral issues the kind of high profile likely to create other significant and adverse political ripples.

The elderly, having big concentrations in the Sun Belt, are a bigger constituency than ever, and now also more volatile than ever because the 1980s may become America's first decade of old-versus-young economics, pivoting, of course, on Social Security. Traditionally, older voters have been more conservative than the electorate as a whole, with their conservatism intensifying in recent years because of inflation and the patriotic and cultural issues of the 1960s. Now they face a threat to Social Security and the political problem of taxing the shrinking relative number of young workers to support the soaring number of retirees. This foreshadows a definite change in the politics of the elderly. Radicalization may be too sharp a term, but when Ronald Reagan announced his Administration's unpopular Social Security cutback ideas in May 1981, his support in the over-65 age group plummeted. Older voters are pivotal in three anchors of the Sun Belt—Florida, Arizona and California—although their greatest relative concentrations are to be found in the Northeast.

So much for conservatism's volatile trend groups. On the other side of the equation, meanwhile, the statistical importance of the youth vote has faded. Even the generation that came of age in the 1960s has since become more conservative, less worried about "social justice" and more concerned about jobs, mortgages and families. Accordingly, politicians have been making few specific appeals to this electorate. But for at least some young people born in 1950 or 1955, the 1980s may stimulate a new kind of radicalism. By the mid-1980s, profession after profession will be overcrowded—doctors, lawyers, dentists. Teachers already face a glut on the market. Major corporations will have too many executive aspirants and too few middle-management positions. Career frustration will be epidemic. The dreams of the 1960s, when mobility was a liberal promise and assurance, will not be fulfilled during the 1980s.

Corporate personnel managers appear well ahead of political strategists assessing the implications. They suggest that the values of a relaxed lifestyle, not those of the success ethic, will become more and more attractive. Politically, that bodes poorly for a conservatism identified with Social Darwinism and the economics of "survival of the fittest." Although traditional values of success may continue to dominate life in the Sun Belt, an alternative future is already apparent in California's "Silicon Valley" and similar high-technology areas. I was struck, analyzing the 1980 presidential vote, by the extent to which these areas gave atypically high support to independent John Anderson and other candidates outside the old two-party system. These trends and their probable continuation may be one of the least recognized and most important phenomena of upcoming American political demography.

In short, there are a number of reasons to be skeptical about the prospect that Sun Belt demographic and geopolitical ascendancy will measure up to conservative expectations and hopes. Not only does the region have a frontier-type, change-oriented history and mentality, but a number of its major demographic groups—religious fundamentalists, the elderly and high-tech workers—are highly volatile groups that could easily move away from the politics demonstrated in 1980. Moreover, the largest caveat to the political-ideological future of the Sun Belt is one that rests on the changing character of population movements during the 1980s and 1990s. The Hispanic population of the Sun Belt is soaring, and in California, Asian immi-

Chart 6

High-Tech, New Lifestyle Areas and Non-Two-Party Presidential Voting,
1980

County	Anderson	Libertarian	Citizens	Total
Marin, Cal.				
(S.F. suburbs)	12.71%	2.46%	2.61%	17.78%
Santa Clara, Cal.				
(Silicon Valley)	13.73	2.33	.58	16.64
Denver, Col.				
(Denver)	13.66	2.12	.65	16.53
Hennepin, Minn.				
(Minneapolis)	11.16	1.32	.76	13.24
Chittenden, Vt.				
(Burlington)	17.92	.87	1.44	20.23
King, Wash.				
(Seattle)	12.68	1.72	.74	15.14

gration—from Korea, the Philippines and elsewhere—is also a major
factor. In 1980, 808,000 immigrants entered the country legally, and
illegal entrants doubtless raised the total to over 1 million. Bear in
mind that much of the 1960–80 conservative trend in the Sun Belt
has reflected the sunward exodus of millions of white middle-class
executives, skilled workers or retirees from New Jersey or Minnesota. Thus, the ideological tide of the 1980s and 1990s could begin
to change markedly if the new wave of immigration from Mexico and
the Pacific Basin begins to have a mushrooming electoral and political as well as numerical impact. Some demographers suggest that if
entry continues at the million-a-year rate, and if immigrant fertility
rates continue to remain high, then by the year 2000 the United
States would have 25–30 million more people due to *immigration*
alone. Much of the impact would be concentrated in the Sun Belt,
with California possibly becoming the first "Third World" (non-
white majority) state by the 1990s.

At the moment the Sun Belt Hispanic population, while already
substantial, is relatively inert from a political standpoint. According
to Census data, less than 30 percent of voting age Hispanics went to
the polls in 1980. But there is also evidence that Hispanic political
power is a sleeping giant about to arise, possibly by the mid-to-late
1980s. If that happens—and I would be inclined to say *when* that
happens—then the geopolitical ascendancy of the Florida–Texas–

California axis could come to stand less for Reagan-style conservatism than for an updated version of the rise of the urban North and
the coming of age of (European) immigrant America in the 1920s and
1930s.

Finally, our political system has been operating for the last two
decades on a declining turnout. In 1960, 64 percent of the eligible-age
electorate went to the polls to chose a President. By 1980, that had
fallen to 53 percent, the lowest in recent memory.* As a matter of
record, past American political realignments have generally occurred in periods of *increasing,* not decreasing voter participation. Of
the watershed elections, 1800, 1828, 1860 and 1932 followed a four- to
twelve-year period of growing turnout. The 1896 election, in partial
contrast, involved high turnout (80 percent), but was a bit short of
the previous peak; after 1896, turnout dropped steadily as blacks were
disenfranchised in the South. So one finds no historical precedent
whatever for long-term realignment occurring during a period—like
that leading up to and including 1980—when turnout was *declining.*
The upshot is that if the nation, instead of being in the *midst* of a
realignment, is poised on the brink of a larger convulsion, still un-
defined, then we may see voter turnout surge during the 1980s. That
itself would have to create new trend groups and change the existing
contours of political analysis. Here, again, we can venture a socioeconomic probability: the decline in voter turnout from 64 percent in
1960 to just 53 percent in 1980 has been most precipitous in low-
income and minority-group precincts, so that any major resurgence
would probably also bulk largest in these same precincts. Unlike
other Western industrial nations, the United States has a huge "miss-
ing" low-income electorate. To some extent, cultural and patriotic
themes—those of a George Wallace, for example—can induce white
low-income voters to turn out for a right-tilted campaign. However,
should these voters be lured to the polls by economic indignation,
any such electoral remobilization would benefit liberal or radical
forces.

Which brings us to the question of the 1980s as an economic
turning point. If supply-side conservatives are correct and the decade produces an American economic renaissance, the influence of
demographic trends would pale, and prosperity would be king. The

*Turnout was a shade lower in 1948, but that was with blacks unable to vote across
much of the South.

critical and volatile trend groups of the 1980 election would become full members of the Republican coalition. Tensions produced by regionalism and age would ease. Prior stay-at-homes would be led to the polls to plunk for the party and the ideology that turned the economy around. A Sun Belt–based conservatism would indeed rule the land.

That's possible—and optimal for the conservative cause. On the other hand, should events confirm Lester Thurow's forecast of a low-growth "zero-sum" game, in which almost everyone's economic gain is achieved at someone else's expense, the current political demography is likely to undergo substantial change. In such circumstances, here are some of the demographic trends to watch for:

1. *Sun Belt/Frost Belt Regionalism:* Free markets, energy deregulation and free trade all work to tip wealth and population toward the Sun Belt, and that would intensify if our economy is relatively stagnant. Throughout the 1980s, unemployment and foreign-trade pressures can be expected to hurt the industrial Great Lakes and adjacent sections of the Northeast the most, thus acerbating regional tension. Like the industrial North of Britain, our industrial North has already become the principal base of statist-welfarist opposition to conservative stringency and economic Darwinism. A backlash against Sun Beltism could be detected in the 1980 presidential election, with Jimmy Carter maintaining or increasing his 1976 majority in a number of major Northern urban and industrial counties.* If the Northern industrial economy does as poorly during the 1980s as many forecasters expect, the backlash against ruling Sun Belt philosophies and programs is likely to intensify. And that backlash could match the force of the reaction against the once dominant moral and sociological thrust of 1960s liberalism.

2. *Religious Fundamentalists/Cosmopolitans:* Strong, expansive economies usually ease cultural tensions. Conversely, if the new economics fails, conservatives may be obliged to escalate their commitment to the cultural and religious legislation needed to hold the loyalties of hitherto Democratic fundamentalist and right-to-life vot-

---

*Carter *increased* his majority in 1980 in these counties: Albany, N.Y. (Albany); Erie, N.Y. (Buffalo); Monroe, N.Y. (Rochester); Genesee, Mich. (Flint); Cook, Ill. (Chicago); Wayne, Mich. (Detroit); Milwaukee, Wis. (Milwaukee); St. Louis City, Mo.; Baltimore City, Md.; and San Francisco, Calif. He maintained about the same ratios in Allegheny County, Pa. (Pittsburgh), and Hennepin County, Minn. (Minneapolis).

ers. Unlike conservatism's *general* return-to-morality agenda of the late 1970s, the *specific* agenda of the early 1980s—from a right-to-life constitutional amendment to aid to religious education and even the teaching of "creationism" in public schools—is extremely controversial and certain to provoke a counterreaction among upper-middle-class cosmopolitans. An antifundamentalist backlash could substantially offset the 1970s explosion in the consciousness and numerical strength of the fundamentalist vote. Alternatively, cultural fundamentalists could be drawn back to economic issues on which they are less conservative.

3. *The Elderly:* In 1900, 4 percent of our population was 65 or older. Today, it is 11 percent, or 25 million people. By the year 2000, it will be almost 13 percent. If the economy of the 1980s is not strong enough to ease the pressures building up in the Social Security system, and if stagflation continues, the politics of being old in the United States may begin to radicalize.

4. *Young Professionals/Lifestyle Liberals:* Many college-educated young Americans in their twenties and thirties, not least those in overcrowded vocations and professions, are opting for a lifestyle that eschews the Social Darwinism of Reagan Sun Belt conservatism for a more easygoing blend of libertarianism and communitarianism. Pollsters like Louis Harris and Daniel Yankelovich have made too much of this constituency, but from New England to the North Pacific Coast, it is finally becoming a force to be reckoned with. Both major parties have cause to fear losing these voters during the coming decade.

5. *Women:* The potential importance of women is less a matter of demographic trends than of the metamorphosis of American conservatism. Since their enfranchisement for the 1920 election, women have generally been more conservative than men in the traditional sense—*Kinder, Küche, Kirche,* as the German saying goes. In recent years, though, that has been changing on several dimensions. First, by dint of the increasing politicization of women on the new family- and sex-related issues; and second, because of their reaction toward the Sun Belt populist conservatism of Barry Goldwater, George Wallace and Ronald Reagan. Women tend to distrust and be offended by foreign policy belligerence, economic Darwinism and hard-boiled attitudes toward welfare and social services. Wallace and Reagan both fared much better among men than women, and Rea-

gan's male-female gap persisted into his presidency—even after his nomination of the first female U.S. Supreme Court Justice. No one can suggest that women are in any sense a bloc, but the politics of the 1980s may be substantially influenced by the extent to which women remain much less willing to support the new conservatism than men.

6. *Third World Immigration:* The Sun Belt states of Florida, Texas and California, emerging as the linchpin of conservative politics in the 1980s, rank among the major U.S. focal points of Third World (principally Hispanic) immigration. As of the early 1980s, Hispanics cast only a small percentage of the vote in all three states, well below their portion of the population. But if immigration continues, if relative fertility rates hold, and if Hispanic political awareness mushrooms, making the 1980s the "Decade of the Hispanic" as predicted, the political equation in these pivotal states could change —greatly.

7. *Minorities and the Poor:* With only 53 percent of those eligible bothering to vote in the 1980 presidental election (and with only 35–40 percent of eligibles participating in off-year congressional contests), the American electorate is disproportionately white and prosperous. Blacks constitute 11 percent of the national population, but cast only 7 percent of the total ballots in 1980. Hispanic turnout rates are even lower. One can reasonably suggest that the economic bottom third of the country cast only 20–25 percent of the total vote, while the top third cast perhaps 40–45 percent. This is a much greater imbalance than exists in any other major Western industrial nation, and could easily begin to change as the effects of a Sun Belt and conservative-dominated zero-sum economic game become fully felt. To protect transfer payments and government spending programs, low-income and minority turnout has the potential to surge. These voters could also come to the polls to protest conservative economic policies tailored to redistribute income toward *upper* rather than *lower* income groups. Of all the trends that will affect the 1980s, this could be the most important.

A generation ago, the forces and trends jostling to shape the politics of the 1970s and the early 1980s were largely noneconomic. The civil rights revolution, the youth upheaval, Vietnam, the sexual revolution, the fundamentalist reaction and the migration to the Sun

Belt all occurred while the nation was prosperous and not torn by stagflationary group rivalry. The result was a conservative hegemony, infused with radicalism, of uncertain duration. With economic issues now pivotal, the trends that would be fostered by a decade of zero-sum competition would be profoundly *un*conservative. And ongoing global inflation makes that possibility all too real.

Part Two

THE PRICE
REVOLUTION AND
THE OBSOLESCENCE
OF LIBERAL
ECONOMICS

8

THE TWENTIETH-CENTURY PRICE REVOLUTION

. . . the rich got richer and the poor poorer. The rewards for the provident, the lucky, the wellborn and the efficient agricultural producer were almost unlimited. But for the poor man, like the dispossessed peasant who worked for a salary, the times were grim indeed. He knew nothing of the subtleties of statistical charts on the standard of living, but he remembered ruefully and in bewilderment that his grandfather—a man no more industrious or thrifty than himself—had more often than not put meat and beer on the table, while he had to scramble to provide even enough black bread for his family.

—Marvin R. O'Connell, describing the great sixteenth-century "price revolution" in *The Counter-Reformation, 1559–1610*[1]

THE REST OF THE 1980s COULD PRODUCE COMPARABLE frustration. Not a few vocational groups, from college instructors to insurance clerks, now feel kindred pressures. For many Americans, real disposable income has been declining for a number of years, their chances of fulfilling the American dream—owning a single-family home—have withered. Yet all around them, others—be they skilled unionized workers, corporate executives or financial speculators—enjoy a standard of living that continues to climb. Such discrepancies have already given rise to a literature on the trend to inequality in an age of stagflation.* Under these circumstances, it is not surprising that frustration has festered and grown, that economic and political loyalties have fractured and become parochial. Forging a stable new political majority will be difficult—or impossible.

The dynamics responsible for such conditions, alas, are not new,

*City University of New York sociologist Paul Blumberg has detailed these trends in *The Future of Inequality in an Age of Decline* (New York, Oxford University Press, 1980).

although they always present themselves in the garb of contemporary historical times. Price revolutions—multigenerational and convulsive—are as old as history itself. That the West was caught up in another price revolution like that of the sixteenth century began to gain attention of analysts during the mid-1970s.[2] If the economic consequences are profound, so too are the political implications, not least of which is the inability of the governments of individual nation-states to do much to stem the military and social upheavals likely to ensue. It is my feeling that no one can understand American politics of the 1980s without first grasping the nature of a global price revolution.

Economic historians can be reasonably precise. The price revolution of our century, the bulk of which has taken place since World War II, represents the *fourth* major period in the last thousand years of peacetime inflation in the West. The first, back in the thirteenth and early fourteenth centuries, was less than severe and so remote in time that it can be passed over. The third and most recent arose during the early Industrial Revolution and peaked during the quarter century of European war, 1790 to 1815. Throughout that period, substantial wartime inflation afflicted most countries, including Britain's Revolutionary American colonies, but there was only a middling long-term rise in the price level—perhaps an underlying average increase of 100 percent between 1750 and 1820. It was a price revolution only by historical courtesy, which measures things in relative terms.

But the second of these four upheavals, known in history simply as "the Price Revolution," most nearly matches our own in magnitude. For a little more than a hundred years, from the early sixteenth century to the early seventeenth century, food prices—the best European consumer price index of the period—rose by 400–600 percent. Since World War II, price indexes in the United States and Western Europe have risen by 300–600 percent. Chart 7, showing British price levels since the year 1275, profiles the unique magnitude of the sixteenth- and late-twentieth-century price revolutions. Chart 8 confirms the broader utility of the British data by showing how price fluctuations in the United States during the nineteenth and twentieth centuries have followed the same general contours. Thus, for the purposes of this chapter, which are general, Chart 7 can be used to look at both American and European inflation.

The graph is almost a history course in itself. The economic explanation of a price revolution, like its social and political ramification, is profoundly simple on one level and extremely complex on another. For at least half of the last thousand years, relative price stability has been the norm. When prices undergo global sea change, action taken by the governments of individual states—whether it be in economic policy making, going to war or suffering a revolution—is not responsible for the inflation. Historically, such activity has caused countless *national* inflations, limited economic epiphenomena, which have been overcome by local recessions, draconian national currency measures or peace treaties. By contrast, global-class inflation occurs only once every few centuries, in watershed periods when the society, economics and politics of the leading nations undergo metamorphoses of enormous magnitude, invariably, and ironically, accompanying what we tend to think of as mankind's great movements forward. True, the expanding role of government throughout the world may be very much a factor producing the global sea change. But the role of *individual* governments, administrations and regimes rarely is. Accordingly, individual nations by themselves cannot attack and solve the general problem. They can, however, buffer the severity of the inflation within their borders.

The question, then, is: Can we assume that the United States and the world are caught up in a fourth price revolution? The answer is almost certainly yes. The comparative circumstances and dynamics of the second and third price revolutions show compelling parallels. The political implications, meanwhile, are unnerving.

Price revolutions occur only at certain times in history—namely, only during the great periods of mankind's economic and political advance: during the full-blown emergence of feudalism and Catholicism in the thirteenth century, again during the Renaissance, the Reformation (and the Counter Reformation) and the rise of capitalism and the nation-state during the late fifteenth and sixteenth centuries, and then once again during early stages of the Industrial Revolution and the rise of Revolutionary North America, and Europe in the late eighteenth and early nineteenth centuries. Whatever we have today—the post-industrial revolution, the microchip revolution, the Third Wave—constitutes one of those great periods of human advancement. If we look at it conversely: no watershed time of the Western economic and political system has *failed* to generate a price revolution in the last thousand years.

Not only have European and American scholars paid too little

English Inflation: 12th through 20th Centuries

Chart 7

Sources: Adapted from "Is Depression the Only Cure for Inflation?" by David Warsh, *Forbes Magazine*, March 1, 1975, drawing on data compiled by E. H. Phelps-Brown.

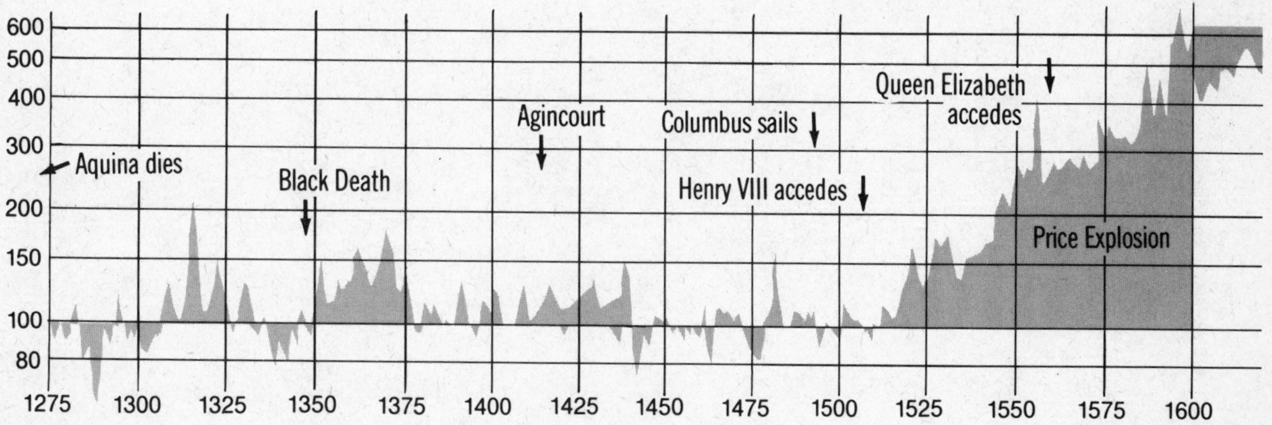

Aquina dies

Black Death

Agincourt

Columbus sails

Henry VIII accedes

Queen Elizabeth accedes

Price Explosion

600
500
400
300
200
150
100
80

1275 1300 1325 1350 1375 1400 1425 1450 1475 1500 1525 1550 1575 1600

| | 1650 | 1675 | 1700 | 1725 | 1750 | 1775 | 1800 | 1825 | 1850 | 1875 | 1900 | 1925 | 1950 | 1975 |

War with Holland →
War with France →
War of Spanish Succession →
7-years War ←
American Revolution →
Napoleonic Wars ←
Crimean War →
First World War ↓
Second World War ↓
Boer War ←
Korean War →

4000 3000 2000 1500 1000 700 600

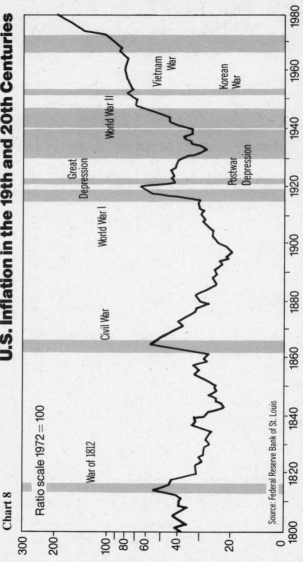

Chart 8

U.S. Inflation in the 19th and 20th Centuries

Ratio scale 1972 = 100

War of 1812

Civil War

World War I

Great Depression

World War II

Postwar Depression

Korean War

Vietnam War

300
200
100
80
60
40
20
0

1800 1820 1840 1860 1880 1900 1920 1940 1960 1980

Source: Federal Reserve Bank of St. Louis

attention to the history of price revolutions, those who have, have produced studies much too specialized or one-dimensional: monetarists attempting to isolate the role of the money supply, and so forth. We Americans are latecomers to world history, and so can perhaps be forgiven for failing to notice historical analogies until recently. But Europeans don't have that excuse. Meanwhile, historical scrutiny suggests that *all* price revolutions to date possess basically similar dynamics, though with the relative importance of this or that factor varying from century to century.

The first instance of common dynamics, and frequently the most fundamental, has been the greatly increasing complexity in the organization of the economy, usually coming in the form of new modes of production (steam engines or microchips) and new instruments of money, debt and commerce. The second has been dramatic growth in the scope and magnitude of world trade. Number three has been a major increase in the money supply and, especially, in the velocity of money. And the fourth has been an expansion in the role of government, along with an increase in government control of the economy and size of the government sector in the economy. Population growth is a fifth critical variable. When these have been present, the result has been price revolution. Chart 9 is an attempt to outline the presence of all five factors in all four price revolutions.

Contemporary politicians and economists should note the multiple causation. Easy answers and explanations are not to be had, be they twentieth-century or sixteenth-century hypotheses. So scholars seeking to explain away the sixteenth-century price revolution as a simple explosion of the money supply—notably the influx of gold and silver from the New World to Spain and thence to the rest of Europe—have only part of the story. From Madrid to London the role of the state grew, as the monarchies of Europe aggrandized themselves, despite intermittent bankruptcies, by finding many new tasks to pursue with new money and by assuming new powers to control the spreading inflation. And more important, private entrepreneurs also figured out new uses and vehicles for the American bullion, and for the fruits of thriving commerce in general. From the initiation of joint stock companies, the use of forward bills, and the *patto di ricorso* to the establishment of the first public bank in Amsterdam in 1609, the 150 years from the late fifteenth century to the early seventeenth century saw an extraordinary number of organizational and procedural innovations in banking and commerce. Fer-

Chart 9

Five Continuing Factors in World Price Revolutions Since the Thirteenth Century

	Period			
	13th Century	16th and early 17th Centuries	1770–1820	Post–World War II
Economic Revolution or Seachange	Manorial System	Renaissance, Reformation and rise of capitalism	Industrial Revolution	Post-Industrial Revolution, shift of major economies to services and technology
Major Expansion of Trade	Early systemization of European trade	Global exploration and opening up of Americas	End of mercantilism, rise of free trade movement	Major post–World War II expansion, global consumer revolution
Expansion of the Money Supply	Increased production of silver in Europe	Inflow of gold and silver from New World, new types of commercial and financial instruments	Expansion of gold and silver coinage, substantial use of paper money	Rapid expansion of paper currency, credit explosion, "plastic" money
Increase in the Role of Government	Emergence of feudalism and strengthening of monarchies	Rise of the nation-state, end of feudalism	Increase of state role to cope with war and revolution	Rise of the Welfare State
Major Population Increase	Substantial population increase in rural areas	50 percent or so increase —large for those times	Rapid (50–100%) expansion of population in Europe after stagnation in seventeenth century	Post–World War II "baby boom," explosion of "Third World" population

nand Braudel, historian *sans pareil* of Mediterranean Europe, has described the farflung ramifications of the arrival in Spain of a South American treasure fleet: "The money from Seville circulated from one money market to another, in settlement of commercial and financial transactions often to a value of ten or a hundred times its own value, and then passed on to the next money market for a fresh period of cash advances and trading settlements. Whether as coin or as bills of exchange, money cascaded from person to person and from money market to money market."[3] The complexity and pace of finance was enormously stimulated. Credit exploded.

Compare that with economic philosopher George Gilder's swirling description of money-supply movement in our own day:

> Today money supply categories M_1 and M_2 multiply like guns, from M's$_3$ through 14, and finally to M_x; they swirl from gold to oil to multinational grease; pop up as embossed plastic; drop briskly underground for a rare irregular run in cash, a monetary limbo; are bet and embosomed, baptized by tellers and statistically reborn in Eurodollars; are semiconducted through silicon to be stored in million-bit bubbles; and then are bounced off a satellite onto a tax-free Caribbean beach, to be glitched by a cosmic ray before leaping to London for an overnight binge in commercial paper. Eventually they may even land in a New York bank seeming perfectly cool and collected and available for discipline by Paul Volcker.[4]

Then and now, such new monetary demand and velocity produces inflation. *Plus ça change, plus c'est la même chose.* Gilder, however, succumbs to an ideological desire, and lays too much blame for the current price revolution on the expansion of the welfare state and too little on the recent growth and complexity of world trade and finance. Gilder oversimplifies, just like the strictly monetarist accounts of the sixteenth-century troubles. Other dynamics are also at work. Price revolutions are unfailingly complex.

Unprecedented economic complexity has an important place, of course, in today's price revolution. Sometime in the future, when students in São Paulo and Singapore, Canberra and Bahrain begin churning out doctoral theses on the massive inflation of the twentieth century, their concerns will be infinitely more complicated—geographically and politically, as well as economically—than the comparable mosaic of the sixteenth century. As International Labor Organization data spell out all too clearly, many of the less developed countries of the world (LDCS)—the Paraguays, Perus, Ghanas and Sudans—have suffered the most, at times experiencing 40, 50, 80 and 100 percent annual rates of inflation during the late 1970s. The rate of increase in the major Western industrial nations has, in general, been a good bit less, but it is to these rates, not those of the LDCS, that scrutiny must be applied. Chart 10 shows the comparative inflation rates for the major Western nations for the period 1960–73 and then for the period 1973–80. Chart 11 shows the comparative 1975–80 consumer-price rises in the major industrial nations, in both the oil-exporting countries and the non–oil-exporting developing countries.

The role of energy costs on the inflation rate is worth a brief aside. The cost of energy is more of a symptom than an underlying cause of global inflation, though it was an indisputably major force in the third stage (1973–80) of the West's price revolution. Intriguingly, those who say that the oil-price surge was a mirror, and not a generator, of inflation can point to Spanish precedent. The pre-

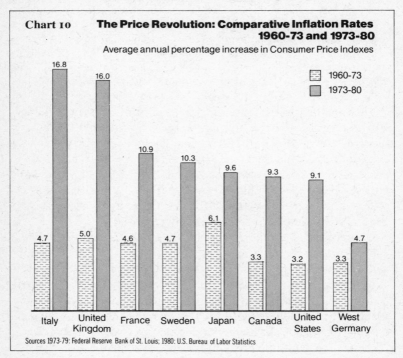

Chart 10   The Price Revolution: Comparative Inflation Rates 1960-73 and 1973-80

Average annual percentage increase in Consumer Price Indexes

1960-73
1973-80

	1960-73	1973-80
Italy	4.7	16.8
United Kingdom	5.0	16.0
France	4.6	10.9
Sweden	4.7	10.3
Japan	6.1	9.6
Canada	3.3	9.3
United States	3.2	9.1
West Germany	3.3	4.7

Sources 1973-79: Federal Reserve Bank of St. Louis; 1980: U.S. Bureau of Labor Statistics

Chart 11

Comparative Consumer-Price Rises Since 1975

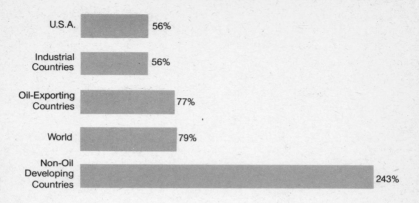

U.S.A.	56%
Industrial Countries	56%
Oil-Exporting Countries	77%
World	79%
Non-Oil Developing Countries	243%

Source: International Monetary Fund

eminent study of the sixteenth-century price revolution shows how the price of Spanish firewood, charcoal and other forest products—wood being the principal fuel of the time—merely kept pace with other prices in the early stages of inflation, but toward the end of the century began to shoot ahead.[5] So sixteenth-century fuel producers did not so much *create* underlying inflationary circumstances as *take advantage* of them. Obviously, OPEC did more than that in the 1970s; even so, price increases have come only on top of an already existing inflationary spiral.

The dynamics of price revolution bears repetition: (1) escalating complexity in the organization of the economy and in the instruments of money, debt and commerce; (2) a major increase in the money supply, and especially in the velocity of money; (3) a massive increase in the scope and magnitude of world trade; (4) an expansion in the role of government, plus an increase in government control of the economy and in the size of the government sector of the economy; and (5) a dramatic population growth. All five factors obtain in Western Europe and the United States in the 1960s and 1970s.

Escalating economic complexity is certainly a way to describe the development of the post–World War II Western economy: the dollar-based Bretton Woods system for international monetary stability, the boom in international trade, the proliferation of multinational corporations (mostly American), the rapid growth of welfare states all over Europe. The first fifteen years or so after the war was a time of relatively simply economic reconstitution. But from 1960 to 1973 —call it stage two—inflation really got under way with half a dozen forces converging. Politicians outbid one another in promising new welfare programs, and from Australia to Scandinavia the public sector mushroomed. New technology launched the "post-industrial" revolution. The postwar baby crop came of age. New communications, especially television, fed global growth in consumer expectations, what the Germans called *Anspruchsinflation*. By the late 1960s, the Bretton Woods system of monetary restraint had broken down with the excess accumulation overseas of dollars printed to fight the Vietnam war. The dollar went from being a force for stability to a vehicle of speculation. Waves of foreign-held Eurodollars began to flow across national borders, responding to interest-rate fluctuations or rumors of currency revaluation. World trade grew dramatically, spurred by new consumer markets, by the multinational development banks, the major American and Western European banks and multinational corporations. All over the West, the money supply exploded, as did credit, with new indices created all too often to measure the new noncurrency forms in which money was being kept. Inflation became a painfully obvious international problem.

The net effect cannot be characterized as anything but a global price revolution. As Chart 10 shows, the inflation rates in the major Western nations have by no means been identical, but they *have* followed a general pattern. In stage one, from 1960 to 1973, average annual growth in the price level came to 3–6 percent. Stage two, aggravated by the failure of Bretton Woods and OPEC oil-price hikes, shows conditions getting worse. Between 1973 and 1980, with the exception of West Germany, major Western nations experienced 9–17 percent average annual rises. The global pattern cannot be stopped by one nation alone, however anxious and deserving the government involved.

That is especially true of the American plight, the dollar being a *world* currency. Back in 1975, before Professor Arthur Laffer drew his famous tax-rate curve, he constructed a statistical series which, in essence, demonstrated a close correlation between *worldwide* inflation and the growth of the *world* money supply (the latter being broadly defined as the U.S. money supply, the money supply of fifteen other major nations, Eurodollar deposits, and exchange-rate variations). Laffer showed that after the breakdown of Bretton

Woods, expansion of the U.S. money supply was no longer the principal force in worldwide inflation. Laffer also argued that with inflation a global phenomenon, the world-currency role of the dollar would make U.S. inflation relatively resistant to money-supply manipulations by our Federal Reserve Board.[6] The events of 1979 and 1980 proved him correct. Furthermore, the global nature of the price revolution has a second troublesome implication, already noted. Because of the enormous postwar growth in European and Anglo-American welfare state spending, public-sector expansion and public-sector borrowing has been a major component of inflation, perhaps the leading one. The larger problem cannot be addressed by any one nation's shift to fiscal conservatism and resultant budget regimen.

Americans are not accustomed to global perspectives. But in any full-fledged price revolution, the historical lesson is that the afflicted must wait for the basic causal forces to attenuate. The early 1980s give us some reason for optimism. The growth of the welfare state has tapered off or reversed itself, even in the Scandinavian nations, where it reached its earliest and largest incarnation. In the mid-to-late 1970s, *Anspruchsinflation* (the push of rising and unreal expectations) began to yield to a recurring historical pessimism about the political and economic decline of the West. The oil prices show signs of stabilizing. So does the high-technology transformation of industry. More and more governments have turned to economic monetarists, to advisers whose remedies may be inadequate (and perhaps in some case quite painful), but whose ideology bespeaks a growing world interest in reining in the money supply.

Is this price revolution about to end? No one can say. However, while historians will not have a clear reading for years to come, prices in the West have already risen as much from the mid-1940s to the early 1980s as they did during the entire span of the great price revolution of four centuries ago. The end may be near, although the political and social ramifications are still gathering force.

9

THE FAILURE OF LIBERAL ECONOMICS, AND THE POPULIST RESPONSE

With his full shock of hair, the bull head squashed down on a five-foot five-inch frame, [Howard Jarvis] had all the charm of an angry Muppet. He insulted everybody, without regard to creed or party. Businessmen were "horses asses; their inventory is cowardice." Republicans, he said, "think like molasses." "It's going to make my trip to Forest Lawn a goddamned joy ride," he proclaimed. "I'll die knowing I really put the hot rod up the butts of those damned stupid politicians."

—Robert Kuttner, *Revolt of the Haves: Tax Revolts and Hard Times* [1]

BECAUSE THE PRICE REVOLUTION AND THE FAILURE of liberal economics are part of a global seamless web, even the most outraged conservative cannot—as some try to—lay all of our problems with inflation at the feet of Lyndon Johnson and his "guns and butter" policy of the mid-1960s. Worldwide phenomena do not issue from American practices alone. Nor was the archetypally populist response of the American people during the late 1970s and early 1980s —the so-called tax revolt—as unique a phenomenon as some would suggest.

This is not to say that Johnson didn't make a mistake. The global role of the American dollar established by Bretton Woods ensured a ripple effect all over the planet. But responsibility for the price revolution can also be traced to Europe's social democrats and welfare-state theorists, the legacy of John Maynard Keynes, Hollywood, television, the Beatles, the semiconductor industry, the space program, Bell Laboratories, Hugh Hefner, Ian Fleming, the gentlemen who launched Eurodollars and money market funds, and to all the people who had so many children in the 1940s and 1950s. To blame bad economic decision making of the 1960s alone for our current woes creates an illusion; namely, that the cure can be effected by good American economic decision making in the 1980s. If it is politically attractive to blame it all on Lyndon Johnson, confidently arousing great hopes based on panaceas also presents political pitfalls.

In any event, inflation did not hit the United States first. Japan, reindustrializing apace in the late 1950s and early 1960s, tolerated a certain level of inflation as an indirect way to pull money out of individual savings to fund rapid industrial expansion. West European prices began to climb in the late 1950s and surged in the early 1960s as pent-up consumer demand broke through the restraints of a decade or more of postwar denial. Britain, for example, had chafed under austerity up through the mid-1950s. The new, swinging Britain that emerged in the early 1960s experienced new, high-flying consumer prices for mini-skirts, Carnaby Street fashions and Merseyside rock music. And West European politicians, including conservatives, launched social welfare programs akin to the Great Society well ahead of the Johnson Administration.

What *can* fairly be said, though, is that the fiscal and monetary consequences of American policies of the time—from wayward domestic finance to the restless Eurodollars market—helped spur a wave of inflation in the West from 1966 to 1972, a wave far more pernicious and encompassing many more levels than the one experienced from 1960 to 1965. Spurred by reaction to Vietnam and by the restiveness of the West's huge postwar "baby boom" generation, the revolt against authority grew. With traditional morality weakening, the public's escalating sense of entitlement, in the United States and abroad, was further inflamed by ambitious politicians. Television, conquering Europe and Japan, began to pave the way for the "me" decade to come. Figures tabulated by the Organization for Economic Cooperation and Development (OECD) show that in its member nations—the major industrial countries—public spending spurted from 28 percent of national output for the years 1955 to 1956 to 34 percent twelve years later and to 41 percent by the mid-1970s.[2] From Washington to Tokyo, the outlays of the welfare state mushroomed.

Even though some politicians have made too much of it, the stagflationary effects of public sector growth seem indisputable. In a few countries like West Germany, which put welfare programs in place only after figuring out how to fund them *and* maintain capital expansion, the growth of the public sector did not produce much inflation. But across much of Europe, welfare state expansion, with its free medical care, generous children's allowances, inordinate unemployment compensation and a host of supporting rules, regulations and taxes, justified the criticism made by many conservatives. Individual taxes rose, through new levies and rates, but also through bracket creep. Incentive slackened. Regulation and taxation of business grew, curbing expansion and undercutting productivity gains. By the mid-1970s the great European economic expansion was slowing, and in some countries coming to a halt.

The United States participated in the larger Western trend, and as "Great Society" deficit finance and inflation worsened in the late 1960s, other nations grew chary of holding large accumulations of depreciating dollars. The trusty postwar reserve currency was losing its stability. Waves of foreign-held dollars began to move across frontiers in response to interest-rate upticks or currency-revaluation rumors. Stimulative and inflationary, these waves caused trouble for the nations thus invaded—and also for the United States. By 1971 Washington could no longer afford to redeem foreign-held dollars with gold at $35 an ounce, and President Nixon "closed the gold window." The Bretton Woods system had come undone. The world's principal currency shed its remaining link to restraint. Inflation was poised for another, bigger surge.

More trouble was at hand. In 1973 the oil-producing states, knowing that they controlled a commodity for which the rest of the world could be made to pay a great deal more, declared the first of a long series of price increases. Between 1973 and 1980 the price of oil increased from $2 a barrel to $35. And in the major OECD industrial countries, the annual percentage increase in the local consumer price index averaged some 10 percent between 1973 and 1980, in contrast to just 5 percent or so between 1960 and 1973. Although OPEC did not start things, actions taken by the group certainly contributed to the painful acceleration of the price level during the mid- and late-1970s.

This book is not an economics tract. I don't want to belabor the breakdown of Bretton Woods, the closing of the gold window or the actions of OPEC save to note that these phenomena stemmed from the same inflationary forces of expansion generated in the 1960s and early 1970s. Conservative theory, in its several forms, puts the fundamental blame for the inflation of the last two decades on *government* —either on state-orchestrated growth of the money supply (the critique of the monetarists) or on the growth of the public sector/welfare state impact on incentive and productivity (the supply-side "inflationary state" thesis). And both are essential components of conservatism's political appeal. Even those who are leery of monetarism or supply-side economics per se are obliged to give credence to the notion that growing government expenditure has been a major culprit behind inflation. History supports that argument, inasmuch as expansion of the role of government has been an active or circumstantial presence in all of the previous price revolutions. In any case, the growth of the welfare state in the years since World War II has taken the public sector of the economy in the OECD nations to extraordinary levels: taxes and social security contributions amount on average to 35–40 percent of individual GNPs. So the expanding economic role of the state *does* seem to have heavily influenced the course of our particular price revolution.

Which brings us to the perceived political and economic culpability of liberalism. True, forces far beyond politics are involved, but if liberalism and the growth of the state's economic role are not completely correlated, the linkage—here even more than in Europe—is much more than well established. Liberalism and the expansion of the state have been philosophically enmeshed. By the late 1970s, however, intensifying inflation had undermined the psychological mindset and many of the political and economic assumptions used by left-liberal politicians since the 1930s: cavalier attitudes toward deficit spending and debt; similarly cavalier attitudes toward tax policy and its effect on investment disincentive; support for increased government welfare responsibilities and outlays; predilection for overregulation of business and individuals; Keynesian belief in spending and demand stimulus; abhorrence of gold as a relic with little or no intrinsic value; an unexamined faith in future economic growth which justified indexing transfer payments, mandating 99.95 percent water and air purity, and so on and so forth. From Stockholm to Washington, this left-liberal thrust held sway. Its loss of momentum after 1973 was sudden and devastating. Much more than economic doctrine only confronted obsolescence; the fundamental worldview of progressivism—in the United States, it can be called "New Deal liberalism"—more and more came to be perceived as part of the problem, not part of any solution.

Because of such perceptions, Western political economics began shifting to the right in the mid-to-late 1970s. Even in Sweden, a Center-Right coalition ended forty-four years of Social Democratic rule in 1976. Anger at tax levels and public-sector aggrandizement ultimately produced either actual reductions or ministerially proposed reductions in punitive top-bracket rates in Britain, Sweden and elsewhere. By 1981, cutbacks in social spending were being implemented or debated from Japan to Britain, Denmark, Germany, the Benelux countries and the United States. And as John Fay, former chief economist for OECD, warned: "Today, the major economic problems that the OECD governments perceive are of a fundamental, across-the-board nature rather than country-specific."[3]

Politically, however, the supranational failure of liberal economics does not mean that a workable conservative alternative can step in and succeed. Even before Ronald Reagan took office in January 1981, Canadian Conservatives had won power and lost it in only a few months, unable to resolve some difficult economic problems, while Britain's Conservatives, mired in stagflation, had lost the promise and luster of their spring 1979 triumph. Still other European conservative coalition governments came undone within a few months of the new American President's inauguration.

Liberal political economics, having failed or become fatally out of date, needs major overhaul. But for all the validity of the conservative *critique,* one has to wonder whether the alternative conservative *blueprint* is viable; basically it's an attempt to roll back the recent growth of government power and the welfare state by easing taxation and restoring incentive. Historically, price revolutions have not succumbed to something quite so neat and easy. On the contrary, as Chapter II suggests, those periods have usually generated radicalism, peasants' revolts, revolution and worse somewhere along the line.

That history is worth keeping in mind. The floundering behavior of major Western governments in the late 1970s and early 1980s is unfortunately quite compatible with price-revolution precedent, as is the tax revolt in the United States. Indeed, the latter phenomenon, which is more populist than conservative, is best interpreted if it is thought of as a response to a price revolution.

From the beginning, the tax revolt had been misinterpreted. For years, public opinion polls had indicated public displeasure with both levels of taxation and some of the more expensive and controversial aspects of the welfare state. Nevertheless, when California's Proposition 13 passed in June 1978, when that long simmering indignation was clearly and neatly registered, the media could not resist the news hook: the tax revolt had arrived. What's more, the phenomenon was billed as "conservative," a victory of the right.

That shift of perception and identification was important. The tax *reform* movements of the 1970s, staffed by young lawyers and political idealists, were essentially liberal-to-leftist in their politics, but had no mass support or following. The tax *refusal* movements—those who declined to pay all or part of their taxes—were also leftish in their orientation. Indeed, so was the history of the tax *revolt* in the United States, from Shays' Rebellion of 1786 and the Whiskey Rebellion of 1794 on down. Mobilization of mass sentiment against one kind of tax or another was left-leaning almost by definition.

Not in 1978, though. California's tax revolt, in a pattern that would be repeated elsewhere, was a triumph of what Europeans would call the petty bourgeoisie, led by right-wing activists whose standing in fashionable circles was almost a joke.* Within a couple of years Paul Gann and Howard Jarvis of California were joined by the architects of Massachusetts Proposition 2 1/2, by Missouri small businessman Mel Hancock, and by Robert Tisch, drains commissioner of Shiawassee County, Michigan, and others. Their visible target, in each case, was the local property tax; their more important concern was the proliferation of bureaucracy, welfare outlays and social ser-

---

*In his book *Revolt of the Haves: Tax Rebellion and Hard Times,* Robert Kuttner makes an important sociological point:

"The corporate tax lobby was distinctly uncomfortable with the crude, unreined populism of a Howard Jarvis and his remarkably similar counterparts in other states: Jim Whittenburg, the leader of Oregon's tax revolt, a convicted bad-check artist; Idaho's Don Chance, a retired insurance-salesman; Bob Tisch, a rural Michigan drains commissioner; and Don Feder of Massachusetts, who contended that the only proper function of the State is to assure the public safety. These were not people whose counsel one sought for legislative strategy, or whom one invited to dinner.

"In its early phase, the tax revolt at its core enlisted that class of people the French call Poujadiste: little people with a tenuous hold in the middle class, vulnerable to economic reverses from events beyond their control. They were the same people who made up much of the 1968 George Wallace constituency, and they were authentically mad as hell."

vice programs supported by the existing revenue structure in high-tax and hitherto liberal states like California, Massachusetts and Michigan.* Few movements better fit the definition of populist conservatism.

Similar movements have occasionally cropped up in Europe, like the antitax voters who rallied behind France's Pierre Poujade in the 1950s. Or Mogens Gilstrup's antitax party in Denmark of the 1970s. But our unique populist traditions, coupled with the relative ease of getting popular initiatives on the ballot in many states, make the United States the hotbed of tax-protest activity.

Four major forces and circumstances dominate the successful tax-revolt movements in California, Massachusetts and Michigan: (1) fierce public resentment of high property taxes (and here it should be remembered that levies on real property are *regressive* and tend to fall most heavily on the lower-middle and middle classes); (2) widespread antibureaucratic, antiwelfare, antijudicial and antibusing sentiment, the latter being most notable in the Los Angeles area vote on Proposition 13; (3) substantial antiestablishment sentiments among the electorate; the major voices of the media (the Los Angeles *Times,* the Boston *Globe,* the Detroit *Free Press,* et al.) backed the existing tax systems and opposed the initatives; and (4) the opposition or standoffishness of major business organizations toward the populist-conservative position on each initiative, showing that these were *not* business-community–backed ideas or measures. To me, this is the stuff of populism.

Somehow or other, though, Proposition 13 and the tax revolt were interpreted to suggest that electorates in state after state were embracing the tenets of conservative economics. They were not. By and large, with Massachusetts something of an exception, leaders of the tax revolt were right-wing populists, not genteel conservatives. Moreover, because the property tax is regressive, their anti–property-tax rhetoric logically attracted a substantial amount of support in low-income and minority neighborhoods. Proposition 13 in California failed to carry a number of upper-income precincts that in 1980 went heavily for Ronald Reagan, the logic of these skeptics being that if Proposition 13 passed, the revenue loss would probably have to be made up somewhere else—presumably in some *progressive* levy.

*The examples in question are, besides propositions 13 and 2 1/2, the multiple 1980–81 ballot sequence in Michigan.

During the same time period, proposed large-scale *income* tax reductions were *rejected* when they appeared on the ballots of Oklahoma and California. Both initiatives were put on the ballot by conservatives; both were defeated, mostly because voters came to realize that the greatest benefits went to upper-bracket taxpayers. The press failed to understand that property tax reduction and income tax reduction have different constituencies. But they can be forgiven for that because Howard Jarvis, the co-architect of Proposition 13, didn't understand what was going on. He tried to follow up his populist triumph by offering Proposition 9, a 50 percent across-the-board cut in state income tax rates, which was defeated in June 1980. Jarvis' miscalculation was substantial. Blue-collar neighborhoods that went two-to-one for Proposition 13 switched and cast two-to-one majorities against Proposition 9. Voters caught up in the pain of price revolution do not pursue abstraction. They pursue self-interest.

Not surprisingly, however, both liberals and conservatives went looking for ideologically pleasing interpretations of what happened. Liberals at first chose to play down the implications of Proposition 13, and suggested that voters merely wanted a more effective delivery of government services without waste, corruption and offensive bureaucracy. But as the tax revolt took hold and as polls in early 1981 showed widespread support for the new Administration's hard line on budget-cutting, even the most dubious began to see that voter disenchantment went beyond matters of bureaucratic efficiency.

The extraordinary thing was that from 1978 to 1980, a number of neoconservatives and supply-side theorists went along with important elements of the liberal analysis—that the electorate had been motivated by straight pocketbook tax-cut sentiment, not by animosity toward liberal programs, sociology or bureaucracy. The ideological interest of these conservatives lay in arguing that voters (1) *wanted* a tax cut and (2) *did not want* spending or program cuts because supply-side doctrine—at least in its earlier, pristine form— insisted that tax cuts and spending cuts did not necessarily have to be made together. In fact, they argued, deep cuts in the federal income tax could be made without jeopardizing federal social programs because reductions in marginal tax rates would generate so much new economic activity that the result would be *more,* not *less* federal tax revenue. This, of course, was the "pot of gold" at the end of the Laffer Curve.

These conservatives were distorting the political meaning of an essentially populist response by the electorate. As the tallies in 1979 and 1980 show in Oklahoma and California, people rejected the sort of sweeping upper-bracket-tilted income tax cuts at the root of supply-side theory. They voted for Proposition 13 and other anti–property tax initiatives for simpler reasons—cutting *regressive* taxes and in the process striking out at unpopular bureaucracies, politicians and programs. Yet many conservative strategists ignored the actual nitty-gritty dynamics of electoral behavior and continued to posit a strong public desire to cut back government by reducing *progressive* income tax levies. Not a few of them have tried to make across-the-board income tax rate reductions a populist cause by raising a standard of shared antigovernment feeling and embracing specific populist mechanisms like initiative and referendum, state legislative calls for a constitutional convention and the like. Yet they have failed to enlist any psychology that moves the public. Like the liberals, conservatives by and large misread the nature of the "tax revolt," which was a response to the expansion of the welfare state and the price revolution. The electorate never expressed unqualified support for massive, upper-bracket-tilted income tax cuts, in part because the public never accepted the Laffer Curve theory, which says that such reductions could be made without substantial program cuts. True, the public favored a number of such cuts, especially in welfare, but not the massive government programmatic rollbacks necessary to offset a huge reduction in future tax revenue.

Down through the centuries, price revolutions have engendered scores of political revolutions, civil wars and peasants revolts, but in my reading of history, they never produced a broadly accepted program of tax relief for the rich. Conservatives and liberals have both misinterpreted the tax revolt, but the conservative error is now the more significant because it is one that wants to transform a substantially populist response to liberal economic policy failure into a mandate that never existed: a return to the conservative economics of the 1920s and its clear bias toward high-income people and groups.

10

THE NEW CONSERVATIVE ECONOMIC THEORY: RENAISSANCE OR REACTION?

So far from being new or revolutionary, supply-side economics is frankly reactionary. "Back to Adam Smith" can fairly be described as its motto . . . It may sound incredible, but supply-side economics really does believe that, if you want an economic education, *The Wealth of Nations* is still the best book to read. Indeed, the publicists of supply-side economics—Jude Wanniski in *The Way the World Works* and George Gilder in *Wealth and Poverty*—will readily allow that their books are but elaborations on themes by Adam Smith.

—Irving Kristol in "Ideology and Supply-Side Economics," *Commentary* (April 1981)

IDEAS ARE IMPORTANT IN THE STRUGGLE FOR POST-Keynesian hegemony. Discredit an economic theory and you discredit its attendant politics. So the characterization of supply-side economics as "reactionary" by an ally like neoconservative Irving Kristol is rather more damning than the expected "back to Coolidge" dismissals of a Lester Thurow or a John Kenneth Galbraith. The fact is, not all that much of the new conservative economics is really all that new.

Neither the meaning of supply-side nor of the new conservative economic package has ever been clearly fixed. Moreover, in a financial climate in which bond prices have fluctuated more in a day than they used to in a year, the staying power of economic doctrines can be just as changeable. The nuances of those doctrines can change, too. Nevertheless, one can say that the Reagan Administration launched its 1981 economic policy with two philosophies that had hitherto been on the periphery of conservative thinking. Supply-side economics was one, of course—the marginal income tax–rate-cutting credo with its ideological roots in Main Street, not Wall Street. The second was monetarism—the theory that economic behavior pivots on the expansion and contraction of the money supply. To curb inflation, you shrink the growth of money. The chief proponents have been a cadre of academicians, most notably Professor Milton Friedman.

Politically, it is important to remember that prior to 1980, *neither* group occupied the cockpit of Republican economic policy making. So their future compatibility was purely speculative. And unfortunately, when supply-side economics and monetarism found themselves yoked together in the new Administration, the operational partnership was a theoretical contradiction. Their economic theories may have differed, but they did share a conservative politics and philosophy. Both doctrines espoused the free market, and both exonerated 1920s Republican economic policy from responsibility for the Great Depression. Each, in political essence, claimed that there was nothing wrong with the expansionist, tax rate-slashing GOP economics of the Coolidge era—blame for the subsequent depression and its prolongation should properly fall elsewhere. Few messages could have been more attuned to the psychologies of party true-believers eager to try a similar economics. I suspect Ronald Reagan, in a quest for conservative theories, had embraced each of these theologies in its own right, without any conception of how the two might or might not complement each other. Furthermore, *both,* in turn, were at odds with traditional GOP emphasis on budget balancing. The saying "Politics makes strange bedfellows" can also apply to economic theories, and in consequence, the Reagan Administration spent much of 1981 mired in fundamental contradiction (about which more later).

Reaganomics as first propounded in 1981 was a Rube Goldberg machine in which everything had to go right: this forecast dropping into that slot at the correct time, triggering something else, and so on. This, in itself, was a very risky, unconservative melding of objectives and methods. But beyond the economic equivalent of a three-cushion billiards shot, the individual economic theories involved drew on a very uncertain theology.

Consider how supply-side theory is glowingly portrayed as a restatement of Adam Smith. This is far from always true. An antiestablishmentarian, Smith took pen in hand to chastise and disrupt the commercial elite of his day. One does find some of that in the books of Messrs. Wanniski and Gilder—small entrepreneurs come off as heroes, the *Fortune* 500 as lumbering bureaucracies. Yet in large measure the repackaging of Smith has been selective, mounted to promote the theoretical notions of classical economics to buttress re-establishing yesteryear's benign economic climate in entirely new and different historical circumstances. By no means a restorationist, Adam Smith in 1776 was not trying to revivify the practices of 1726. His laissez-faire was innovation in the time of late mercantilism.

This is not mere quibbling, not if we are to take the larger vistas of supply-side thinking seriously. It is, for example, a central component of popularized supply-side economics that a high margin of profit is useful and necessary to promote investment and thus supply of goods, though high wages are inflationary. "In reality," Smith wrote in *The Wealth of Nations*, "high profits tend much more to raise the price of work (that is, goods) than high wages." Vital enterprise, he thought, ran on very thin margins: "The rate of profit . . . is naturally low in rich and high in poor countries, and it is always highest in the countries which are going fastest to ruin." Inasmuch as hardly anyone reads *The Wealth of Nations*, hardly anyone is aware of the extent to which supply-side economics is only a partial and selective restatement.[1] That does not dispute the substantial validity of much of what is being restated. Nevertheless, for the purposes of political suasion, or of the judgment of economic history, theories that are essentially restatements of past thinking are usually less powerful than their proponents want.

This chapter cautions precisely that. Philosophically, politically, and even historically, the new economic conservatism is a muddled affair. This doesn't mean that it is doomed; one fervently hopes not, because even a muddle is a source of useful, even essential, perception and corrective in the wake of liberal failure-cum-obsolescence. Yet the contradictory dynamics here suggest limitations, technical and political, and these should be understood.

As previously noted, the operational conservatism empowered by the 1980 election—supply-side economics—is a curious mix of populism and elitism. While that reflects the odd political coalition of 1980, neither the doctrine's clarity nor its long-term chances of success are thereby enhanced. The newest New Economics is populist in that it opposes an expansion of government power, regulatory and fiscal interference with the enterprising public, the so-called Inflationary State. But the New Economics is also profoundly elitist in that it bathes in fiscal memory of Coolidge-Hoover Treasury Secretary Andrew Mellon, espouses tax relief aimed at upper-income brackets, believes in "trickle down" economics, and exalts the gifted and entrepreneurial over the common man—an economic survival of the fittest.

Now a politics that at once invokes populism *and* Andrew Mellon suffers from a fundamental contradiction. To be sure, past waves of American populism have glorified entrepreneurs. Jacksonian Democracy certainly did, and even William Jennings Bryan portrayed the farmer as a small businessman. But such forms of populism always pitted the entrepreneur against a powerful financial elite, be it Nicholas Biddle's Bank of the United States or the Wall Street of J. P. Morgan. The unprecedented challenge and strategy of the supply-side populist-conservative synthesis has been to mobilize the populist mood and electorate by postulating a new oppressive *public sector* economic elite—the bureaucrats and managers of the Inflationary State. By this thesis, *government* has become the dominant (and also inefficient and abusive) means of production, extorting the price of its goods and services through taxes.

In many respects, that argument is perceptive and plausible, with the workings of the current price revolution offering support. Moreover, two of the recent political figures of undoubted populist appeal —George Wallace and Howard Jarvis—have laid the groundwork of antigovernment feeling. Bureaucratic socioeconomic arrogance *has* become the prime populist bogeyman, giving the political right an edge bidding for populist fusion. Even so, one must remember that Wallace and Jarvis led their crusades with the corporate-financial establishment either against them or on the sidelines. By contrast, the new conservative economic strategists have been trying to mobilize the antibureaucratic, populist electorate using a reduced-federal-aid and reduced-taxation economic agenda that corresponds nicely to the agenda of the national corporate and financial community. The 1981 White House–business alliance was widely publicized. But no significant historical precedent exists for so mobilizing populist electorates. In the present instance, political opponents have mounted a relentless barrage of charges claiming that the new conservative economics favors the rich, with public opinion polls confirming substantial voter agreement.

The contradiction has definite strategic implications: for Reaganomics to harness low-middle-income populist constituencies on behalf of upper-income groups and the corporate sector, employing a larger set of cultural and nationalistic themes becomes necessary. In fact, these have been apparent in other elements of the Reagan Administration's blueprint. Along with restoring a respect for business, investment and production is a parallel effort to rehabilitate respect for work, faith, family and flag. Our country is to regain strength *spiritually* and *militarily* as well as economically. This larger context has important ramifications well beyond economics (more on which later).

If the appeal of uncompromised supply-side economics is probably too narrow to succeed politically, its reading of economic history is also flawed. John Kenneth Galbraith overstates the matter when he says that no one any longer believes in the theories of Jean-Baptiste Say, a major eighteenth-century architect of supply-side economics. Nevertheless, one can argue that Say's Law—the thesis that *supply* (production) creates its own demand—took a terrible intellectual beating in the years following the Great Depression. The common wisdom is that the crash showed that Say's Law was unreliable, demonstrating that overproduction—when linked to overinvestment and excessive speculation (*too few* people had *too much* of the money)—can indeed fail to generate sufficient broad-based demand. The point is that when the decade's speculative bubble burst, too little of the money needed to support a sustained high level of demand was available. A few hundred thousand families had most of the nation's discretionary income. The transient profits generated from building too much capacity had facilitated the creation of a minimally regulated, minimally taxed, speculatively overextended economy that could not sustain demand. Chart 12, adapted from *Business Week,* illustrates the concentration of wealth and the resulting speculation fueled by the economic policies of the 1920s, which included multiple tax cuts.

Accept this interpretation of the Great Depression, as most economists did by the end of the 1930s, and the political durability of supply-side economics—which, far from ducking its past, has openly embraced and boasted of the stimulative approaches to the decade by Harding and Coolidge, witness in particular Ronald Reagan's frequent, unblushing expression of admiration for Calvin Coolidge —*should* have elicited calls for a great national economic debate. Consider the following: if supply-side revisionists can really prove that basic Republican pro-business, pro-investment and (candidly)

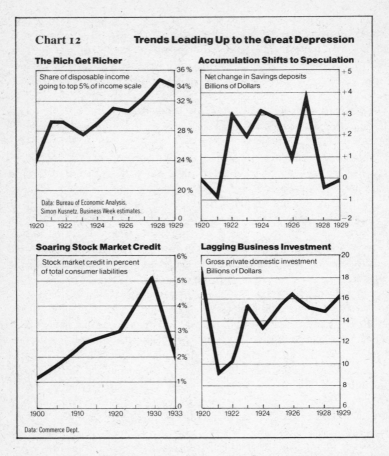

Chart 12   **Trends Leading Up to the Great Depression**

The Rich Get Richer

Share of disposable income going to top 5% of income scale

Data: Bureau of Economic Analysis. Simon Kusnetz. Business Week estimates.

Accumulation Shifts to Speculation

Net change in Savings deposits Billions of Dollars

Soaring Stock Market Credit

Stock market credit in percent of total consumer liabilities

Lagging Business Investment

Gross private domestic investment Billions of Dollars

Data: Commerce Dept.

pro-speculation economic policies did *not* play a major role bringing on the Depression, then the successor liberal economics, notably Keynesian demand-management, which assumed that those policies did, can be even more effectively impugned. On the other hand, if the Republican tax cuts and the laissez-faire philosophies (Coolidge's "The business of America is business") can in fact be shown to have played the central role liberals claim they did, then supply-side theory can legitimately be seen by some as doctrinal camouflage for a dubious political attempt to restore a golden yesterday. One would have thought Republican politicians would have wanted to ponder the risks involved—privately if not publicly.

Most supply-side theorists, for their part, have preferred not to dwell on the Republican dynamics of the Great Depression. George Gilder, in *Wealth and Poverty,* passes over its causes in a single short paragraph asserting that the debacle occurred largely because of U.S. tariff legislation and the collapse of the international trading system, along with a severe contraction of the money supply thanks to bank failures and misjudgment by the Federal Reserve.[2] No mention of massive stock speculation, of holding company pyramids, or of the call money market, of September–October 1929 margin calls, of the other dominoes that tumbled as paper profits vanished. The one supply-side theorist who *does* address himself to the economic convulsion attributes the stock market's decline to anticipation of, and then reaction to, passage of the far-reaching Hawley-Smoot Tariff Act of 1930. This is the analysis of Jude Wanniski, the former *Wall Street Journal* editorial writer who played a central role in the tutoring of chief congressional supply-side advocate Jack Kemp.[3] The late 1929 and 1930 collapse of the stock market is linked to some daily development on the tariff front. The market went down nine points? That was the same day a congressional committee tentatively decided on a half-cent increase in chemical tariff rates.

There is much to be said for Wanniski's analysis. Given the uncertainties plaguing the commodity markets and the international banks, the enactment of the Hawley-Smoot tariff undoubtedly made the Depression worse. But as a way to exculpate Harding-Coolidge-Hoover economics, Hawley-Smoot comes up more than a little short. Like the 1929 panic and collapse, the other panics of the preceding century—1837, 1857, 1873, 1893 and 1907, to name the most notable —had occurred within a familiar national context of protective tariffs *and* unsound or speculative financial practices. The latter were invariably held responsible. Why should the panic of 1929, occurring after by far the greatest speculative binge in American history to that point, have originated not in the unprecedented financial and speculative abuses, but in the rumors of tariff legislation still over a half-year from enactment? The mind boggles. Yet if the arch–supply-siders are wrong about 1929, their whole theoretical construct loses credibility.

This analyst, at least, is inclined to see the Depression principally resulting from a mix of world instabilities and 1920s economic policies, including some of the same policies once again being recommended by supply-side advocates. Chronicler Frederick Lewis Allen summarizes a widely held post-crash view that strikes at the conceptual core of those who now reaffirm Say's Law—that supply creates its own demand:

> During the nineteen-twenties, industry had become more mechanized, and thus more capable of producing on a huge scale than ever before. In the bullish days of 1928 and 1929, when installment buying and stock profits were temporarily increasing the buying power of the American people, innumerable concerns had cheerfully over-expanded; the capitalization of the nation's industry had become inflated, along with bank credit. When stock profits vanished and new installment buyers became harder to find and men and women were wondering how they could meet the next payment on the car or the radio or the furniture, manufacturers were forced to operate their enlarged and all-too-productive factories on a reduced and unprofitable basis as they waited for buying power to recover.[4]

Or consider the kindred point made by writer Caroline Bird in *The Invisible Scar:*

> In 1928 and 1929, investment bankers had literally forced money on manufacturers to expand capacity. The sober light of the Crash disclosed that industry was dangerously overbuilt. Industrial production had been leveling off since June 1929. Most lines were down in September and further off in October, before the Crash. In November, steel users told *The New York Times* that they would have been buying cautiously even if there had been no Crash. The stock-market drama simply publicized what astute observers had been whispering for months: everyone who could afford a house, a car, or a radio had one already.[5]

John Kenneth Galbraith puts it only a little differently:

> In a mature view, the speculation of the late '20s and the stock market collapse were matters of importance. As earlier noted, the prosperity of the '20s was strongly skewed in favor of the earnings of business and the incomes of the rich. In consequence, continued prosperity depended on continuing high investment expenditures by business, continuing high consumer expenditures by the affluent. The stock market crash struck a mortal blow at both. As share values came rushing down, prudence in all investment decisions rose as a reciprocal. Solid enterprises began to reconsider their investment commitments. The jerry-built structures of Hopson, Kreuger, the Van Sweringens, Insull and Foshay were forced

to retrench, for soon their creators were without the cash to pay interest on the huge bond issues by which they had constructed their pyramids. Banks were suddenly cautious. Borrowers had been caught in the market. Soon depositors might take fright.[6]

But being too cynical about a pro-investment economics would be as unwise as being too naïve. A supply-side focus of the 1920s on upper-bracket tax cuts, investment and production can hardly be fatal to its current utility. Sixty years ago the policies of Andrew Mellon carried matters from the proper to the extreme. In the 1980s, investment and production, much farther down the Mellon curve, can clearly use more tax stimulus before any threat of another 1929 is encountered. And much of the personal income tax reduction of 1981 can be justified by bracket-creep alone. What does constitute grounds for concern is the shallowness of supply-side political history: How could advocates so casually cite the policies of Andrew Mellon and Calvin Coolidge as precedents favorable for their own, dismiss widely held expert opinion that those same policies led the nation to economic disaster and Republicans to political rout, all the while assuming that the country would go along with their visionist disregard of the events of 1929? How long have Democrats run against Herbert Hoover and the Depression?

If supply-siders, brandishing a 1920s revisionism, are the cutting edge of the conservative New Economics, monetarists—the second major economic school marshaled on the political right—have also played a central role, not least in shaping policies for the conservative governments in the United States and Great Britain. The great appeal of monetarism to conservative strategists and regimes has come from (1) its simplicity—no vast governmental mechanisms are needed because the shape of the economy (and inflation) can ostensibly be manipulated by increasing or decreasing the supply of money; (2) its compatibility with the free market—no Keynesian demand management, redistributionist tax strategies or central economic planning is required if almost everything can be done by expansion and contraction of the money supply; and (3) its exculpation of 1920s Republican economic policy, with Federal Reserve Board mismanagement charged with turning a panic into a depression.[7]

Although both supply-siders and monetarists blame the Great Depression on something other than expansionary, tax-cutting Coolidge economics, their current policy positions are often at variance.

Supply-siders give monetarists some credit for perceiving money supply-inflation relationships *in some circumstances* and for imposing needed discipline, but they fear monetarism in its more stringent applications. It is an important contention of supply-siders that the money supply, both here and around the world, is too elusive to be effectively controlled. When the Federal Reserve Board attempts to control it with tight money and high interest rates, the central bank too often winds up choking elements of the private sector, in the process aggrandizing the very force—the state—whose expansive mechanics and escalating tax levies are the *true* spur to inflation. Only four months after Ronald Reagan's inauguration, Professor Arthur Laffer warned:

> The Administration's attempt to fashion a new monetary policy based on curtailing the growth in the money supply is in trouble. The all-too-evident turmoil in the financial markets is the inevitable consequence; an acceleration in inflation will be the result; and President Reagan's economic program is the most likely casualty.[8]

Therein lay a fundamental problem of the New Conservative Economics: in early Reagan Administration practice, its two major component theories proved incompatible and even hostile. This, in turn, obliged the supply-siders to renew their longstanding demand for a theoretical antidote to monetarism and high interest rates, a return to the gold standard.

Metallism—holding down inflation by linking the expansion of the money supply to the supply of gold—is the third major economic component of the new conservatism. For decades now, this thesis has been associated with the far-right wing of the Republican Party and the publishers of doomsday newsletters. However, the accuracy of "doomsday" forecasts made around 1970 that inflation would send gold prices soaring and the dollar skidding have made both gold ideologists and gold itself more respectable. More recently, support for a return to a modified standard has been growing. Prominent supply-side theorists like Arthur Laffer have long been among the staunchest gold standard theorists, for the logical reason that gold-linked money would limit the power of government to inflate the currency and its tax revenues while also establishing effective control of the hitherto slippery money supply. Without a gold standard, Laffer argued in 1981, high interest rates doom expansion.

Alas, the big problem with gold-backed dollars, another casualty of the New Deal, is that they, too, produced severe crises in their time. Champions of gold maintain that for well nigh a century after 1815, the gold standard gave the world its greatest spell of price stability and prosperity. But Edward M. Bernstein, the first research director of the International Monetary Fund, has pointed out that in the United States alone, there were twelve financial crises between 1815 and 1914. According to Bernstein, "The great depressions that occurred twice in the 19th Century and even more destructively in the 1930s resulted from the interaction of wartime inflation and the gold standard."[9] In any case, most economists around the world dismiss the gold standard as an archaism. Its strong advocacy by supply-side theorists in 1981 and 1982 struck some as a desperate move, aimed at trying to get supply-side theory off the hook of failure.

Fourth on the list, and often not mentioned, are the regulatory rollback advocates—men like Murray Weidenbaum, chairman of the Council of Economic Advisers, and James C. Miller III, chairman of the Federal Trade Commission. Supply-siders and monetarists alike share their concerns about overregulation and the need to eliminate unnecessary burdens on business and productivity. In the course of the decade, benefits are expected to be counted in the tens of billions. Yet here, too, one finds more than a slight whiff of politically naïve nostalgia-cum-restorationism. For example, in *Agenda for Progress,* an early survey of potential reductions in the federal role that might be made by the incoming Reagan Administration, outside contributors writing for the Heritage Foundation advocated the termination of involvement in multinational development banks, abolition of the Strategic Petroleum Reserve, sale of national parks to private owners, an end to Federal Housing Administration and Farmers Home Administration loans, discontinuation of federal mass-transit outlays, abolition of the Interstate Commerce Commission, elimination of the Federal Maritime Commission, and so forth.[10] Deregulation of this magnitude struck most observers as impractical and provocative. Repatriation to the states of federal program responsibility, and ultimately even parts of the federal revenue base, was spelled out in 1981 as part of a kindred objective—restoration of the old federal system despite the enormous growth of burdens of a sort requiring coordination on the national level.

Lastly, the ideology of the new conservatism also includes an attempt (1) to create a theology and philosophy of the corporation and democratic capitalism; (2) to infuse politics with the concepts and methods of business—Reagan Republican National Finance chairman, businessman Richard DeVos, proposed that the GOP organize itself like a corporation, raising money from its members and convening shareholder meetings around the country; and (3) to re-establish links between business, capitalism and religion, not least the new revivalism. All this, too, constitutes an extraordinary blueprint. Nothing like it is being tried anywhere in the industrial West, not even in Margaret Thatcher's Britain.

The ardent attempt to develop a religious framework to support the corporation—and democratic capitalism—has been the particular province of Michael Novak, resident scholar in religion and public policy at Washington's American Enterprise Institute. In an intriguing series of lectures delivered in 1980 and then reprinted in pamphlet form under the title "Toward a Theology of the Corporation," Novak traces the origin of the corporation to pre-Christian religious communities in New Kingdom Egypt (1300 B.C.) and the lineage of the multinational corporation to the medieval Benedictine monasteries. Having done so, Novak suggests that "The corporation mirrors God's presence also in its liberty, by which I mean independence from the state." Because economic and political freedom go hand in hand,

> I advise intelligent, ambitious, and morally serious young Christians and Jews to awaken to the growing dangers of statism. They will better save their souls and serve the cause of the Kingdom of God all around the world by restoring the liberty and power of the private sector than by working for the state. I propose for the consideration of theologians the notion that the prevailing moral threat in our era may not be the power of the corporations but the growing power and irresponsibility of the state.[11]

George Gilder also conjoins faith, altruism and capitalism:

> Capitalist production entails faith—in one's neighbors, in one's society, and in the compensatory logic of the Cosmos. Search and you shall find, give and you will be given unto, supply creates its own demand. It is this cosmology, this sequential logic, that essentially distinguishes the

free from the socialist economy. The socialist economy proceeds from a rational definition of needs or demands to a prescription of planned supplies . . . Under capitalism, the ventures of reason are launched into a world ruled by morality and Providence. The gifts will succeed only to the extent that they are altruistic and spring from an understanding of the needs of others. In such a world, one can give without a contract of compensation. One can venture without the assurance of reward. One can seek the surprises of profit, rather than the more limited benefits of contractual pay. One can take initiative amid radical perils and uncertainties.[12]

Not all pro-business sermonizing is so abstract. Dixie preachers are a lot pithier. After all, the theological legitimacy of the corporation is important not only to justify the increased role the new conservatives hope business will play in politics, but to strengthen, ideologically, the alliance of conservative politics, free enterprise and fundamentalist religion. This is especially apparent in the South, where prominent fundamentalist leaders and electronic evangelists, from Virginia's Jerry Falwell, leader of the Moral Majority, to Texas' James Robison, are close allies of antibureaucratic, pro-growth, pro-enterprise conservative and New Right politicians. The economic growth of the Sun Belt over the last two or three decades, a phenomenon political analyst Samuel Lubell has called "the mechanization of the Southern Baptists," has made the country's most religious and fundamentalist region ripe for such a philosophic confluence. Across the South and Southwest, individual economic opportunity awaits one in the new factory or shopping center down the street, just as the opportunity for personal religion or individual salvation awaits one in the chapel just around the corner. In June 1981, according to the Los Angeles *Times,* Herbert Ellingwood, deputy counsel to President Reagan, told a "Financial Success Seminar" in Anaheim, California, that "Economic salvation and spiritual salvation go side by side."[13] Similar evocations were commonplace during the Coolidge years.

As for the scope of its ambition, we are talking about an upheaval comparable to the New Deal and unique in its reversionary and restorationist intentions. As hard-headed politics, the new economic "conservatism" strikes me as a precarious undertaking, not least because of its collective contradictions and risks. Individually, all of the themes involved—the supply-sider's focus on investment, production and innovation; the monetarist's emphasis on restraint of credit and money growth; the metalist's call for the discipline of gold; the deregulationist's position that government regulatory burdens have become costly and stifling; and the theologian's insistence that capitalism is a credo of faith and freedom—are important correctives to the sterile expansion of the public economic sector that has characterized the Western experience since the mid-1960s. Irving Kristol is surely right when he says that the significance of supply-side economics and conservative economic reform in general lies in an affirmation of human and irrational qualities—faith, religion, ambition, innovation—against the type of "mathematical-mechanical" analysis offered by liberal rationalists and Keynesian demand managers. And some deregulation is clearly in order. But a desire to deregulate, for example, does become absurd when the deregulators want to abolish both the Federal Trade Commission and the concept of a national park.

Therein lies the enigma. In mild and tempered form, ideas of the new conservatives *could* be the stuff of a renaissance. Yet taken together as an economic policy base for a government of the United States, the strands of the new conservatism take on collective overtones of inadequacy, confusion and revolutionary restorationism-archaism. They are inadequate because the impetus of the Inflationary State and the broader late-twentieth-century price revolution seems so massive. Confused, because although supply-side economics and monetarism share a conservative logic of political coalition—conveniently blaming the 1929 crash on something other than basic Republican economics and business expansion—they have found themselves at operational loggerheads. When both are simultaneously pursued, the result—as exemplified in the Britain of 1979 to 1981—can be chaotic, counterproductive and disclaimed by purists on both sides.

Meanwhile, the case for early Reaganomics as restorationism-archaism is easy to make. I suspect that the real conceptual bond of supply-side economics, 1920s revisionism, remonetarization of gold, substantial elimination of federal regulatory agencies and their responsibilities, and reglorification of the corporation as the mainstay of America is not logic but reverie—an attempted re-creation of what Frederick Lewis Allen called "the Indian Summer of the Old Order."

Many of the new policy thrusts deserve to succeed, and perhaps they will—especially as early-stage Reaganomics yields to a second-stage outlook less rigid in adherence to supply-side and monetarist shibboleths alike. But in their first blush, the new economics went beyond conservatism to adventurism, and if the larger attempt fails, the public's preference in economic policy could begin to move in directions conservatives now dismiss as corporatist, statist or worse.

11

POLITICAL ECONOMICS OF THE 1980s: A ZERO-SUM SOCIETY?

> As we head into the 1980s, it is well to remember that there is really only one important question in political economy. If elected, whose income do you and your party plan to cut in the process of solving the economic problems facing us.
>
> —Lester Thurow, *The Zero-Sum Society*

IN THE END THE NEW CONSERVATIVE PROGRAM, LIKE others that preceded it, will prove partially successful and partially unsuccessful. That much is obvious. Yet in one respect at least, the process of dissipating the prior decade's penchant for escalating outlays, entitlements and regulations, the Reagan Administration consummated a sea change in mood simply by forcing budgetary restraint on Congress. Even if statism and economic regulation gather force again, fiscal profligacy and regulatory extremism are gone for the rest of the 1980s, if not beyond. Moreover, the trend here is reassuringly part of something transnational. Similar battles are being fought, and in some instances won, from Europe to Japan. Progress *is* being made. The excesses of the 1960s and 1970s are being curbed and the tide turned in most of the major Western industrial nations.

But the political question, raised in Chapter 9, is whether the sort of conservatism epitomized by Ronald Reagan in the United States and Margaret Thatcher in Great Britain—free-market–oriented, an-

POST-CONSERVATIVE AMERICA

ti–welfare-statist, monetarist, restorationist—can carve out long-term supremacy for itself or whether its role is merely transitory: undermining an economic liberalism turned profligate and irresponsible. All the results are not yet in, but odds on the former seem unencouraging. Milder attempts at restoration have already failed in Canada, Sweden and several other West European nations. One has a sense, from both foreign election returns and from a reading of history, that the economics of revolutionary conservatism are an ideological spasm of sorts, promoted most forcefully in Britain and the United States, the very nations that brought the world the Industrial Revolution, modern market theory and global trade, and in general the most advanced forms of relatively pure capitalism. After all, if the unfettered capitalist past cannot muster a nostalgic spasm in Britain and the United States, where can it? Restorationist policies, however, have not been known to build effective new political-economic systems. My surmise is that revolutionary conservatism is a species of last-stage "conservatism," likely to be remembered as what happened after last-stage "liberalism."

In using such terminology, I don't mean to endorse either Robert Nisbet's "twilight of history" or Daniel Bell's "end of ideology." But conservatism and liberalism are *both* terms whose genesis lies in the Industrial Revolution, and there is no reason to think their semantic utility will outlast the era already coming to a close.* Liberal economics have already demonstrated an inability to manage the societies of the West as they confronted post-industrialism and the price revolution. When these economics miscarried, and other liberal policy hopes failed along with them, conservative forces, waiting in the wings, moved front and center with their old theories and verities,

---

*"Words are witnesses which often speak louder than documents. Let us consider a few English words which were invented, or gained their modern meanings, substantially in the period of sixty years with which this volume deals. They are such words as 'industry,' 'industrialist,' 'factory,' 'middle class,' 'working class,' 'capitalism,' and 'socialism.' They include 'aristocracy' as well as 'railway,' 'liberal' and 'conservative' as political terms, 'nationality,' 'scientist,' and 'engineer,' 'proletariat' and (economic) 'crisis.' 'Utilitarian' and 'statistics,' 'sociology,' and several other names of modern sciences, 'journalism' and 'ideology,' are all coinages of this period. So are 'strike' and 'pauperism.' . . . To imagine the modern world without these words (i.e., without the things and concepts for which they provide names) is to measure the profundity of the revolution which broke out between 1789 and 1848 and forms the greatest transformation in human history since the remote times when man invented agriculture and metallurgy, writing, the city and the state." E. J. Hobsbawm, *The Age of Revolution, 1789–1848* (1962), p. 17.

many of considerable merit. Yet for all their utility and value in an earlier time, it is hard to see now how these ideas can effectively address and solve national problems when we face an "advanced," "mature" and even "over the hill" political economics. My own pessimism is further intensified by the legacies of misguided liberal economic optimism so pervasive in everything from entitlement programs and budget deficits to zero-risk environmentalism.

And at the same time, conservative restorationism is a muddle-headed phenomenon, simultaneously pursuing balanced budgets, massive tax cuts, far-flung deregulation, money-supply restraint, return to a gold standard and other hallmarks of bygone, better days. Lester Thurow likes to compare his predicted zero-sum economics of the 1980s to the stand-off described in Robert Ardrey's *The Territorial Imperative,* where to subdue an animal of the same species on his home turf, the invader must be twice as strong as the defender.[1] In a kindred biopolitical sense, the contest between the last defenders of profligate liberalism and the advocates of revolutionary conservatism is perhaps like the last fight between two old bull elephants, *neither of whom* will survive the encounter to lead the herd.

The likelihood is that revolutionary conservativism will work only to the degree that historians will call it a successful transition to another kind of politics—one in which both Franklin D. Roosevelt and Calvin Coolidge will be political memories, not ongoing sources of inspiration for public policy. As of the early 1980s, the price revolution is probably moving into its final stages, but little likelihood exists that inflation will ease enough to produce a "soft landing," thereby giving the new conservative economics the full triumph it covets. Short of that, some degree of the zero-sum economic-political dilemma seems to me inevitable.

Moreover, from restorationism's basic thrust it is possible to predict at least some of the reactions it will engender. For starters, if the economy shows little of the promised improvement, American business, having been perceived as both a cheerleader and formulator of Reagan Administration economic policy, will lose much of the prestige it regained during 1980 and 1981. The public and the politicians would almost certainly continue to express concern over productivity, investment, job creation, increased exports, and the like. But the idea of *unleashing* business to attack the problems would go by the boards. Attempts to restrain corporate political activity would grow, while the notion of hiring professors of religion to develop a theology of the corporation would shrivel.

On a second front, public support of income redistribution, muted since the late 1970s, could easily come to the fore again. Modeled on the economics of the 1920s, supply-side economic theories were enacted into law by the massive 1981 federal tax cut and reduced tax rates in the upper brackets; this, to free up more money for investment. And so, between 1982 and 1986, large tax reductions are blueprinted to flow to the upper quintile of American families. The politics of all this is simple: So long as "trickle down" economics—the label once again being trotted out by foes—works, as in 1923–29, the population at large will pay relatively little attention to income distribution. In such circumstances, the left howls in vain. But should conservative policy fail, as it did in 1929, the 1981 tax reductions benefiting the rich will probably soon give way to a subsequent reaction in favor of *downscale* income redistribution. Here, one must presume that conservative restorationists know enough about the political economics of the 1920s and 1930s to know what happened. Chart 13 A presents one consulting firm's estimate of the negative and positive impacts of Reaganomics in different income groups. Chart 13 B, meanwhile, illustrates the contrary, downward shift over the last half-century in the percentage of total U.S. income going to the various quintiles of American families, as well as to the top 5 percent.[2] Redistribution after 1929 was substantial. Liberal economists like Thurow would like to see that trend play off Reaganomics to resume its former direction in the 1980s.

Politically and economically, the stakes of the new fiscal policy are great. If Reaganomics in the end proves to be a nostalgic grab bag of unworkable policies, then by the mid-1980s the upper-quintile redistribution of wealth launched by the 1981 tax law—see the estimates—is likely to be a source of bitter controversy.* In that event, the less affluent four fifths of our population, encompassing the great middle class, may find itself rallying behind tax "loophole" and redistribution rhetoric almost diametrically opposite to that of 1981. The thing to remember is this: if the new economics does not greatly

---

*I have not detailed the changes involved—in basic rates, gift and estate taxes, unearned income, pension arrangements, and the like—because most readers of this book will presumably be aware of the 1981 law, its opportunities and its upper-bracket implications.

Chart 13A

The Effect of Reagan's Fiscal Policy by 1985

In billions of dollars

Household Income

	below $11,500	$11,500–$22,900	$22,900–$47,800	$47,800+
Spending Cuts	($38.5)	($65.5)	($42.5)	($12.0)
Tax Cuts	$13.7	$59.6	$136.3	$151.8
Net effect	($24.8)	($5.9)	$93.8	$139.8

Source: A. Gary Shilling and Company

Chart 13B

Changing U.S. Income Distribution

% of Total U.S. Income	1929	1941	1947	1977	1985 (Est.)	1980s (Thurow Ideal)*
Top 5% of families	30.0%	24.0%	20.9%	17.0%	21%	
Top 20% of families	54.4	48.8	43.0	41.5	45	36.7
Middle 40% of families	33.1	38.6	40.2	41.7	41	41.7
Bottom 40% of families	12.5	13.6	16.8	16.8	14	21.6

*Taken from *The Zero-Sum Society*, p. 201.

"enlarge the pie," as the term goes, it will in the meantime have redistributed some of the existing pie to the most prosperous 5–10 percent of American families. The politics of the mid-1980s would then presumably shift to a debate in which the bulk of the population would demand a re-redistribution.

On a third front, if attempts to return economic decision making to the "invisible hand" miscarry in the early 1980s, the failure could easily provoke renewed emphasis on economic planning and business-government partnership. The thrust of Reaganite thinking has been quite clear—to strip away regulatory agencies and restraints so that more allocation and reward can be made by the marketplace. If the larger economics of "reprivatization" do not work, because of policy contradictions or whatever, pressure is likely to mount for state economic mechanisms and political processes that can manage the task of allocating economic resources, sacrifices and rewards. Conservatives would have a point of sorts if they complained in such circumstances that market mechanisms never got a fair try. In political terms, though, their complaint would be overmatched by the roar of the crowd.

Given the obstacles to a free-market renaissance, inept conservative attempts to bring it about could in the end help further several contrary trends. Corporate autonomy and authority could be diminished. Attempts at income redistribution could return with a vengeance. Support could grow for a business-government partnership or a national industrial policy in the European, but not Japanese, manner. Conservatives of the breed who mutter about "statism" while attending hard-money seminars in New Orleans would protest, of course. By contrast, the chief executive officers of the Business Roundtable might even be relieved. Notwithstanding the welfarist or Ralph Nader–like tenor of much of the economic regulation of the 1970s, a new mid-1980s business-government partnership would probably be far more corporatist than liberal. The terms "liberal" and "conservative" would become irrelevant, just as they are currently now nearly irrelevant when one tries to understand the difference between the corporatist political economics of "conservative" John Connally or the views of "liberal" Felix Rohatyn.

Nor is it clear that any such political economics would have to await the passing of the Reagan Administration. Substantial elements of his Republican coalition would favor moving in just such directions if the larger fate of center-right politics confronted real trouble in its economic policy making. Prior to Reagan's nomination, much of the corporate community favored John Connally's brand of government-business alliance, and elements of the New Right, more interested in economic growth and economic nationalism than in free-market philosophy, were also sympathetic to Connally's approach. Observers forget that New Right fund raiser Richard Viguerie ran 1980 direct-mail fund raising for John Connally *and* the Religious Right simultaneously. Conversely, if the Reaganites fail and put the Democrats back in power, the latter have become heavily dependent on the declining Frost Belt industrial electorates, and so would probably move toward the state capitalism-industrial redevelopment model of Felix Rohatyn. Indeed, if one were to speculate using trends elsewhere apparent in the industrial West, the precedents clearly favor an aggrandized state role.

That is certainly true of practices in Germany, the Benelux countries, France, Scandinavia and Japan—indeed, almost everywhere. Public-sector aggrandizement is also a product of global inflation, a phenomenon with political precedents in earlier price revolutions. True, the analysts of the left may be too pessimistic when they predict that the political economics of the 1980s will be a zero-sum game, a loser for every winner. Supporters of the case for the resumption of *some* meaningful economic growth are also persuasive. Nevertheless, there are sure to be a large number of economic losers, coupled with substantial public appreciation of just that. As a result, further politicization of economic decision making seems likely. Thurow suggests that Americans faced with losses from stagflationary economics "retreat to government" and try to use politics to stem those losses, often with considerable luck.[3] Historically, as it happens, price revolutions have almost always involved a growth in the role of government—in multiple stages, really, first as a partial cause of inflation, then as an effect. For the great price revolution of the sixteenth century, English historian J. H. Plumb has described the process as follows:

> Indeed, one of the ironies of inflation is that it forces governments to attempt complex remedial measures that rarely have any effect except to intensify class bitterness on the one hand and distrust of government on the other . . . Almost every financial action taken by any government in the sixteenth and early seventeenth centuries led to social and political discontent. Ministers were hated, vilified, and used up with remarkable

rapidity by monarchs who increasingly felt that all criticism was iniqui-
tous. Representative assemblies, no matter how limited their social base,
became anathema to kings and rapidly began to disappear. Even in
England, Parliament had to wage war to maintain its privileges, and
elsewhere parliaments vanished, replaced by absolute monarchs backed
by increasingly efficient bureaucracies. In an inflationary world the nos-
trum is always authority—the power to impose. And yet, Philip II of
Spain, who had more direct power, perhaps, than any other monarch of
his time, was as powerless to check inflation as Elizabeth I of England,
who had to share some of her authority in finance with Parliament.
Nevertheless, the mood among men of property and authority, then, as
now, was that only a great increase of power at the center could check
the rot that inflation was creating in the social fabric.[4]

More worrisome still is the weighty evidence that past price revolutions and the economic upheavals surrounding them have brought
on war, revolution and civil turmoil. Not surprisingly, academicians
have documented abnormal political volatility in the later stages or
aftermaths of global inflations. Take the years from 1600 to 1660,
during which, as Chart 7 shows, the great sixteenth-century price
revolution was coming to an end or over. During that period, Europe
was torn by religious warfare (the Thirty Years' War), while even
relatively stable England executed a king, staged a civil war and
indulged her one national bout of center extremism. As for the third
generally accepted price revolution, that of 1770–1820, its later stages
produced the French Revolution and Napoleonic Wars, laying the
historical groundwork for the period from 1815 to 1848, frequently
called "Revolutionary Europe." David Hackett Fischer, chairman of
the history department at Brandeis University, has sketched the
social disintegration, war and revolution following each of the West's
four price revolutions since medieval days in a fascinating article[5].
It is a doleful survey. Fisher leaves the reader feeling that our current
bout with inflation may be regarded as nothing compared to what's
coming next.

At the very least, there is certainly no reason to anticipate the sort
of stability posited by either a Burke or a Coolidge to prevail during
the later stages or aftermath of a price revolution. History is almost
never a progression of soft landings, especially at critical junctures
—and not least because inflation unleashes the worst in human
nature, feeding a host of other religious, cultural and national frustrations.

Part Three

SOURCES AND PROSPECTS OF MIDDLE AMERICAN RADICALISM

12

AMERICA
IN THE 1980s:
A WEIMAR ANALOGY?

In 1972 a conclave of distinguished American historians debated
whether the United States was going the way of Germany's ill-fated
Weimar Republic. (The colloquium proceedings were published in
Social Research, Summer, 1972.) They concluded that it was not, that
the differences outweighed the similarities. But a few participants, such
as Geoffrey Barraclough, were already worried, and today reappraisal
seems overdue.

—Robert Alan Cook, "American Weimar," *Worldview* (July 1980)

ONE OF THE MORE DISCONCERTING ASPECTS OF
American politics of the 1980s is its vulnerability to yet another
failure of regime. Surveys taken during the 1980 presidential campaign indicated that 40 to 50 percent of the public believed resort to
force might be necessary to straighten out our political system. Even
though public faith was thereafter bolstered by the election of a new
President, confidence in national political institutions remains precarious. Moreover, the consequences of earlier historical intervals of
global inflation were war and revolution, strife and strongmen: the
Thirty Years' War, the American and French revolutions, the revolutions of 1848, the advent of leaders like Cromwell and Napoleon.
Not auspicious. And as Chapter 2 suggested, the two-decade breakdown, followed by the ensuing Balkanization of the national spirit,
has left a skittish populace beneath a patina of suburban affluence.

If the economy fails to respond as hoped during the 1980s, the
social and political yeast in the system will begin to ferment. Available indices range from the obscure to the stereotyped. Applying one

of the former, potential turmoil lies in the electoral data produced by the Reagan revolution and its precursors. Both draw an extremely disproportionate amount of its support from men. From Barry Goldwater and George Wallace to Adolf Hitler and Pierre Poujade, only populist and revolutionary conservative movements have demonstrated that pattern.[1] The establishmentarian variety of conservatives usually do better with women. Pollsters and political scientists have been struck by the unprecedented polarization—racial and sexual—in measurements of Reagan approval ratings. Social commentators cite other yardsticks. Anti-Semitism is increasing both in the United States and Europe. So are signs of youth movement to the right—from British "skinheads" to campus chapters of the Ku Klux Klan. Some analysts even see growing authoritarian predilections in mass culture, from the resurrection of old superheroes (Superman, et al.) in movies and comic books to the suprarational cult of *Star Wars* and the enormous fascination theatergoers have shown for old films about Napoleon and Hitler. In times less happy, these psychological inclinations could lose their peripheral, epiphenomenal political character.

It's odd that back in the 1960s so many professors could spend so much time thinking about a possible American analogy to Weimar Germany, thanks to the disquiet and disturbances in the universities, only to miss the much more significant American-Weimar parallels of the late 1970s and early 1980s. Likewise, the academics who two decades ago published books and articles by the score on the "Radical Right" in America—spotting potential fascists behind every White Citizens Council in Mississippi or John Birch Society chapter in Orange County, California—have been strangely mute during the last few years. Perhaps having cried wolf so often in 1963 or 1972 when there was none, they don't think the country would listen to them today when liberal ideology stands discredited.

Yet whereas the case for comparing the United States to Weimar Germany in 1970 was hardly very strong, the case for entertaining such a comparison as the Carter Administration left office in 1981 was significantly stronger. To be sure, the dissimilarities between the American (or Anglo-Saxon) mind and culture and that of the German are enough to vitiate any clear, working parallel. The United States will never experience what followed Weimar. However, surface similarities were more clearly apparent in 1980 than in 1970—the fact is, the underlying German reaction to Weimar was *right-*

ward, a direction also emphatically taken by the American electorate in 1980. A good case can be made that Americans in 1980 were responding to many of the same psychologies influencing German voters in 1930.

Kindred causes, congruent psychologies, do not always produce similar historical outcomes. But they *do* suggest a potential for turmoil. Of the major factors behind the Weimar malaise, all four— inflation, skepticism of political institutions, cultural anomie and nationalist frustration in the wake of the nation's first lost war—exist in the United States today. And their convergence goes a long way to explain why a nation (any nation) so buffeted could fall prey to a politics of frustration and bygone glories, one of Arnold Toynbee's nationalist-archaist digressions. Even though Florida and California are not Franconia or Schleswig-Holstein, the Weimar-American eighties parallel merits scrutiny.

As for inflation, the Weimar analogy has become a cliché. Massive inflationary destabilization of the middle class (1921–23), followed after some years by a severe slump (1930–33), is that fact of Weimar life most often and rightly blamed for the rise of Hitler. Everyone knows that as the 1923 German inflation peaked, suitcases of currency, *Billionen* of marks, were needed to buy groceries. Other European and Asian countries that experienced runaway inflation also wound up with authoritarian regimes—Austria and Hungary in the 1920s, China in the 1940s. And many Latin American nations have exchanged double-digit inflation for new military juntas. Neither the experience of the United States nor of the other English-speaking countries has been so severe.* But the first wave of peacetime U.S. double-digit inflation, from 1973 to 1975, moved even sober publications like *Business Week* to run features on the decline of the middle class. The second wave, occurring from 1979 to 1980, was as bad, but triggered fewer such thoughts. And while the books are not yet closed on our inflationary binge, the economic dislocation here will in no way match Germany's. However, the inflation we have had has been insidious, wearing down morality, productivity and support for existing institutions—as it always does. As chapters 8 and 11 show, no one can safely assume that inflation must reach the levels of Weimar to lay the groundwork for political upheaval.

*Anglo-Saxons are not immune, though. Modern Britain's one flirtation with a strongman—Oliver Cromwell—came in the wake of the sixteenth- and early-seventeenth-century price revolution.

The second major parallel is a congruent public loss of faith in political and governmental institutions. Here again, the Weimar case was more fierce because the Germans had little experience with democracy before 1919. Many of those who expressed contempt for the new, parliamentary republic were unrequited monarchists on one hand or recently minted Communists on the other. By contrast, we have two centuries of direct democratic experience, buttressed by an Anglo-Saxon historical legacy. Even so, a parallel cannot be dismissed out of hand. It is true that the city of Washington will not see a putsch orchestrated out of the Alpenhof restaurant on 19th Street or wake up one morning to hear the rumble of tanks on the Memorial Bridge. Yet up through 1980, the collapse of the American public's faith in its major institutions—the presidency, the Congress, the Supreme Court, the executive branch, the political parties—was frightening (see Chart 4, in Chapter 2). A 1979 CBS News poll found 66 percent support for a leader who would bend the rules to get things done.[2] The controversial New Right, leaders of which are on record as "working to overthrow the power structure of this country," is more often than not hostile to the existing party system, impugning the elites of both parties as bankrupt; it leans toward a plebiscitary and interest-group democracy. If the election of November 1980—which put government on a new course and initially reduced popular discontent with our institutions from 80 percent to somewhere between 40 and 50 percent—fails to bear fruit, public demand for a greater political and institutional change could easily surge once more. We should remember that populist reaction to the right in 1932–33 Germany occurred not against a left-leaning government in power but against the ineffective traditional right-center coalition of Franz von Papen.

Americans might also do well to reconsider the cumulative historical impact of events from the assassination of President John F. Kennedy in 1963 to the impeachment and forced resignation of President Richard Nixon in 1974. In 1973 and 1974, several observers—columnist Stewart Alsop and British historian Hugh Trevor-Roper—likened the toppling of Richard Nixon to the overthrow of England's King Charles I and France's Louis XVI.[3] Both regicides were the culmination of grudges held by organized groups in the societies of the time. That's what usually lies behind regicide. And if one accepts the notion of Nixon's overthrow as a republican form of regicide, a whole ghastly series of historical analogies swing into play. All of the major Western powers have seen the popular over-throw or execution of kings at some crucial point in their history: England in 1649 (Charles I), France in 1793 (Louis XVI), Russia in 1917 (Nicholas II), Germany in 1918 (Wilhelm II) and Spain in 1931 (Alfonso XIII). In each case, there followed a relatively short period, from a year or so to a decade, of attempted democratic rule through a legislature: the Rump Parliament, the National Convention, Kerensky's Duma, the Weimar Republic, the Spanish Republic. None of these worked. The final phase invariably produced an authoritarian regime and the great symbolic strongmen of modern history: Oliver Cromwell, Napoleon Bonaparte, Nikolai Lenin, Adolf Hitler, Francisco Franco. Arguably, the United States has already pursued a very limited version of such progression: from figurative regicide in 1974 through a period of a weak presidency and a strong Congress, the Ford and Carter Administrations, to a Reagan Administration whose initial efforts demonstrated a strong, even plebiscitary presidency able to coerce Congress brandishing the popular will or the presumed ability to mold that will. The emergence of a new politics after perceived failure on the part of the Reagan Administration to solve our problems—or if the Reagan Administration itself takes an approach increasingly plebiscitary—could move the American version of the historical process further down the road.

As for a third major parallel, the offense many Americans have taken at the perceived excesses of sociologists, egalitarians, drug advocates, sexual liberationists, permissive educators, pornographers, modern artists, media programmers, and such, is disturbingly like the reaction of many Germans of the 1920s to the famous "cabaret culture" of Berlin—its transvestites and cynical attitudes, the plays of Bertolt Brecht, the cocaine use of the famous, the antitraditionalism of the Bauhaus, and the contempt for the ordinary German and German patriotism in the cartoons of George Grosz and others. In both instances a small metropolitan elite was thought to have run away with national culture, producing a tone many traditionalists regarded as immoral, antipatriotic or antireligious. In each case, a political opportunity was created. Hitler's National Socialists first criticized and then banned modern art, replaced antiwar films with epics about Frederick the Great, and called for a Germany of family, work and Fatherland. All this struck a chord too popular to be dismissed as the Nazi regime's own tastes in petty-bourgeois cultural kitsch. Ronald Reagan struck a similar chord in 1980 when he urged

Americans to return to the values of family, neighborhood and work.

A nation's spasms of cultural ultramodernism, creative as they may be in the memory of literary and art history, all too often signal ill health in the wider body politic. And nothing is so conducive to that kind of spiritual anomie as the loss of a war which strikes at the heart of a nation's and a culture's self-esteem and faith in old verities. Which brings us to a fourth parallel. Germany lost a war in November 1918. Until then, the story of Prussia was one of unbroken geographic and military advance, from the days of the Teutonic knights through the wars against Denmark, Austria and France in the nineteenth century. From an obscure duchy on the eastern marches of Western Europe, Prussia had expanded to become—in the form of the German empire—the most powerful nation on the European continent in the early twentieth century. Until 1918. Later the Allies imposed on Germany a peace treaty and war reparations that further inflamed the fires of national indignation and bitterness. For left-leaning artists and playwrights, the collapse of German imperialism was cause for a decade of celebration; for many other Germans it was an embarrassment and betrayal to be avenged.

Here during the late 1960s, the collapse of national confidence in the Vietnam war effort—and in America's global role—occurred in rough tandem with the "trashing of America," as described by sociologist Robert Nisbet and as satirized by writer Tom Wolfe. The two phenomena—war and reaction at home—were related. Historically, any major war breeds great social change of all sorts. How much more social dislocation can be expected from a nation that had never before lost a war, loses its pride, and sees long cherished beliefs and verities trodden down? The American belief in Manifest Destiny, honed by centuries of westward advance toward the Pacific and then by over a half-century of global advance from Manila Bay to V-J Day, was shaken during the 1970s much as Germany's self-image was after November 1918. The question becomes, How severe will the American reaction be?

A few scholars, albeit not many, have sounded a klaxon. In mid-1980, just as Ronald Reagan was sweeping to the Republican nomination, Canadian writer Robert Cook suggested that an "American Weimar" was in the making.[4] After citing the parallels of inflation, skepticism toward institutions, and public revulsion at the despair apparent just beneath the gloss of high culture, Cook suggested that Americans resent failure in Vietnam, Cuba and elsewhere just as

POST-CONSERVATIVE AMERICA

their German counterparts of the 1920s resented the "betrayal" of the German army in the 1918 armistice. As we will see in Chapter 13, there are reasons to believe that we have not heard the last of Vietnam.

Aside from four major similarities, other, perhaps less important criteria show diminished parallelism. Helmut Thielecke, a West German theologian who as a young pastor resisted Hitler, discussed the preconditions for American fascism in *Between Heaven and Earth: Conversations with American Christians.*[5] Religious belief and desire for a redeemer figure can go together, he warned. Thielecke noted that Hitler freely used Christian vocabulary and talked much about the Almighty's blessing. The Christian confessions, Hitler promised, would become pillars of the new state. In 1978, *Christianity Today,* a magazine for evangelicals, reprinted a lengthy excerpt from Thielecke's book, along with an analysis by Professor Robert Lindner of Kansas State University who suggested that while not all of Thielecke's preconditions for a popular extremism were in place in the United States, a number were. And he specifically said that the forty million U.S. evangelicals might readily find a popular extremism appealing. So have other evangelical scholars.

This overreaches. Perhaps a case can be made that American Protestant and Catholic fundamentalists are potential supporters of an antiliberal politics, especially one promising a restoration of morality. But given the opportunity, any excess which the Moral Majority might pursue would take Anglo-Saxon form, more in the tradition of Oliver Cromwell and his "New Model" Puritan army than that of any recent totalitarian strongman. (Indeed, the religious New Right of the 1980s *is* in many ways another "New Model" *political* army.) In this light it may seem reasonable to think that religious fundamentalism, inflamed by a perception of an amoral larger world, may augment, not restrain, a radical politics. Yet I think there is no Weimar analogy to be made with respect to religion and the religious. Germany's Catholic Center Party, however dubious of Weimar liberalism, presented a major obstacle to Hitler, and National Socialism's "Bavarian heartland" was not really a heartland at all. It took religion too seriously for that.

The rightward radicalization of young people, especially in the universities, was another characteristic marking the disintegration of the Weimar Republic. Here, too, an American analogy is strained, though less strained now than in the late 1960s. The movement on campus is clearly to the right, and some forms of extremism have taken root. From the *Harvard Political Review* of spring 1981:

> Once confined to the rural South, racial terrorism has spread to north-eastern college campuses. The list of such incidents of intimidation has continued to grow. In November of last year, the president of the Black Students Association at Harvard University discovered that someone had defaced her office calendar with racial slurs and threats: "Ten Days to Kill" was written under one date, "KKK Unite" under another. The vandalism was followed by a series of obscene phone calls and rape threats. At Purdue University a wooden cross was set afire outside a black fraternity house. At Williams College a cross was burned near a Black Student Union gathering during homecoming weekend last fall, followed by a wave of racist letters, phone calls and threats—all anonymous. At Wesleyan University an anonymous letter containing obscene racial slurs and anti-Semitic references was placed into the mailbox of the Afro-American Studies Center. The catalogue goes on and on, dealing a steady flow of overtly racist threats and acts at schools as diverse as Cornell, the University of Massachusetts-Amherst, Iowa State, and SUNY-Buffalo.[6]

Meanwhile, and perhaps more important, working-class and lower-middle-class youths, both in Britain and the United States, have taken some liking to swastikas and the nihilism of punk rock music or membership in roving gangs. The Boston *Globe* printed the following lyrics from "Youth Corps," a song by Unnatural Axe, the toughest punk band in Boston:

> We're apolitical, antihistorical
> We don't care about the past . . .
> We're moving' in for sure
> An Aryan culture takeover
> Lightin' fast . . .
> Our thoughts are soarin'
> And there's no ignorin' the potential
> In our minds . . .
> We've got the idea
> So you better hide dears
> Hurry up there's no time,
> We've arrived, we'll survive,
> We're the Youth Corps.[7]

Anti-Semitism presents another shaky potential parallel. In the United States today as in the Germany of the 1920s, Jews were very much part of the cultural revolution anathema to much of the Christian majority. Back in 1975, Harvard sociologist Nathan Glazer let himself wonder what had happened, given the European experience, to the predictable wave of anti-Semitism:

> In the 1960's and early 1970's the United States went through revolutionary social change; sexual mores were transformed, pornography became open and legal, abortion suddenly became legal, the women's movement transformed the domestic family scene. In many of the battles over these issues one saw the classic confrontation of Jewish liberals and radicals versus Catholics and fundamentalist Protestant conservatives. Such radical social change affecting the most intimate aspects of life, it seemed, must lead to an unsettling frustration, and a parallel aggression; and if it did, would not the classic scapegoat of Western Christianity, the Jews, be held responsible, particularly since Jews were so prominent in causing these frustrations?
>
> Once again, it didn't happen. The sexual revolution took place, and Middle America did not fight back. Indeed, here is one of those mysteries that social scientists should explore. What has happened to that great reservoir that fed the Know-Nothings, the American Protective Association, the Ku Klux Klan, the Coughlin movement, and the rest? Of course, one can argue it is still there in the Wallace movement, and yet it appears to me remarkably reduced. Perhaps Watergate served to channel the anger in another direction, against the Republican party, so that there was no way of directing the frustrations over Vietnam and social change into anger against liberals and radicals. In any case, no such anger has developed.[8]

Conceivably, Glazer's forebodings may yet materialize. Pessimists can argue that the early 1980s present renewed danger. However, though the number of anti-Semitic incidents did rise from 1979 to 1981, the religious element in recent right-wing populism has made possible what may constitute a unique historical phenomenon—a grass-roots, right-tilting populist Christian movement that is simultaneously pro-Zionist. This is based on the fundamentalist belief that the Bible calls for the Jews to be gathered in Israel. Much was made, after the 1980 election, of the fact that Moral Majority leader Jerry Falwell and Israeli Prime Minister Menachem Begin, closely tied to

Israel's religious right, were friends and political allies. Meanwhile, low- and low-middle-income Hasidic, ultra-Orthodox Jews of Brooklyn's Boro Park section gave Reagan as high a vote as the West Texas Baptist Bible Belt.

Overall, two points must be made about an American-Weimar analogy. The first is that anyone who thinks that the United States might really become a Germany of Hitler is going to be proven very, very wrong. Recent evidence of anti-Semitism and American Nazi activity is a minor component to a different kind of movement to the right. Yet that raises the second, and contrary, point: Anyone who ignores the idea of some kindred underlying dynamics between the German political and cultural reaction of the 1920s and the emerging American reaction to the political and cultural trauma of the last two decades is also making a big mistake. The stimuli and pathologies are similar enough to warrant concern. In the Germany from 1929 to 1933, the stimuli and pathologies produced a Teutonic ripeness for one of the movements historian Arnold Toynbee has described as a nationalistic archaism, a culture's attempt to restore a past glory and mythology. Elements of the Reagan revolution suggest a related attempt may be occurring in the United States. Both involve a movement to the right, a politics increasingly nationalistic, a return to folkways and traditional values and the rejection of avant-garde culture. The important thing to remember is that there is an enormous difference between an attempt to restore Frederick the Great, the god Wotan and German-Teutonic supremacy over Europe and an attempt to restore Calvin Coolidge and the Indian Summer of the old American financial order. The Weimar-U.S. analogy can be usefully pondered when one compares parallel feelings of frustration in the social order; for anything beyond, the analogy breaks down.

So taken, the key here may well be whether or not the American public takes a second look at the war in Vietnam during the 1980s.

13

VIETNAM:
AN UNEXPLODED BOMB?

Several years [ago], we brought home a group of American fighting men who obeyed their country's call and fought as bravely and well as any Americans in our history. They came home without a victory not because they had been defeated but because they had been denied permission to win.[1]

—President Ronald Reagan, 1981

THESE ARE EXTRAORDINARY WORDS OF RECRIMINA-tion for a sitting President of the United States to voice, and Ronald Reagan voiced them in a Medal of Honor presentation ceremony for Roy P. Benavidez, a retired Army sergeant who had served in Vietnam. In 1976 the Joint Chiefs of Staff had refused to award the medal to Benavidez because only one witness corroborated his act of heroism. Just as the Joint Chiefs changed their minds in 1980 when another witness was found, the American people may yet also revise their views of the war in Southeast Asia.

For Ronald Reagan's verdict on Vietnam to become the nation's —and the stuff of politically charged revisionism—would consummate over a decade of little-publicized recriminationist oratory, taking in Reagan and George Wallace on the right to the Social Democrats U.S.A. (formerly the U.S. Socialist Party) on the left. All have maintained that the war in Vietnam was lost not on the battlefield but in the media, in Congress and on the nation's campus quadrangles.

The principal thrust, of course, has been on the right. On August 22, 1980, Reagan, as the Republican presidential nominee, told the American Legion that the war in Vietnam was "a noble cause"—a poor choice of phrase even by conservative measures and one he did not reiterate. Throughout his 1976 presidential bid, however, Reagan frequently sounded the theme that American troops had been denied victory in Vietnam by the restraints imposed on them at home. No other President—before or after election—has outdone Reagan sounding recriminationist themes. Much the same point was made in a book published in 1976, *A Soldier Reports*—by General William Westmoreland, who served as U.S. commander in Vietnam from 1964 to 1968 and then as Army Chief of Staff through 1976. According to Westmoreland, from mid-1965 until our withdrawal seven and a half years later, "no American unit in South Vietnam other than a few companies on the offensive or an occasional small outpost ever incurred what could fairly be called a setback. That is a remarkable record."[2] Asked whether he thought the American effort in Vietnam was a success, the general said, "The military effort was, but the general effort was characterized by a series of blunders. The military did what they were told to do, and they did it, in my opinion, admirably, under very, very difficult circumstances. So it was not the military who failed, it was the political mechanism that failed."[3]

Four years earlier, in the election of 1972, support for an honorable military conclusion in Vietnam and condemnation of politicians charged with undercutting the war effort had been a conservative staple. Incumbent President Nixon positioned himself as the candidate of achieving peace through the application of more power—bombing North Vietnam and mining the waters off Haiphong. Democratic nominee George McGovern, a disengagement advocate, had gone so far as to suggest that he would crawl to Hanoi to achieve peace, something that offended millions of voters in the conservative and George Wallace wings of the party. On the very day that Wallace was shot in Maryland, he had provoked his greatest response from the crowd with an attack on the "no-win" nature of the war in Vietnam. Press reports record that a tense approval mounted in the audience when the Alabamian denounced Senators George McGovern and Hubert Humphrey for backing the Gulf of Tonkin Resolution in 1964. "Those liberals got us into the war," Wallace charged, "and then they wouldn't let us win it."[4]

Wallace's assertion has had a place in the nation's subconscious for some time, a minor chord of enormous potential importance. Yet by and large, media discussion of our policy in Indochina from 1965 to 1975 has ignored the nationalistic subcurrent, the ongoing thesis of a kind of betrayal as proposed by Nixon, Wallace, Westmoreland and Reagan. Instead, the press portrait of American involvement swung from a naïve drumbeating—in 1965–66, even James Reston, Walter Cronkite and company proclaimed the war a necessity—to one of American guilt, brutality and failure—of corrupt imperialism and inevitable embarrassment and defeat. The "Marine Hymn" yielded to the antiwar lyrics of Joan Baez and Pete Seeger, and national pride yielded to Watergate. By 1975, when the collapse of South Vietnam fulfilled the predictions of liberal opinion, public support for the U.S. military and even for defense spending in general had reached a post–World War II nadir. Because most of the press ignored the persistence of Reagan's views on Vietnam, their powerful re-emergence in 1980 took pundits by surprise.

This is not the place for a debate on the merits of the war in Vietnam, except to structure a way to look at its probable impact on the politics of the 1980s. American public opinion toward the war was two-edged from the beginning: "Win or get out" probably summed up the feelings of the majority in 1965 and 1966. By the early 1970s, when victory no longer seemed possible, majority preference swung to a respectable egress, as represented in 1972 by Richard Nixon.* Only well after the negotiated U.S. withdrawal in January 1973, as the debris of Watergate began to accumulate, can it be said that public opinion swung (briefly, I think) and blamed Nixon, the military and the conservatives for the debacle. Here Richard Whalen and others were percipient in calling Watergate a disguised political civil war to allocate blame for the failure in Southeast Asia. It was, and from 1974 to 1976, Watergate did. But the preliminary allocation was not permanent, and the question now is whether we can expect a reassessment.

Arguably so, and for two principal reasons. First, our political history suggests that our country's wars do not end—not their final national impact—until they've been refought in the political arena, and the refighting can go on for more than a decade. We have not

*For a detailed analysis of how the public's desire for toughmindedness and a face-saving outcome in Vietnam was a major force working for Richard Nixon in the 1972 election, see Chapter 5 of Samuel Lubell, *The Future While It Happened* (New York, Norton, 1973).

yet had a no-holds-barred review, the recurring hints of conservative politicians notwithstanding. With an American-soldiers-were-denied-permission-to-win rhetorician elected President, however, that day may be drawing closer. Second, the circumstances of our defeat in Vietnam are as unique as the fact of defeat itself. In the critical years, from 1964 to 1968, the war was fought using unusual academic theories and political constraints imposed by an essentially liberal leadership elite. And the role of the news media, widely commented upon, *was* absolutely unique. All this has really yet to be evaluated—at least in a national debate.

As a political analyst here, I find myself embracing the role of a lawyer who wants to establish not that a statement is *true,* but simply that it was in fact made. Thus, when I note assertions that liberal theorists of the war were responsible for our defeat, I do not want to establish the validity of these statements, but to heighten and underscore a thesis held by many American conservatives: that our soldiers in Vietnam were defeated in the Congress, the National Press Club, the network television newsrooms, the tables of the Paris peace negotiations, and the universities, *not* on the battlefield. In short, all that is necessary for a post–World War I, German-style recrimination is in place.

The critique made by military people is simple enough. In 1974 Brigadier General Douglas Kinnard, a soldier turned political scientist, sent out a questionnaire to 173 generals who had served in Vietnam, as had Kinnard. Sixty-four percent sent back replies, for the most part rendering a severe indictment of political-military tactics and media influence.[5] Fifty-eight percent of the generals thought that "search and destroy" tactics were either "not sound" or "sound when first implemented, not later." Fifty-three percent expressed the belief that in view of the casualties and disruption of our politics and society, the war either had not been worth the effort or should not have been pursued beyond an advisory stage. More than 70 percent, according to Kinnard, held a negative opinion of how Washington ran the war. Much of the blame fell on Secretary of Defense Robert McNamara, who presided over our early build-up and strategy in Indochina. Kinnard argues that "McNamara was a great peace-time secretary and a lousy war secretary," and although McNamara deferred to the military when it came to the actual fighting, he constrained them in ways that made solid performance impossible.

General Westmoreland presents a comparable indictment in his own memoirs, criticizing the McNamara concept of escalation which allowed the enemy "to adapt to each new step and absorb the damage." And he deplores the civilian "whiz kids" in the Pentagon, State Department and White House who refused to take bold decisive measures and who were constantly chasing after chimeras, lights at the end of various tunnels, that existed only on computer print-outs and within their own minds. In describing Pentagon refusal to authorize bombing Russian-made missile sites in North Vietnam, Westmoreland laments: "It was all a matter of signals, said the clever civilian theorists in Washington. We won't bomb the SAM sites, which signals the North Vietnamese not to use them. Had it not been so serious, it would have been amusing."[6] *Clever civilian theorists*— three very pregnant words.

On June 28, 1970, *Newsweek* ran a photo literally worth a thousand explanatory words. Captioned "A council of war in Honolulu, 1966," the photo showed three past and future global eleemosynarians sitting around the table with Lyndon Johnson: Secretary of State Dean Rusk, former president of the Rockefeller Foundation, later a university professor; Defense Secretary Robert McNamara, former president of the Ford Motor Company, later president of the World Bank; presidential assistant McGeorge Bundy, former Harvard dean, later president of the Ford Foundation. These policy architects chose not to employ the traditional way to fight a war, i. e., the fullest necessary application of military power; they—and the lesser of "the best and the brightest"—instead applied concepts of limited war, including the deadly notion of a "favorable body count" and other chimeras cited by frustrated Army commander Westmoreland. We even saw an element of global New Dealism: Lyndon Johnson could speak of a TVA on the Mekong, and Vice President Hubert Humphrey could with his usual enthusiasm say that the war was "a great adventure, and a wonderful one it is."[7] Centrist liberals gave the war its essential shape—a computerized, politically restrained attempt to apply limited military power. If the conflict in Indochina was the first American war to be fully condemned by the university community and the intelligentsia, it was also the first to be largely blueprinted by people within these same circles. That duality of failure has the potential to be a great source of embarrassment. So our defeat in Vietnam appears to lend itself to plausible conservative attempts to blame the intelligentsia—for formulating misshapen military policy directives *and* then protesting the war itself, with each indictment feeding on the other. As defined and fought from 1964 to 1968, Vietnam was the Liberal Foreign Policy Establishment's war. Barry Goldwater, had he been elected in 1964, would have bombed North Vietnam into oblivion, another kind of problem entirely.

If Vietnam is to be revisited, the intellectual community has a second Achilles heel—the role of the media. Kinnard's survey of general officers who served in the war turned up massive antipress indignation: 89 percent thought that newspaper coverage was either partly or completely irresponsible and had disrupted military efforts; and 91 percent thought that television coverage tended to present matters out of context or went for the openly sensational. In 1977 Peter Braestrup, former Vietnam correspondent for the New York *Times* and later for the Washington *Post,* published an extraordinary two-volume study, called *Big Story,* of major media coverage of the war.[8] His key findings focus on the coverage of the January–March 1968 Tet offensive, generally regarded as the turning point of the war. The national media, Braestrup says, drastically misinformed the country about the events and meaning of Tet, told the American people that Tet was a disaster for the United States and South Vietnam, when, in fact, it was a major setback for Hanoi. So much has been confirmed by troops in the field at the time. The press thereby directly contributed to public loss of confidence in Lyndon Johnson and to his decision to abandon his candidacy for re-election in 1968. "Many commentators," Braestrup writes, "promptly claimed for Hanoi an important 'symbolic' and 'psychological' success which . . . Hanoi itself did not claim."[9] Magnified in media commentary and recycled in the pivotal New Hampshire primary, the press coverage of Tet had a devastating impact, although Braestrup suggests that, ironically, "the Tet offensive, as portrayed in the media, appeared to have a far greater effect on political Washington and the Administration itself than on the U.S. population's sentiment on the war." The American public lost confidence in LBJ's leadership but continued to support the war itself in polls for a long period thereafter.

Braestrup was by no means the first newsman to castigate media war coverage. One of the bluntest statements came back in the early 1970s from ABC newsman Howard K. Smith, who said: "The networks have never given a complete picture of the war. That terrible siege of Khe Sanh went on for five weeks before newsmen revealed that the South Vietnamese were fighting at our sides . . . And the Vietcong's casualties were 100 times ours. But we never told *that.* We just showed pictures day after day of Americans getting the hell kicked out of them. That was enough to break America apart. That's also what it did . . . Lyndon Johnson was actually politically assassinated."[10]

Of course, if revisionism does become part of the politics of the 1980s, the antiwar groups will also possess powerful arguments. Today, as ten years ago, the left-liberal case against the war derived no small validity from the lies and misrepresentations of both the Johnson and the Nixon Administrations, to say nothing of inept military tactics (like defoliation). Moreover, many military officers came to regard Vietnam as a tour of duty to be milked in every way for current and future promotion. Any discussion—like this one—that only presents the critiques of Westmoreland, Kinnard, Braestrup and Smith can hardly give full scope to the weakness of our policy in Indochina. Yet if the war is a still-unexploded sociopsychological bomb buried in the psyche of our politics, the two theses I have cited—that the military wasn't allowed to win, and that the media and intelligentsia were mostly to blame for that—are the pivotal ones: these two, and not the other side of the debate, call up an analogy to the political currents of Weimar Germany and the notions of a betrayal of the German army.

European analogies aside, the second reason to anticipate further impact of the war on our politics is unique to our own traditions. All previous wars have been refought to some extent or another in the arena of political recrimination, something that seems to be as American as apple pie. Perhaps through Watergate and the onus which came to rest on conservative Republicans we have already refought Vietnam. But the Watergate and the post-Vietnam politics of 1973 to 1976 appear to violate the basic postwar pattern which has obtained from the days of James Madison through those of Dwight Eisenhower. At the risk of too much generalization, three rules seem to apply:

- Whenever an American political party has let itself appear sympathetic to a enemy (whether foreign or confederate), or unwilling to provide necessary support for troops on the battlefield, it has been decisively defeated in the next presidential election (1816, 1864, 1900, 1952).

- Whenever certain groups within our population have been perceived as unpatriotic, they have become victims of an extremely unpleasant postwar backlash (the years after the War of 1812, the Mexican War and the Civil War, the "Red Scare" after World War I, and the post–World War II McCarthy era).
- Although war, by its waste and fundamental inhumanity, always produces significant demand for political reform, postwar politics in our history has usually swung toward repression or reaction, and it is impossible to find a single postwar period that produced a clear victory for what can be regarded as reform.

Judged by the politics of 1973 to 1976, public reaction to Vietnam would appear to breach all these precedents. Yet before jumping to that conclusion, it may be well to look at the actual historical patterns involved. I have omitted the American Revolution, although the hostility to Tories and loyalists, many being obliged to flee to Bermuda, the Bahamas or Canada, may have helped create a precedent for taking wartime patriotism seriously indeed.

Wartime patriotism certainly was taken seriously after the second American confrontation with Britain—the War of 1812. The hostilities were extremely unpopular in New England, especially among leaders of the Federalist Party, the political vehicle of regional maritime and mercantile interests. Much of the objection was economic, because the British blockade throttled New England shipping and commerce. Samuel Eliot Morison, in his *Maritime History of Massachusetts,* writes that Federalist villages on Cape Cod openly welcomed British naval landing parties, while Democratic towns fought them off.[11] Federalist politicians derided the conflict as "Mr. Madison's War." Massachusetts refused to allow her militia to be used outside the state borders. Celebrations were held to cheer English victories over Napoleon. The island of Nantucket went so far as to declare its neutrality in August 1814, and Newburyport's Sea Fencibles would fly only a five-starred New England flag, not an American one. Many local ships traded with England and Canada under license from the British fleet. Finally, the Federalist-controlled General Court (legislature) of Massachusetts summoned a New England convention at Hartford late in 1814 to discuss war, politics and possible secession from the Union. Meanwhile, some Federalist newspapers openly advocated secession, preferring to reconstitute New England as a small pro-British maritime nation. But cooler heads prevailed.

Although the January 1815 report of the Hartford Convention threatened nullification if the Administration resorted to military conscription, the idea of secession was repudiated.

Elsewhere in the land, the war, even as it was often badly fought, stirred patriotic sentiments and ended in a blaze of glory as Andrew Jackson smashed the best regiments of the British army at the Battle of New Orleans. When the peace treaty was signed in 1815, patriotic hallelujahs swept the land, and the Federalists paid dearly for their defeatism and near-treason. In the elections of 1816 and 1818, the Federalists were all but wiped out, and in 1820 the party of Washington, Adams and Hamilton didn't bother to offer a presidential nominee.

Three decades later, many New Englanders again objected to the Mexican War of 1846–48, which they regarded as a creature of the expansion-minded Southern slaveocracy. The Massachusetts legislature declared the war "hateful in its objects . . . wanton, unjust and unconstitutional."[12] Ohio's Whig Senator Thomas Corwin said that if he were a Mexican, he would greet the Americans "with bloody hands" and welcome them "to hospitable graves."[13] Other Whig politicians—heirs of the Federalists—shared these views. Whig Congressman Abraham Lincoln of Illinois sneered at Democratic President James K. Polk's assertion that the war was justified because Mexico had shed American blood on American soil. Congressman Lincoln introduced the celebrated "Spot Resolution" demanding that President Polk point to the spot where this occurred. Although quite a few Americans shared Whig (and Free Soil Democrat) doubts about the war, public opinion soured on those Whigs who seemed to have gone beyond the pale in opposing what was, after all, a very successful military foray. Lincoln was among the Whig congressmen not returning to Washington after the 1848 election.

Meanwhile, President Polk hurt his cause by trying to tie the hands of important generals who happened to be Whigs. One of them, General Zachary Taylor, complained that "Polk, Marcy and company have been more anxious to break me than to defeat Santa Ana."[14] In his book *The Mexican War,* historian Otis Singletary says: "This was the theme that gained widespread popular support: An aged and courageous commander, victorious in spite of being stripped of his troops in the face of a powerful enemy. It was this image that made Taylor the next President of the United States [in the 1848 election]."[15]

However Abraham Lincoln may have felt about homefront defeatists in the Mexican War, the shoe was on the other foot during the Civil War. By then Lincoln was a Republican, and the Northern Democrats—some of them Copperheads, Knights of the Golden Circle, and so forth—were the party of antidraft riots, peace resolutions and collusion with the foe. From 1862 to 1864, many Northern Democratic politicians brazenly opposed "Mr. Lincoln's War," treating every Confederate advance as a new reason for a hurried peace. Lincoln grew so angry that he ordered one Peace Democrat, Ohio Congressman Clement Vallandigham, deported to the Confederacy. The climax came in 1864. Meeting in Chicago on August 29, the Democratic National Convention adopted this antiwar plank in its platform:

> Resolved, that this Convention does explicitly declare as the sense of the American people, that after four years of failure to restore the Union by the experiment of war, during which, under pretense of a military necessity, or war power higher than the Constitution, the Constitution has been disregarded in every part, and public liberty and private rights alike downtrodden, and the material prosperity of the country greatly impaired, justice, humanity, liberty and the public welfare demand that immediate efforts be made for a cessation of hostilities . . .[16]

Well into September, Democratic politicians sabotaged military conscription and hoped for a forced peace, but Sherman's capture of Atlanta and Sheridan's Shenandoah victories turned the tide. Republican strategists counterattacked with their big campaign issue: treason. Peace Democrat after Peace Democrat was linked to secret antiwar and pro-Confederate societies. In Illinois, Democratic gubernatorial candidate James Thompson was found to have accepted $40,000 from Confederate agents operating out of Canada.

The Republicans won the elections in November 1864, and the North won the war in April 1865. Subsequently, even after the Compromise of 1876 brought a Republican rapprochement with the Confederate South itself, GOP orators continued to attack and label Northern Democrats as somehow treasonous. Professor Woods Gray, in his book *The Hidden Civil War,* puts it this way:

> Although few of those who gave aid and comfort to the Confederacy either through political maneuvering or revolutionary plotting were ever

directly punished for their activities, the Democratic Party suffered severely for the extent to which it permitted itself to be used as an instrument of the Copperheads. Disloyalty during the War of 1812 had given the death blow to the Federalist Party, and opposition to the Mexican War played a part in the demise of the Whigs. Had it not been for its (patriotic) strength in the South . . . the Democratic Party might have disintegrated as a result of the Civil War.

Republican campaigners were keenly aware of the weapon they held and used it for half a century . . . Antiwar speeches or activities during the course of the conflict were disinterred years afterward to besmirch the reputations of Democratic candidates for office.[17]

The pattern should be taking shape: *not an American war has been fought without recrimination coloring postwar politics.* Nevertheless, with the coming of the Spanish-American War in 1898, the Democrats raised the antiwar, antimilitary theme once again. After taking the Philippines from Spain, American troops quickly faced a new rebellion aimed to achieve Filipino independence. At first the pacification campaign went poorly, and Democrats, attacking McKinley "imperialism" and "militarism," urged the withdrawal of our troops. Republicans complained that the Filipino rebels were abetted by Democratic sympathy, and by Congress' successful gutting of Army appropriations. On February 16, 1899, President McKinley spoke in Boston on the policy in the Philippines. He disclaimed imperial designs and reaffirmed Administration intentions of guiding the Filipinos toward self-government. He attacked the domestic "prophets of evil," blasting the Democrats who had led the pressure for war with Spain in 1898, only to cry out a year later against the consequences of their own making.[18]

Unaccustomed to jungle warfare, U.S. troops in the Philippines continued to do poorly through 1899. Democratic politicians expected political dividends as the first militia returned from the islands, bloodied by ambush and exhausted by lethal sun and tropical rains. After reviewing Pennsylvania's militia in Pittsburgh, McKinley made a speech. Without them, he said, "Our flag would have had its first stain and the American nation its first ignominy . . . They had no part or patience with the men, few in number, happily, who would have rejoiced to see them lay down their arms . . . Who resisted the suggestion of the unpatriotic that they should come home?" The President read the name of the units ("The First California, First Idaho, Fifty-first Iowa . . .") and waves of cheers from the Tenth Pennsylvania regiment dispelled Democratic hopes.[19]

In 1900 the Democrats nominated William Jennings Bryan for President, trumpeting "imperialism" as the "paramount issue" of the campaign. Bryan denounced GOP militarism and promised a special session of Congress to bail out of the Philippines. But the war issue failed, and the Republicans won their greatest victory since the "Bloody Shirt" days of 1872.

Postwar reaction to our intervention in Europe in 1917 and 1918 took place on several fronts. Though many German-Americans agonized over the World War, defeatism or sympathy for the enemy was rare except among a small number of radicals, socialists and anarchists. Public hostility toward such attitudes quickly led to Redbaiting, and the years 1919 and 1920 were years of pronounced reaction. On the other hand, ethnic Americans—Germans, Italians, Irish and others—reacted strongly in the 1920 election against Woodrow Wilson's plan to involve the United States in European enmities and a League of Nations.

After World War II, no discussion of the postwar backlash can isolate the larger war from its Korean sequel. Even before 1945, many conservative Republicans accused the Roosevelt Administration of taking a view too conciliatory toward Soviet Russia. As the Cold War flared in 1947–48, Roosevelt war policies were examined anew for evidence of softness toward the emerging Russian enemy rather than the weakening German foe. Yalta (referring to the 1945 conference at which FDR acquiesced to Russian dominance in Eastern Europe) became a symbol of alleged Democratic softness toward Communism. Four or five years passed before the issue came into full political focus.

Coming hard on the heels of the 1949 Communist takeover of China, outbreak of the Korean War in June of 1950 brought the "Soft on Communism" issue to a head. Even while announcing his support for the war, Senate GOP leader Robert Taft of Ohio said that the Democrats had "invited" North Korea's attack on South Korea by their "sympathetic acceptance of Communism."[20] By and large, congressional Republicans wanted to go "all out" in Korea, while the Truman Administration pursued a policy of limited warfare. GOP allegations reinforced similar queries about the acumen and fortitude of American anti-Communism in the last years of World War II. Meanwhile General Douglas MacArthur, the U.S. military commander in the Pacific, soon came to regard Washington's prosecution of the Korean War as wishy-washy. He wanted to use more military force for a clear victory. Believing this would be too dangerous, President Truman removed MacArthur from command in April 1952. Soon thereafter MacArthur told a Joint Session of Congress: "Why, my soldiers asked of me, surrender military advantages to the enemy in the field?" He paused, and then said, "I could not answer."[21] The Republican Party took up MacArthur's cause, its leaders raising the bitter argument that our will to win in Korea was being sabotaged by "a pro-Communist State Department group." In the 1952 presidential elections, the GOP won a smashing victory with a "K(1) C(2)" strategy: the issues of Korea, corruption, and Communism in government.

The history of American postwar political reaction to war is instructive because for over a century and a half, the pattern is steady and clear. Whenever one of the major political parties has become identified with seeming sympathy for the enemy, defeatism or insufficient support of American troops committed to battle, the American people have rebuked that party with a vote for what they construed as patriotism. Far from being a ticket to political victory, peace resolutions have subsequently brought their proponents to the brink of partisan collapse—the Federalists after 1815, the Whigs after the Mexican War, the Democrats after the Civil War.

These past patterns show just how striking an exception was the immediate postwar reaction to the war in Vietnam. The question is whether it can remain an exception, or whether the pre-Vietnam norm of a backlash against "defeatism" will soon enough appear. Supporters of the latter view have history on their side; there is also evidence that Americans really only began to confront the war on a cultural basis in 1977 and 1978 *after* the first-wave, Watergate-linked reaction. The years 1977 through 1981 brought an outpouring of war-related books and movies, as well as savage proof—in Vietnam and Cambodia—that a Communist takeover would be ruthless and murderous, just as supporters of our role in Indochina had always maintained. Only in the late 1970s, then, did the framework for a genuine Vietnam (as opposed to Watergate) post-mortem begin to fall into place, more or less in tandem with a larger national political trend to the right.

Here the election of Ronald Reagan in 1980 did more than merely empower a President who felt that our troops weren't allowed to win in Vietnam. The 1980 Republican platform called for intensified internal security activities, pledging that "establishment of a Congressional and Executive capability to oversee our internal security efforts will no longer be neglected."[22] And the early actions taken by the Reagan Administration, not least rekindling federal preoccupation with the threat of subversion and internal dissidents, are entirely compatible with a 1980s recriminatory post-mortem of "Who lost Vietnam?" So is the growing attempt to draw analogies between 1960s military intervention in Southeast Asia and early 1980s policy in Central America.

A modicum of intellectual groundwork is being laid as well. By 1980 and 1981 there was an effort on some campuses and on the part of a few bold professors to promote a revisionist interpretation of the nature and consequences of American involvement in Vietnam. The key academicians cited in press analyses were Robert A. Scalapino, director of the Institute of East Asian Studies at the University of California (Berkeley), Harvard historian Oscar Handlin, Boston University sociologist Peter Berger, and University of Massachusetts political scientist Guenter Lewy.[23] The principal catalyst, logically enough, was the Hanoi government's actions after 1975 from institution of re-education camps and the invasion of Cambodia to the handling of the boat people. Not only did Communist mass murder make involvement morally justifiable in retrospect, the revisionist argument goes, but events after 1975 also partially substantiate yesteryear's argument that military defeat in Vietnam would have repercussions elsewhere in Southeast Asia: weakening faith in American commitments, encouraging Communist forces and motivating other governments to review military agreements with the United States, as Thailand and the Philippines have in fact done.

How far the new debate can or will progress remains to be seen. Many revisionist arguments are highly rebuttable. As critics of American involvement suggest, the war in Indochina probably *was* an end-of-empire excess, destined for failure. And much of Vietnam's aggression after 1975 *can* be tied to historical apprehension of China and rivalry with Thailand for domination of Indochina—two long-standing realities only partially linked to the outcome of the war. Yet I wonder how much these intellectual caveats matter in American *political* terms. Even though most historians may scoff at the brand of revisionism described above, quite a few nevertheless expect it to gather force as young historians try to make a name for themselves, and as the changing tide of American public opinion supports a shift to the right in historical analysis. Besides, if the United States *is* in an end-of-empire stage of history, that sensitivity-cum-frustration may only serve to make the public, if not the academic community, even more amenable to a revised interpretation of our involvement in Southeast Asia, one that would simultaneously facilitate retrospective citizen pride in our imperial role and intentions while scapegoating an unpopular and allegedly unpatriotic minority for the *collapse* of that role. Measured by Gross National Psychology, the 1980s could be a decade ripe for revisionism.

A revised interpretation of our defeat in Vietnam would most probably have rightward implications in conventional political parlance. But H. L. Mencken also put his finger on something important back in 1921 when he suggested what it would take to shake the American "boobery" out of their bourgeois optimism: "Only one thing will ever damage that structure: unsuccessful war. The day that the United States is beaten on land and sea, and the unbroken hope of 144 years suddenly blows up—that day it will be high time to look for the birth of radicalism."[24]

One doubts that he was talking about the radicalism recently exemplified by Joan Baez, David Dellinger and Jane Fonda.

14

A FOURTH U.S. "GREAT AWAKENING"?

The life and heart of the [1980 Reagan presidential] campaign are not to be found in elite concerns with economic and foreign policy, but in mass concerns with social and moral issues . . . Political scientists have devoted great attention to political realignments in American history but have not taken fully into account the extent to which these seismic shifts in partisan loyalties were accompanied by, and perhaps stimulated by, the shockwaves of religious and quasi-religious revivals.

—James Q. Wilson, in "Reagan and the Republican Revival," *Commentary* (October 1980)

MARTIN MARTY, UNIVERSITY OF CHICAGO PROFESSOR of the history of modern Christianity, made a mistake in the mid-1970s when he asserted that the 1964 Goldwater nomination represented the "high tide" of fundamentalism and neo-evangelicalism in American politics.[1] That high tide either occurred in 1980—or is yet to come in some future year for which results are still only a gleam in the electorate's eyes. As James Q. Wilson, Samuel Lubell and others have observed, few omissions are as recurrent in the political literature of the last two decades as the failure to comprehend the importance of fundamentalism, revivalism and the realignment of Southern Baptists. Surging religious radicalism is a significant component of the politics of the 1980s.

The United States is a unique nation and polity in two ways: *both* populism and fundamentalist revivalism have shaped its history. Indeed, the two have often seemed to go hand in hand, much to the unhappiness of the political establishment of the country. The First Great Awakening, lasting from roughly 1730 through 1760, emphasized the individual nature of religious experience, offending the gentry not only by uncouth revival practices—moanings, seizures, and the like—but by rejection of the established order in religion, society and, ultimately, politics. Most historians feel that the First Great Awakening helped lay the groundwork for the American Revolution.

The Second Great Awakening (1800–1830) again emphasized the common man, gainsaying hierarchial religion and politics alike, and supplying a moral framework for the posture assumed by Jacksonian Democracy. The Third Great Awakening, beginning in the late nineteenth century and ebbing shortly after World War I, once more linked Protestant revivalism—the tents, baptisms and river gatherings—with the politics of the common man. The candidate most associated with turn-of-the-century revivalism, three-times (1896, 1900, 1908) Democratic presidential nominee William Jennings Bryan, epitomized rural democratic politics at its simplest. His 1896 famous "Cross of Gold" speech extolled farmers and small townspeople "crucified" on the hard-money, business-interests' doctrine of the gold standard. But others, less bucolic and agrarian, made the ideas of the Third Great Awakening an effective tool for opposing Social Darwinism and industrialist laissez-faire economics. In no sense, however, can populism and the sort of religious revivalism characterized as "great awakenings" be treated as identical. Each has had many facets unrelated to the other, though the overlap of religious revivalism and populist politics, mostly a phenomenon of the hinterland, *has* been a recurrent force in American history.

Thus the importance of the growing number of observers who make the case that another such great awakening is under way. In 1977 George Gallup reported growing evidence "that the United States may be in an early stage of a profound religious revival, with the evangelical movement providing a powerful thrust."[2] Brown University Professor William G. McLoughlin, in a book published in 1978 entitled *Revivals, Awakenings, and Reform,* suggests that the events of the 1960s and 1970s amounted to a Fourth Great Awakening.[3] A decade ago, futurist Herman Kahn saw the nation in the throes of a 1970s counterreformation after the reformation of the 1960s.[4] Meanwhile, New Left activists Jeremy Rifkin and Ted Howard published an intriguing book in 1979 called *The Emerging Order: God in an Age of Scarcity,* which stated that the American evangelical movement had "the potential for a Second Protestant Reformation.'"[5] Tom Wolfe saw a Third Great Awakening getting under way —he didn't count the one led by Bryan—around the selfish dynamics of the "me" decade.[6]

Not all of these analysts employed religious criteria. Some assumed that the secular moral trend would be the key to the new great awakening. But most looked to denominational measurements, and signs of a fundamentalist resurgence were widespread by the mid-1970s.

In 1980 the Washington *Post* published a well-documented article by Tony Thomas, an editor of the *Economist,* suggesting that leading media, academicians and opinion-molders had by and large missed one of the most important stories of the prior decade: the new-time rise of old-time religion.[7] Since the upheaval of the mid-1960s, the more fashionable Protestant denominations, those that had chosen to move toward secularism, doctrinal tolerance and social liberalism, had been rapidly losing adherents while many, many converts were being made by churches more fundamentalist, charismatic, nonpermissive in doctrine and authoritarian in nature. Chart 14 provides vivid substantiation of Thomas' point: the ebbing Methodists, Episcopalians and Presbyterians, the growing Southern Baptists, Mormons and Seventh-Day Adventists.

In point of fact, as he himself acknowledged, Thomas was largely reiterating—with fresher, even more imposing data—the case made by National Council of Churches official Dean Kelley in his 1972 book, *Why Conservative Churches Are Growing.* Kelley argued that "strong" churches—those that insisted on high membership, commitment, intolerant of dissent, absolutist in belief, missionary in zeal, expecting obedience to the commands of charismatic leadership— were growing, while "weak" churches—the permissive, noncharismatic, middle-class and upper-middle-class institutional variety— were losing ground.[8] With moral, sexual and general cultural rebellion mushrooming, Americans either fell away from religion—joining, as so many upper-middle-class professionals did, the church of the Sunday-morning newspaper—or embraced religion more fully, turning to the reassurance of the strict doctrine.

Other religious scholars and sociologists provided some important amplifications. In 1976 University of Texas political scientist Steve Hendricks published data derived from samplings by the University of Michigan Survey Research Center and the University of Chicago's National Opinion Research Center, suggesting that the fashionable

Chart 14

Surging Fundamentalist Membership

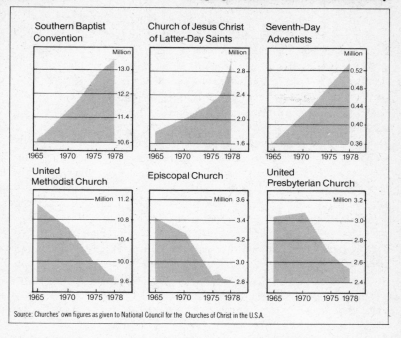

Southern Baptist Convention

Church of Jesus Christ of Latter-Day Saints

Seventh-Day Adventists

United Methodist Church

Episcopal Church

United Presbyterian Church

Source: Churches' own figures as given to National Council for the Churches of Christ in the U.S.A.

denominations were mistaken in assuming that fundamentalists and evangelicals would shift direction once they prospered and moved in middle-class circles, as had been the case historically. Hendricks found that, to the contrary, "We are seeing a tremendous change in the composition of fundamentalist churches. They are becoming massively middle class."[9] Successful young fundamentalists, far from leaving their churches, were attracting socioeconomic peers raised in other, "softer" denominations. What's more, highly trained, technically oriented individuals were especially likely to join fundamentalist churches. Even New England, generally regarded as the least fundamentalist and evangelical region of the country, has been part of the surprising trend. No data is available for the mid-1970s, but as of spring 1981, a survey by the Boston-based Evangelistic Association of New England found that of the 350 to 450 churches founded in New England in the previous decade, almost all were evangelical or fundamentalist. Moreover, of the 8,000 churches in New England, roughly half identified themselves as fundamentalist or evangelical: 70 percent in Maine, 60 percent in New Hampshire, 60 percent in Rhode Island, 58 percent in Vermont, 52 percent in Massachusetts and 49 percent in Connecticut.[10] The extraordinary thing is that large numbers of Bostonians and New Yorkers (to say nothing of Boston–New York–Washington opinion leaders) have little or no comprehension of these numbers and trends. The religious-moral gap between the larger American public and the leadership elite is large —and probably still growing.

Though the two terms are often used interchangeably, the difference between evangelicals and fundamentalists is worth an aside. The term "fundamentalist" refers to a view of the Bible as literal truth. Fundamentalists need not necessarily be "born again," though many are. By this criterion, the fundamentalist group, conservative almost by definition, is distinctly more conservative than the evangelicals— the "born agains," those who assert they have had a personal experience of Jesus Christ as Savior. Although many evangelicals are conservative in culture and politics, many are not. Quite a few are liberal members of progressive denominations. So, measurements of fundamentalists in polls or elections are not the same as measurements of evangelicals. Not at all.

Far from being peripheral, religious trends are of central importance to U.S. politics and society. By anybody's statistics, America is the most religious of major Western nations. Recent Gallup data showed 94 percent of Americans believing in God or a universal spirit as compared to 89 percent in Canada, 88 percent in Italy, 80 percent in Australia, 76 percent in the United Kingdom, 65 percent in Scandinavia and 38 percent in Japan. Also, 56 percent of Americans say that religion is very important in their lives, as compared to 36 percent in Italy, 25 percent in Australia, 22 percent in France and 12 percent in Japan.[11] George Gallup calls the United States "unique in that we have both a high level of formal education and display a high level of religious belief and practice."[12]

Yet somehow, over the last two decades, judges, educators and philosophers have thought it not just politic but proper and even constitutionally obligatory to remove more and more of religion's role in public life—far more, for example, than secularists have sought to strip away in most of Western Europe, where state-recognized churches and state aid to church schools are common. The result has been a festering build-up of resentment against so-called secular humanism, especially on the part of the nation's 45 million or so evangelicals and fundamentalists. Sometimes, to be sure, elements of this debate have verged on the inane. Conspiratorially minded conservatives place fear-ladened emphasis on the threat posed by 1973's Humanist Manifesto II and 1980's Secular Humanist Declaration, though these documents have had little national exposure or support, as befits their appeal to a very small number of Americans. Conversely, liberals insist on painting politically active fundamentalists as a threat to the separation of church and state, though any serious legal analysis will make clear that the church-state intrusion of the last two decades has been almost entirely on the part of the state. That encroachment has been substantial, driving prayer from the classroom, Christmas manger scenes from the courthouse lawns, and involving IRS determination of what is and what is not religious activity. Those involved—on both sides—take the issue seriously. In the Supreme Court's fall 1980 term alone, the justices heard thirty-four cases pertaining to religious matters. Held in the spring of 1981, a Washington conference on government interference in religious affairs drew nearly four hundred participants ranging from fundamentalist Baptists to Sikhs and Scientologists.[13]

As official encroachment has escalated over the last two decades, adverse reaction at the grass roots has swelled not only the ranks of Christian fundamentalism but the political awareness and importance of what observers have been wont to label collectively the Religious Right. However, before turning to the significance of the Religious Right's political involvement, it may be useful to summarize the group's two major philosophic thrusts-cum-complaints. First, they perceive, and deplore, "humanism" gaining force in society. The essence of that credo—launched, they contend, by fifth-century Greek philosopher Protagoras' observation that "Man is the measure of all things"—is to assert that the human being is the measure of value, with man occupying the center of his own universe. Thus morals, being man-made, become malleable, not absolutes grounded in the divine authority of the Bible.

The second fundamentalist complaint is against "secularism," against the trend toward a godless society given to political relativism and divorced from any system containing clear moral purpose.

In Stanford University's 1980 Hoover Institution series on America's third century, sociologist Peter Berger called on Americans to halt the trend to establish "secularism as the quasi-religion of the republic." He condemned "the belligerent attitude of some liberal groups, increasingly supported by the federal courts, to deny tax support in any shape or form to education that takes place under religious auspices." Berger says the "attitude [is one] of extraordinary sociological blindness," given the dependence of the American creed and state on the "moral values that the churches embody and mediate."[14] Spokesmen for the Religious Right have been less delicate in their phraseology.

Even though the diatribes hurled against "secular humanism"— as the composite bogeyman is labeled—have often seemed harsh and sweeping, elements of their critique seem almost unassailable if one wants to learn what drives the sociocultural trend. To many Americans who believe that moral standards have their root in religion and the Bible, the moral-cultural climate, judicial decisions, legislative retreats and general politics of the last two decades have been quite literally revolting, in that they have helped stimulate a spreading fundamentalist political revolt. God and Bible have been chased from the classroom. Abortion has been legalized. Amorality has been enthroned. Religion is under legal, bureaucratic and fiscal attack. These are the points made again and again by the political preachers. Not surprisingly, the religious electorate in the United States, larger by far than that of any other Western nation, has been aroused: the role of the Moral Majority and the rest of the religious right in the 1980 election bears witness.

Yet if the rise of the fundamentalist churches did not happen overnight, neither did their involvement in politics. As with so many aspects of conservative politics, the election of 1964 was a major watershed. Erling Jorstad, in his *The Politics of Doomsday,* claimed: "The Fundamentalists of the far right had consciously and enthusiastically involved themselves for the first time in a national campaign."[15] Four years later, George Wallace provoked an unusually large turnout—and received heavy ballot support—in fundamentalist states across the South. By 1972 it was obvious to many political strategists and some academicians that the fundamentalist electorate had achieved pivotal status. Two percipient researchers, Lowell Streiker and Gerald S. Strober, in a volume entitled *Religion and the New Majority: Billy Graham, Middle America and the Politics of the 1970s,* argued that:

> The only type of Democratic candidate who could possibly defeat Nixon would have to begin with centrist appeal. This appeal . . . must have some relation to the theological and social positions of Billy Graham. Unfortunately, Democratic candidates tend to have liberal, Eastern-based advisers on matters religious who automatically wrote off the fundamentalist potential. It is our belief that in 1972 a candidate who has not allied himself with the radical movement in America can build a coalition which includes all of the 1968 Democratic groupings as well as significant numbers of fundamentalists.[16]

It didn't happen, of course. Republican Richard Nixon had not only Billy Graham in his political orbit, but also a panoply of country music singers, while Democratic nominee George McGovern was tagged by conservatives as the triple-A candidate: acid, amnesty and abortion. McGovern's Biblical invocations, mostly of the liberal social gospel variety, were duly received in some evangelical areas, the Middle West principally, but he failed almost completely in the fundamentalist strongholds of the South and Southwest. The white Southern fundamentalist vote went overwhelmingly to Richard Nixon, marking the fourth straight election of mounting Democratic weakness. The closer the national Democratic Party got to Manhattan, Harvard and Beverly Hills, the less it appealed to Calhoun County, Alabama. And the more the Democratic Party promoted the culture and philosophy of Manhattan, Harvard and Beverly Hills —a convenient pejorative—the more the Calhoun counties moved toward political revolution.

After the 1972 election, analyst Samuel Lubell pointed out that "Surprisingly, little attention has been paid to the one ethnic element that is currently having the most explosive political impact in the country—the Southern White Baptists."[17] And as Chart 15 shows, data from the 96 heaviest Baptist counties in the country, all located in the South and in border states, bear him out:

Baptists are by far the largest of the fundamentalist denominations. Albert J. Menendez, author of *Religion at the Polls,* speculated in 1977 that evangelicals and fundamentalists had probably given about 13 million votes to Nixon and only 3 million or so to McGovern

Chart 15 *Baptist Presidential Voting, 1956–80*

Year	Democratic Candidate	Democratic Percentage of Vote in 96 Counties
1956	Stevenson	49.9%
1960	Kennedy	47.6
1964	Johnson	48.7
1968	Humphrey	24.2 (Wallace, 37.5)
1972	McGovern	25.5
1976	Carter	58.0
1980	Carter	40.0

Source: Albert J. Menendez, *Religion at the Polls,* 1977.
Albert J. Menendez, "Religion at the Polls, 1980,"
Church & State (December 1980)

in 1972.[18] Democrats did not do too much better among all Baptists, drawing only a quarter of the total vote in both 1968 and 1972. A major shift of loyalties was under way. Menendez notes that while Democrat Adlai Stevenson ran 7 percentage points *better* among Baptists than among Americans as a whole in 1956, thereafter the relationship changed. Baptists gave John F. Kennedy 2 percentage points *less* support than the country as a whole in 1960. They gave Lyndon Johnson 13 percentage points less in 1964, Hubert Humphrey 19 points less in 1968 and George McGovern 13 points less in 1972.[19]

During 1973 and 1974, however, notions of fundamentalists as a strong new conservative and Republican constituency dissipated—like so many other new perceptions—in the face of Watergate. By 1976 the victory of Jimmy Carter would stir up the mud on the baptismal creek bottom, clouding trend perceptions. The fundamentalist Christian vote was more important than ever, as election data showed, but in 1976 the Democrats had the sort of nominee Strober and Streiker had suggested back in 1972: a "born again" Baptist Sunday school teacher from Georgia, a man who frequently drew on the Bible in speeches, who spoke of a "government of love," and who promised the American people "I'll never lie to you." To top it all off, his sister was a prominent faith healer–cum–revivalist—Ruth Carter Stapleton.

Confronted by such a nominee, the forces advocating a "return to morality" found themselves divided politically, and the Democrats benefited handsomely. Jimmy Carter doubled the 1972 Democratic percentage among Baptists (to about 50), and he more than doubled the Democratic share of the vote among fundamentalists and evangelicals, raising it to 40–45 percent. Most of the improvement occurred in the South, where Carter won ten of eleven Confederate states, when McGovern had lost all eleven. Yet Baptist strength, along with strong representation of other fundamentalist denominations, also reaches well into the North—into the southern parts of states like New Jersey, Pennsylvania, Ohio, Indiana, Illinois and Iowa. Shortly after the November 1976 election I decided to check which counties, in each of these states and in border states from Maryland and Virginia to Texas and New Mexico, had given Jimmy Carter his largest gains over George McGovern. The results were revealing. Running 11 points ahead of McGovern's 39 percent nationally, Carter scored much more impressive gains in these high-trend counties—often 20–40 percentage points. Religion was a factor. From Maryland's Eastern Shore to Ohio's Scioto Valley to "Little Texas" in eastern New Mexico, Carter's highest-trend counties were often poor-white, frequently those with high proportions of Baptists or fundamentalists. Albert Menendez, in his study of the 1976 vote, also says the fundamentalist swing was decisive even in states like Pennsylvania and Ohio.[20] No one can be sure how much of the trend was directly related to Carter's "born again" Southern Baptist religion and how much of it was simply the responsiveness of local Democratic traditionalists to the precedent-shattering presidential candidacy of a middle-of-the-road Democrat who spoke with a Southern accent. But it does seem reasonable to say that religion was a major factor in Carter's victory.

For the religious right, however—or at least what would soon be labeled the religious right—Jimmy Carter proved a blessing in disguise. "Born again" Southern Baptist as he might be, Carter did little to live up to the sociocultural expectations induced by his campaign. Few evangelicals and fundamentalists won appointment to federal office. And while the new President deplored abortion personally, he avoided any fight on behalf of right-to-life proposals. Meanwhile, federal departments and agencies continued to push ideas repugnant to the religious right from school busing to barring girls' basketball teams under antidiscrimination laws. Moreover, the Internal Revenue Service continued to move against Southern private academies, not a few of them set up by new Christian religious denominations. As the years went on and a clear pattern of federal appointments and regulations emerged, Jimmy Carter's stock dropped among Southerners generally and among fundamentalists in particular. Not a few suggested that even a born-again Southern Baptist made no difference when elected President by, and required to collaborate with, the largely liberal national Democratic Party. In a sense, the Watergate fluke paved the way for the *ultimate* demonstration: (1) that a Southern Democratic President could not deliver—could not really even try to deliver—on the cultural demands of his home region; (2) that the election of 1976 was the electoral aberration, not the one held in 1972; and (3) that fundamentalists and other angry religionists could not expect to change policy in Washington without a far more sweeping degree of political involvement and mobilization.

Nor was that mobilization long in coming. In 1976, many antiabortion groups and conservative fundamentalists had seen little reason to involve themselves politically on either side. Richard Viguerie and his New Right allies so distrusted Republican incumbent Gerald Ford that they contemplated launching a third party. A year later the New Right's first attempt to fan the fires of anti-Carter discontent focused on mobilizing opposition to the Panama Canal treaties. But the 1978 elections showed that abortion remained the potent local issue in a number of states, with religious-connected one-issue groups demonstrating a surprising electoral prowess. And so, in 1978 and 1979, the three key national New Right strategists, Richard Viguerie, Paul Weyrich and Howard Phillips, took bolder measures. In the words of Viguerie's own *Conservative Digest,* they

> decided that the millions of fundamentalists in America were a political army waiting to be mobilized. The two leading groups, the Moral Majority, headed by the Rev. Jerry Falwell, and the Religious Roundtable, led by Ed McAteer, came out of meetings attended in early 1979 by Weyrich, Phillips, McAteer, Falwell and others. According to McAteer, who introduced Phillips to Falwell, the term "moral majority" was coined by Phillips and first used publicly by Weyrich in a presentation to Falwell and his associates.[21]

The results exceeded expectations. Weyrich and Viguerie are ardent, archtraditional Catholics, and I have always been amazed at how few have appreciated their striking achievement, having put together for the first time in American history a political coalition of militant Protestants and Catholics united around religious and moral issues. Early on, Moral Majority leader Falwell noted that the various religious groups, long at each other's throats, were putting aside doctrinal conflict to battle common foes: "Religious organizations are marching together who never worked with each other. Evangelicals, fundamentalists, conservatives, Catholics and Mormons are all working together now."[22] Just how right he was would become apparent in another fifteen months when Oklahoma and Alabama, two Democratic and solidly Baptist states with some history of political anti-Catholicism, would elect two Catholic Republican candidates to the U.S. Senate that were backed by the Moral Majority: State Senator Don Nickles and Admiral Jeremiah Denton (USN, Ret.). So the fundamental goal of the religious right is not simply to produce a great awakening in the old-time Protestant spiritual sense, but also one in *new political* terms—the mobilization of the nation's estimated 75 million right-leaning Christians, everyone from Mormons and Southern Baptists to traditionalist Roman Catholics.

That the 1980 election constituted a giant step toward that goal has become a truism. I am not so sure it was. There is simultaneously less and more than meets the eye in coming-of-age of the religious right. On the affirmative side of the ledger, the 1980 election results produced a triumph greater than expected. The millions of new voters registered by the Moral Majority and their allies made an enormous difference in two ways: in the Senate races, especially in the South, and according to pollster Louis Harris, in the presidential vote. Harris has estimated that white, fundamentalist, Moral Majority–type voters accounted for two thirds of Reagan's surprise 10-point margin over Jimmy Carter. County-level electoral data suggest much the same thing.

At the same time, however, the acceptance of the religious right by the new Republican Administration fell far short of what these groups deemed to be their electoral due. From the start, Reagan aides were quick to downplay the difference that the religious right had made on election day. Moreover, prominent Republicans like Vice President George Bush and Arizona Senator Barry Goldwater scoffed publicly at the New Right, Moral Majority and such groups, and denied their true conservatism while privately suggesting that fundamentalist positions—not least an antiabortion constitutional amendment—are offensive to the Episcopalian, Presbyterian and Congregationalist upper-middle-class Republican elites.

In short, there is good reason to wonder whether the "Reagan

Revival," as understood by James Q. Wilson and others, can maintain itself—and fulfill the hopes of those who plunked for a moral revolution. If the religious counter reformation is as massive in depth as partisans suggest, it could seek a vehicle of its own. Or, if it is as superficial a phenomenon as critics allege, the revival could merely subside, with some political-moral impact, but leaving the 1980 election as a high-water mark. All in all, the jury is still out on the question of a Fourth Great Awakening. Should it arrive, that revival will have an enormous and profound impact on the calculus of future Middle American radicalism.

15

MIDDLE
AMERICAN RADICALISM

There is a distinct force for activism in American society that is both volatile and pivotal. The word *radical* has many connotations, and orientation toward the left is only one of them: its basic meaning is going to the root of the problem. From this central idea of action emerges the paradoxical reality of this decisive force—the Middle American Radical (MAR). His perspective does not readily fit the traditional molds of liberal or conservative ideologies . . . The Middle American Radical sees all levels of government—local to national—allied simultaneously with minority and idealistic groups against his own interests and social survival. Since he feels himself thus threatened, the MAR is an unpredictable force in American political life, an uneasy ally for either the left or right.

—Donald I. Warren, "The Middle American Radicals,"
The *Nation* (August 17, 1974)

ONE OF THE BIGGEST MISTAKES MADE BY MOST POLITical scientists, journalists and sociologists during the late 1960s was the assumption that the dominant alienation, radicalism and populism in American politics was encompassed and defined by the *left*. So misled, these commentators dwelt on antiwar demonstrators, Ralph Nader–type activists, marijuana lobbyists and other predominantly middle-class left-liberal groups. Accordingly, they downplayed the much more important demography composed of people who applauded Spiro Agnew, hummed along with Merle Haggard's "Okie from Muskogee," or spent Sunday mornings listening to fundamentalist preachers. Caste and class—the fact that many opinion-molders come from backgrounds that parallel those of the left-trending elites—presumably helped to undermine statistical reality. Yet the numbers were always there—in the George Wallace vote of 1968 and 1972, in the dramatic growth of fundamentalist church membership, in the proliferation of radio stations featuring country-and-western music. And the converging typologies of majority apprehension—middle-class fear of inflation, racial and ethnic hostility, frustrated nationalism, religious fundamentalism—bespoke a right-tilted radical potential.

In 1972, analysts could fool themselves into thinking that South Dakota's George McGovern, "the Prairie Populist," came from the tradition of Andrew Jackson and William Jennings Bryan, even though 40 percent of the delegates at the Democratic National Convention that nominated him had master's degrees or better. By 1976, though, any hopes for a left-leaning populism-cum-radicalism collapsed with the electorate's nonresponse to the presidential campaign of former Oklahoma Senator Fred Harris, who could only engage a few middle-class housewives and college students.* Blue-collar interest was negligible, largely because the historic constituencies of American populism were not looking left. As historian C. Vann Woodward admitted in 1981: "When the [liberal] neopopulists went to the people to offer leadership, they found the whites lined up behind George Wallace, and the blacks, in time, behind the hostile nationalists."[1]

The confusion of the liberals was understandable. Throughout those years, "Middle Americans," from restive farmers to anxious insurance clerks, were unhappy about the shape and direction of our society and politics. Precious little in our past suggested that such frustration or alienation would find vent in traditional *conservatism;* prior movements composed of the alienated had usually been populist to radical, though sometimes the radicalism involved tilted right (as with the nativism of the 1850s, the Ku Klux Klan sentiment of the 1920s, or McCarthyism of the 1950s). The notion of popular

---

*Perhaps the most telling portrait of left "populism" in the mid-1970s can be found in this description by reporter James Perry in the April 5, 1975, *National Observer* of a Fred Harris presidential campaign rally in Boston's historical Faneuil Hall:

"I *know* this crowd, even if the faces and the names have changed. This is the old McGovern constituency: students, teachers, upper- and upper-middle-class housewives, Brahmin-type WASPs, high-income Jews. Good, decent, high-minded folks, each and every one of them—but not a hungry belly in the lot.

"In Boston, the New Populists were asked to spread out and join any one of 11 'interest' groups that interested them most. Interest groups included Women's Rights, Tax Reform, Minority Rights and Economic Structure. Said Alice Cohen to Martin Cohen "Whaddya like—women's rights?' At the minority-rights session, an earnest young college student explained: 'one reason we have poor people is that we have rich people.' The 'expeditor' for the foreign-policy panel wore a button that showed a smoking cigarette. 'Yes,' the button said, 'I do mind.' Popular, too, this election year are Dutch sailor caps. The biggest, toughest issue in Boston is school busing, but there was no panel to discuss that."

frustration breeding conservatism seemed hardly credible. Yet only a small number of pundits and academicians saw the obvious variation on the theme: a wave of "right-wing populism" or "conservative populism," perhaps the most important such wave in American history.

It is beyond dispute that inflation, cultural and moral revolution (and counterrevolution), the first American wartime defeat and consequent frustrated nationalism produced a reaction toward the right in the late 1970s. And as that happened, many of radicalism's old constituencies were mobilized. Skeptics have only to pick up old electoral tabulations to see how the Lower East Side and Brooklyn Orthodox Jewish neighborhoods, where Reagan did so well in 1980, were Socialist and American Labor Party strongholds of the 1920s or 1940s. In parallel fashion, the rural Southern fundamentalist counties, where Reagan improved 20 and 30 points on Gerald Ford, were William Jennings Bryan strongholds in 1896, and were later bastions of Huey Long, "Pitchfork" Ben Tillman and George Wallace. The Wheat Belt, including many counties where Reagan scored 30–40 points better than Ford, is the volatile core of Farm Belt radical tradition. And who can remember that rural Oklahoma, allied with the Moral Majority in 1980, turned in this century's highest Socialist presidential percentages just before World War I? Meanwhile, the arch-Catholic counties of the northern Farm Belt, also strong Reagan trend areas in 1980, led support for Congressman William "Liberty Bell" Lemke, Father Coughlin's splinter-party candidate for President in 1936. Ronald Reagan may not have done well in the ersatz, middle-class radical strongholds of Manhattan, Fire Island, Aspen and San Francisco, but he did extraordinarily well for a Republican in areas of genuinely radical populist traditon.

Where this all will lead remains to be seen. The Reagan electorate is an extremely unusual Republican constituency. My own feeling is that a large and decisive minority of the Reagan vote was mobilized not just by economic, cultural and patriotic frustrations but by a desire for bold measures to be taken. Successfully fulfilling such electoral hopes is likely to be difficult. Hence, Reagan's coalition is most probably unstable.

If one wants to understand the radical nature of the Reagan coalition and the "conservative" politics of the early 1980s, several theories and analogies strike me as especially useful. The first is Seymour Martin Lipset's notion of "center extremism": the idea that under certain circumstances, when traditional politics breaks down, previously centrist electorates move toward a radicalized set of issues and beliefs that is neither "right nor left." In practice, "center extremism"—the radicalization of the electoral middle—has been closely linked to various degrees of fascism, Caesarism or authoritarianism. A second theory, closely related, is Donald Warren's notion of "Middle American Radicals," who number 25–30 percent of the American electorate. A third tack worth noting is the idea of a reborn "revolutionary conservatism," a phenomenon akin to the emergence in the late nineteenth and early twentieth centuries in France, Germany and Italy of activists and intellectuals who attacked the institutions of secular liberalism and called for the reassertion of religion, ethnicity and nationalism. As we shall see, some parallel exists between these movements and the rise of the New Right in the United States and in several other Western nations.

The evidence does indicate that the multiple failures of mutated "liberalism" of the 1970s in the United States have generated some radicalization of centrist American constituencies. Accordingly, Lipset's concept of "center extremism," developed two decades ago and applied principally to Hitler's Germany, Mussolini's Italy and Perón's Argentina, also seems to apply to the United States of the 1980s.[2] With an obvious caveat: frustrated radicalism of the center here has a very different kind of non-European thrust, thanks to the legacy of a populism unique to us and the current involvement of fundamentalist religious leaders. Judging by past examples, a movement big enough and intense enough to become a form of "center extremism" often tries to re-create some mythical past for itself. In the United States the radicalized middle could, as suggested, try to re-create a prosperous, pre-inflation, pre-Vietnam America.

Center extremism, by definition, means that a radicalized "ism" politics doesn't have to come from the extreme right or left. It can, of course—and often does. Communism, for example, is a form of extremism on the left, composed of the working class and allied intelligentsia. By contrast, and in Lipset's view, European conservative extremist movements of the twentieth century have been based in the church-military-economic right wing: the Horthyites in Hungary, the Christian Social Party of Dollfuss in Austria, the *Stahlhelm* and other nationalists in pre-Hitler Germany, Salazar in Portugal, the pre-1958 Gaullists and the monarchists in postwar France and Italy.[3] Several political regimes more broadly based, like those of

France's Charles de Gaulle and Spain's Francisco Franco, shared some of these characteristics, drawing heavy support from the aristocracy, the Catholic Church and the military.

The remaining "ism," that of the center, is built on the frustration and ideological values of the *middle classes:* small businessmen, farmers, artisans, white-collar workers and some professional elements. That "ism" of the center, a mix of yesteryear's liberalism and populism, is suspicious of big business, big labor and big government alike. Radicalize that value framework, Lipset says, and the result is fascism or some variation of it. So the rise of Adolf Hitler was basically a phenomenon of middle-class radicalization. "Fascism and populism," according to Lipset, "propose to solve the problems [of the middle classes] by taking over the state and running it in a way which will restore the old middle classes' economic security and at the same time reduce the power and status of big capital and big labor."[4]

In the United States of the 1970s, the ongoing political revolt of the lower-middle and middle classes was overt in two elections, 1972 and 1980, and confused in two others, 1968 and 1976. But if one looks at the four elections taken together, several patterns emerge rather clearly. Democratic Party loyalties held up relatively well among the left quarter of the electorate: the intelligentsia, minorities, working-class electorates of stagnating industrial areas. Generally speaking, Republican strength maintained itself in affluent suburbia, old conservative Northern rural areas and among business executives. By contrast, lower-middle and middle-class voting streams—small businessmen, rural Southerners, artisans and prosperous workers, farmers, service workers, retirees, white-collar employees—showed great volatility. Precision is hard to come by, but these voters moved in a massive fashion toward the two GOP presidential nominees—Nixon in 1972 and Reagan in 1980—who very successfully enunciated populist, antiestablishment themes, voiced overt appeals to Middle, Silent or Forgotten Americans, and deployed slogans about family, work and neighborhood. Cumulatively, the presidential elections held between 1968 and 1980 severely eroded the one third or two fifths of the New Deal coalition composed of the rural and small-town white South, rural and small-town Catholic Farm Belt areas, and lower-middle-class suburbia especially in new high-migration Sun Belt metropolitan areas. So a huge slice of "Middle America" has come loose from its electoral moorings.

A radicalization of the center of the American electorate is hardly unprecedented. One could also see the process going on in other times of national convulsion—during the 1850s, 1890s and 1930s as frustrated centrist constituencies radicalized and switched party affiliation. By the 1970s, when George Wallace rightly warned us of a middle class again radicalizing, the dynamics were new and more dangerous. Back in the mid-1970s I briefly collaborated with Patrick Caddell—George McGovern's pollster in 1972, and Jimmy Carter's from 1976 to 1980—on a research project. Caddell very much believed that the nation was caught up in a politics of antiestablishment frustration, and in late 1974, when Watergate was fresh in the nation's psyche and when unemployment was climbing toward a post-Depression high, he conducted a survey using two-and-a-half hour interviews designed to bring to the surface political beliefs and pathologies missed by more superficial inquiries. The results were striking. Two years earlier, in 1972, Caddell had discovered that 18 percent of those sampled were willing to back George Wallace for President—9 percent really wanted him in the Oval Office, and the other 9 percent would back him in protest. By late 1974 Caddell found 18 percent eager to put Wallace in the White House, while another 17 percent were willing to cast a protest vote for him. That came to 35 percent, double Wallace's 1972 strength and almost triple his actual 1968 vote. Along with these data, Caddell found voter ideology churning. A growing number of people simultaneously favored radical, socialistic economic solutions while backing a hard-line, even authoritarian position on social issues. "The people smack in the middle—the people who are the least ideological—are the most volatile," he said. Forty-one percent thought that "the true American way of life is disappearing so fast we may have to use force to save it." "The middle class is coming unhinged," Caddell wrote, "Center Extremism is correct."[5] The difference between us was that Caddell thought the popular alienation could be channeled into left-liberal politics given the right candidate; hence the attraction he soon felt for the self-proclaimed Georgia populist Jimmy Carter. My own belief, based on the patterns of 1964 to 1972, was that the radicalizing centrist constituencies would have to move toward a rightist, Middle American ideological view of things.

At least a few others were reaching conclusions akin to mine. Michigan sociologist Donald Warren proposed a similar thesis, arguing that the convulsions of the 1960s and early 1970s had turned 20 to 30 percent of the electorate into what he called "Middle American radicals"—men and women whose ideology fitted neither liberal nor conservative prescriptions but linked the economics of frustration with indignant social conservatism and suspicion of rich and poor alike. Said Warren:

> For many white Americans, the rejection of the blacks and poor is only one part of a larger rejection of the government and the rich. Preliminary data from a national cross-section probability sampling of 1690 white Americans indicate that 30 percent of the population thought that the blacks had too much political power; 63 percent said that about the rich. Approximately 30 percent said that poor blacks were getting more than their fair share of government aid; 56 percent said the same thing about the rich. Eighteen percent said that blacks have a better chance than whites to get fair treatment from courts, while 42 percent said that about the rich. In other words, hostility toward the rich is extensive; it may equal, or even exceed, hostility toward blacks.[6]

At this point—and once again, it's difficult to draw any parallel without straining credulity and engaging in pejoratives—American center extremism must lead us to compare its workings with the political dynamics of Germany in the early 1930s. As Lipset shows, Adolf Hitler's National Socialist Workers' Party (NSDAP) greatly benefited from the radicalization of the middle classes and the collapse of the old center parties. Despite the Nazis' climb from 2.6 percent of the vote in 1928 to 43.9 percent in 1933, the entire Communist electorate and two thirds of the Social Democratic electorate remained in place on the left. The German National People's Party (DNVP)—vehicle of the industrialists, military elite, aristocracy and upper-middle classes—also maintained about two thirds of its prior strength on the right. What pushed Hitler into power was the collapse of the bourgeois, agrarian and small business (non-Catholic) center parties. From 28 percent of the total vote in 1928, these parties plummeted to 2.5 percent in 1933.[7] Theirs was the principal support base the future dictator won over. Political scientist Harold Lasswell summed up the cultural-political dynamics of the Nazis as follows:

> Insofar as Hitlerism is a desperation reaction of the lower middle classes, it continues a movement which began during the closing years of the nineteenth century. Materially speaking, it is not necessary to assume that the small shopkeepers, teachers, preachers, lawyers, doctors,

farmers and craftsmen were worse off at the end than they had been in the middle of the century. Psychologically speaking, however, the lower middle class was increasingly overshadowed by the workers and upper bourgeoisie, whose unions, cartels and parties took the center of the stage. The psychological impoverishment of the lower middle class precipitated emotional insecurities within the personalities of its members, thus fertilizing the ground for the various movements of mass protest through which the middle classes might revenge themselves.[8]

There is obviously some parallel between the dynamics of center radicalization in Germany between 1928 and 1933 and the radicalization of Middle America between 1968 and 1980. Kindred constituencies have been involved, as well as kindred psychologies. Middle-class radicalization, which takes a decade or more to occur, also requires great sources of external stress. Once radicalization reaches critical proportions, the phenomenon cannot be taken lightly.

As they see center extremism and right-wing populism, Lipset and Warren tend to emphasize the reaction of the larger electorate and ignore the role of the elites. The approach has much to it, but it does not entirely account for people from elite groups taking a right-wing populist or "conservative revolutionary" approach to politics in the late 1970s and early 1980s—and not just here but pretty much throughout Europe. As we saw in Chapter 3, the American "New Right," with its heavy emphasis on the mobilization of antiestablishment constituencies around cultural, moral and nationalist issues, fits the mold of a right-wing populism, perhaps even "center extremism." However, the cultural, religious and political beliefs and values of its leadership elites also bear some resemblance to those of the "conservative revolutionary" theorists and publicists of late-nineteenth- and early-twentieth-century Europe, the men whose critiques of secular and rationalist liberalism were a force in the upheavals of the 1920s and 1930s.

Part of history is repeating itself here. In his useful treatise called *The Politics of Cultural Despair,* Professor Fritz Stern profiles the earlier development of revolutionary conservatism as exemplified by such men as German's Paul de Lagarde (1827–1891) and Moeller van den Bruck (1876–1924).[9] Although many of their views of German culture and politics have been recognized as legitimate or at least prescient, the conservative revolutionaries were caught up in a paradox. Like today's New Right, they proclaimed themselves revolutionaries out of conservatism, yet in Stern's words, they "sought to destroy the despised present in order to recapture an idealized past in an imaginary future. They were disinherited conservatives, who had nothing to conserve, because the spiritual values of the past had largely been buried and the material remnants of conservative power did not interest them. They sought a breakthrough to the past, and they longed for a new community in which old ideas and institutions would once again command universal allegiance."[10] Van den Bruck, scarcely known in the United States, is important because he was the leading German theorist of revolutionary conservatism in the 1920s. His last and best-known book, *Das Dritte Reich* (in English "The Third Reich"), would help to set up the 1930s—it was the blueprint for a utopia in which Germany would recover its old spirit, values and sense of community.[11] Chart 16 shows the substantial similarity of mood and outlook between the conservative revolutionaries of fifty and a hundred years ago and the present-day New Right. Doubtless I have generalized too much, but for the purpose of facilitating comparison, the list presented is a reasonable one. There are important differences, yet the large number of similarities reflect the related origins of the two movements in periods of what can reasonably be called eras of "cultural despair."

Chart 16   *Parallels Between European Conservative*
Revolutionaries of Late 19th and Early 20th
Centuries and Late 20th Century
European-American New Right

Conservative Revolutionaries	*New Right*
Nationalist, patriotic	Nationalist, patriotic
Ethnic, Folk-rooted	Ethnic, Folk-rooted in Europe, more populist in U.S.
Anti-secular	Anti-secular, pro-religious (in U.S., populist-fundamentalist)
Anti-liberal	Anti-liberal
Supportive of restoration of "Old Morality"	Supportive of restoration of "Old Morality"
Anti-commercial	Hostile to "Big Business"
Anti-parliamentarian, anti-political party	Involved with rightwing parties (in U.S., skeptical of Republican-Democratic two-party system)

Many of the key features of early 1980s American political life—disenchantment with the welfare state, inflationary malaise, reaction against extremes of equality, and a general move to the right—have also been at work in Europe. So it is no surprise that the New Right has spread to Europe. So has the term—in official and unofficial parlance. Not only are right-wing youth movements growing in Germany, Britain and elsewhere, but young intellectuals have begun to restate many of the old ideas of revolutionary conservatism. The most widely publicized European version of the New Right is French, built around the Club d'Horloge and the Research and Study Group for European Civilization (GRECE), which espouses "an attempt to rehabilitate certain values that we feel are necessary to maintain civilization. Among these are courage, dynamism, a respect for differences that precludes egalitariansim and a restoration of hierarchy and order."[12] France's New Rightists support ethnic separatist movements in Brittany and Corsica, oppose race-mixing and show a surprising interest in the cult of the Aryan-hero, pre-Christian mythology and Wagnerian music. The groups include a number of university professors, some journalists and bright young men in Jacques Chirac's right-populist Gaullist party.

In Germany, where the radical right is also growing, the revolutionary conservative intelligentsia seems to have less political influence. Even Russia has produced a "New Right," which may be fitting in light of Feodor Dostoyevsky's role as one of the first conservative revolutionaries of the nineteenth century. In "The Russian New Right: Rightwing Ideologies in the Contemporary USSR," the principal analysis of these new currents in Soviet life, Professor Alexander Yanov argues that Russia, too, is witnessing a religious revival and a resurgence of nationalist sentiment from Pan-Slavism to xenophobia.[13] Abraham Brumberg, guest scholar at Washington's Kennan Institute for Advanced Studies, feels that Russian nationalism is "far more pervasive—and more responsive to *popular* yearnings" than the liberal dissident movements given so much attention in the Western press. Brumberg, restating Yanov, sums matters up as follows:

> Today's Russian nationalists, of whatever stripe, have no use for the Stalinist "Soviet-Russian" symbiosis. Their nationalism represents a complete repudiation of standard Communist ideology. Even those of them who dream (not unlike some late 19th-century Russian Slavophiles)

of a new imperialism based on a fusion of Russian Orthodoxy and the existing social and political order have nothing but contempt for the libertarian and universalist strands of Marxism. If they admire Lenin and Stalin, it is because they see them as heirs to the autocratic traditions of imperial Tsardom, rather than to Marxism, that loathsome spawn of Western civilization and Judaic philosophy.[14]

A Russian New Right, indeed. Despite my own probable overindulgence, I am nevertheless skeptical of drawing too many close parallels between the economics, politics, culture and religion of Europe and those of the United States. Among other things, the democratic legacies of both populism and the past religious "Great Awakenings" in the United States—both of which less influenced European history—force one to acknowledge the limited utility of past or current European parallels. Yet there *does* seem to be a *larger* movement throughout the West toward nationalism, ethnicism and irrationalism that matches the rise of populist or revolutionary conservatism in the United States. Besides the intriguing developments in Russia, it is probably no coincidence that as "conservatism" has become Reaganite revolutionary and populist in the United States, similarities can be noted in the British Conservative Party of Margaret Thatcher, the French Gaullists of Jacques Chirac, and the West German Christian Democratic wing of Franz Josef Strauss, to say nothing of the Israeli Right under the leadership of Menachem Begin.*

Setting aside European parallels, we should note that American far-rightists, plumbing troubled depths, chalked up extraordinary and unprecedented percentages in a number of elections: Harold Covington, leader of the U.S. Nazi party, got over 40 percent of the vote in the May 1980 Republican primary for attorney general of North Carolina; Thomas Metzger, leader of the state Ku Klux Klan, won the Democratic nomination for Congress in the June primary in the suburban 43rd Congressional District of California; and former Nazi party member Gerald Carlson, who quit to found the National Christian Democratic Union, won the Republican primary

*Begin's conservative politics may, in fact, be the archtype. Militaristic, ethnocentric, religious, based on the *least* affluent sectors of the population, Begin's coalition is populist nationalism writ large. Not only has Begin's brand of politics been likened to Hitler's, but the Israeli Prime Minister has close ties to the United States Religious Right, and ardently pro-Begin Orthodox Jews in New York City were strong 1980 Reagan supporters.

in the suburban 15th District of Michigan, and then scored heavily in the general election as well. In both California and Michigan, party officials were afraid that the radical votes were cast deliberately, and that the more publicity Metzger and Carlson got, the more support they would get.[15]

So to my mind, some of the elements necessary for American center extremism were in place in the early 1980s. Besides the increase in the activities of the (still negligible) American Nazis, a clear growth was apparent in the size of the Ku Klux Klan from 1978 to 1981—its membership doubled, and Klans became active on the high school and college levels.[16] Analyses prepared by the Congressional Research Service showed a parallel escalation of violence directed against minorities.[17] Sales of patriotic insignia soared. In California, state Attorney General George Deukmejian described the growth of paramilitary groups as "phenomenal," and said that "California has become a haven for paramilitary groups and cults, most of which view themselves as separate societies above the laws of the state."[18] And in November 1980, as the country elected Ronald Reagan President, the Washington *Post* profiled "the latest and unlikeliest folk hero on American college campuses"—convicted Watergate burglar and Teutonophile G. Gordon Liddy, whose political autobiography, *Will,* draws heavily on fascist themes: patriotism, leadership, loyalty, will, force. Extolling these, Liddy drew standing ovations on campus after campus.[19] In the meantime, American mass culture, epitomized by Hollywood and the movies, was turning to a kindred emphasis on force, will, power, irrationality and mythology in a series of sword-and-sorcery movies, beginning with *Star Wars* in 1977 and then going on to *Excalibur, Clash of the Titans, Raiders of the Lost Ark* and *Conan the Barbarian.*

The die is hardly cast. The larger question is whether the United States can regain yesteryear's easygoing middle-class confidence and optimism, both enemies of radicalism and the politics of cultural despair. So if our national leadership elites over time can restore our economy and our belief in the future, Middle American radicalization will slacken and ease. But if not, a major convergence of various radicalisms is possible. Whereupon the public mood could support a politics of national mythology, Social Darwinism and charismatic leadership.

Part Four

THE SEPARATION OF POWERS AND ITS OBSOLESCENCE

16

SOFT LANDINGS AND OTHER INSTITUTIONAL MYTHS

In parliamentary terms, one might say that under the U.S. Constitution it is not now feasible to "form a Government." The separation of powers between the legislative and executive branches, whatever its merits in 1793, has become a structure that almost guarantees stalemate today. As we wonder why we are having such a difficult time making decisions we all know must be made, and projecting our power and leadership, we should reflect on whether this is one big reason.

—Lloyd Cutler, "To Form a Government," *Foreign Affairs* (Fall 1980)

AMERICANS, MORE THAN OTHERS, DON'T LIKE TO BE-lieve that the passage of time—history—changes things; hence our constitutional arrangement of government, drawn up and ratified two hundred years ago, can never become obsolete. Newly elected Presidents, upon coming to the White House, think they have a clean slate and can right whatever has gone wrong. And why not? While campaigning, they promised to do exactly that. So a new Administration assumes office with an economic blueprint that ignores the recurrent reality of the business cycle. Precedent, being of little importance, can be safely pushed aside. Whatever the difficulties, a soft landing—economic, social and otherwise—becomes an immediate certainty. Doomsayers be damned.

But despite our Fourth of July rhetoric, the American people have never escaped history. Even the United States could not make it through the multiple crises of the last two decades without severe dislocation. Indeed, the public has been expecting a Big Crisis for years, as it consumed books and movies about the upcoming economic crash, giant earthquake or Armageddon. Doomsayers, in fact, have prospered. From time to time, members of the opinion-molding elite add their gray thoughts. White House Counsel Lloyd Cutler and domestic policy chief Stuart Eizenstat did in 1980, urging that the United States consider a modified form of the parliamentary system because our own system no longer works. But every time a new Administration is inaugurated, hard-learned lessons of the previous one are lost; time is lost, too, while a new cadre of officials learns the limits of institutional power.

But then again, no nation, recently pre-eminent, can go through a major moral and religious upheaval, a technological and communications revolution, an unprecedented peacetime inflation and a first defeat in war without a major loss of public confidence in existing institutions. And that's exactly what happened to the country in the 1970s. Polls show the public's loss of confidence in governmental and political institutions to be beyond dispute. To be sure, the election of Ronald Reagan in 1980 elicited from the public renewed signs of optimism, but really no more than had been apparent after the inauguration of new Presidents in 1974 and 1977.

Some commentators have written that the Watergate crisis proved that the American political system of powers, as laid down by the founding fathers, works. My own analysis, very much to the contrary, is that the *failure* of the system in many ways produced Watergate. The separation of powers between Congress and the presidency helped nurture the breakdown of the U.S. war effort in Vietnam and the perceived breakdown of national security. Meanwhile, the inability of the Nixon Administration to effectively control the machinery of Washington—in sharp contrast to what a new government under a European parliamentary system would encounter—helped encourage the White House's siege mentality and use of political espionage and surveillance. And as Seymour Martin Lipset and Earl Raab have noted (see Chapter 5), that use was amateurish. Other administrations had moved much more effectively. A decade earlier, when the Democratic Senate was reluctantly investigating the Bobby Baker scandal and the trail led to the Johnson White House, the lines of investigation were promptly narrowed, although recent allegations suggest that Lyndon Johnson, of all recent Presidents, may have been the ripest for impeachment. In that instance, checks and balances did not work at all. Partisan political loyalties overrode the constitutional arrangement. Indeed, the constitutional arrangement has again demonstrated its fallibilities under Ronald Reagan.

In the summer of 1981, after Reagan had pushed his budget cuts and tax package through a surprised and awed Congress, we heard once more that the system worked, that the presidency again firmly occupied the saddle and that bold leadership could surmount the separation of powers and the "iron triangle" of Congress, bureaucracy and interest groups. The braggadocio was extremely short-lived, however. To secure interest-group support on tax policy, the White House had engaged congressional Democrats in "bidding war." That war, like others before it, was made possible by the constitutional separation of powers and the parallel lack of a solid White House coalition in the House of Representatives. This particular war reduced tax revenues by $150 billion over five years, creating an enormous (and poorly anticipated) deficit prospect. The financial markets thereupon went into a nose dive, and within six weeks or so cast renewed doubt on the efficacy of our system recently praised so fulsomely.

As one who believes that the events of the last ten years or so have reflected more the system's faults than its virtues, I regret that the President and some of his key advisers, dazzled perhaps by the 10-point victory of 1980 and by the election of a Republican Senate, began their White House tenure with the business-as-usual assumption of partisan power and reaffirmation of existing institutional arrangements. During much of 1980, proposals to reform the system were made and most of these still stand up.* But a notable opportunity to act may have been lost; reform will come harder now than in early 1981.

The difficulties our governmental system faces go far beyond a single national election or its results. The dubious doctrine of "American exceptionalism"—based on the idea that this country is uniquely blessed, or that God takes special care of babies, drunks and the United States of America—is a misconception that may soon lead us to our undoing. The origins of exceptionalism are many, among them the belief that we possess a peerless Constitution and brilliantly structured political system, designed by candlelight in 1787

*Much of this chapter is adapted from my article "An American Parliament?: Overcoming the Separation of Powers" (*Harper's*, November 1980). But I have held these views for some ten years now, dating back to a precursor analysis penned for *Newsweek* in early 1973.

for the ages. Yet our ability to cope with the 1980s may depend on the speed and intelligence with which we can reform a number of obsolete, even crippling political institutions, mechanisms and relationships.

Oliver Wendell Holmes's "one-hoss shay," which, going along nicely, suddenly collapsed, presents an unpleasant parallel to the 1970s' breakdown of American presidential leadership, of the party system, of the relationships between the executive, legislative and judicial branches, and between Washington and the fifty states. So the political issue and challenge of the 1980s may not involve the realignment of the party system, which may be impossible, but the larger recasting and regrouping of the governmental institutions with which the parties necessarily interact.

Although a surprising number of political leaders, commentators and analysts are beginning to think in these terms, the movement interested in governmental reform has yet to coalesce—in part, I suspect, because liberals believe they have lost the nation's leadership and cannot hope to profit, while conservatives must overcome their post-1932 inexpertness in governance, to say nothing of their post-1980 hubris. Yet in 1980, important and encouraging signs appeared. Although the negotiation between Ronald Reagan and Gerald Ford at the GOP convention over what amounted to a restructuring of the federal executive branch failed to bear fruit, its mere occurrence bespoke a critical recognition. Astute senators, meanwhile, had begun proposing ways to improve communications between Congress and the executive branch; Lloyd Cutler was advocating a quasi-parliamentary system; Harvard professors were writing books about judicial usurpation (Raoul Berger's *Government by Judiciary*), and even liberal Democratic governors were calling for re-emphasizing states' rights and revitalizing federalism.

Of all the ways in which the American political system malfunctions, the most obvious and the worst is the relationship between the White House and Congress. Here the very essence of the counterproductive has become entrenched. The theory of "separation of powers" was first formulated by one Charles de Montesquieu, an eighteenth-century French philosopher. He mistakenly perceived an executive-legislative division in Britain because the king and the parliament were often at loggerheads, not seeing that the legislative branch was in fact closely knit to the *operational* executive branch —the prime minister and cabinet. John Adams, among others of our

Founding Fathers, was heavily influenced by Montesquieu's tripartite mode of thought. So much for history. Meanwhile, the ongoing crisis of our own time stares us in the face.

Unlike the parliamentary legislatures elected elsewhere in the West, our Congress not only operates independently but does so in a way to frustrate and twist executive policy. If the White House has a national-security apparatus, a budget bureau and a technology office, Congress must have its own counterparts—and Congress does with a vengeance, with some 19,000 employees to man its turf-protecting battlements and fortifications. The legislative branch also has various quasi-executive functions, exercising control over major segments of the federal bureaucracy through auxiliaries of Senate committees, House committees, and allied lobby groups. Effective government often becomes impossible.

Part of the predicament—the nominal separation of powers—is written into the Constitution. Much of the problem, though, is only a matter of paper, people and procedures; it can be changed without resorting to a Constitutional Convention—not easily, but it can be done.

New York Senator Daniel Patrick Moynihan's suggestion of putting members of Congress in the Cabinet is one such nonconstitutional reform:

> My thought is that the time is at hand to involve the legislative with the executive, and that this could be done by the practice of appointing members of the House and Senate to the Cabinet . . . the essence of the problem, clearly, was the constitutional decision to separate the executive from the legislative in a way not found in any other government, much less any other democracy . . . The president (by appointing members of Congress to his Cabinet) would have the advantage of devising legislative proposals that would be seen by Congress as partly legislative in origin, and the president's proposals would have advocates in the committees and on the floor.

At the time, commentators thought that the senator's suggestion would require a constitutional amendment. Not so. That *would* be necessary for a sitting senator or congressman also to hold office as Secretary of Defense, Secretary of Labor, or whatever. Those are "offices under the United States," which members of Congress cannot occupy concurrently. But no prohibition exists against giving elected legislators Cabinet status as ministers without portfolio. The Cabinet itself has no legal or constitutional status—anyone can be appointed. In such fashion, leaders on Capitol Hill could help the President devise legislative proposals, just as Moynihan suggested in 1980, without assuming the administrative burdens of a Cabinet department. Several might also serve as Administration floor spokesmen in their areas of competence. Wisconsin Congressman Henry Reuss, chairman of the House Banking Committee, proposed going further and amending the U.S. Constitution to allow members of Congress to serve, without additional compensation, in the executive branch.

As the Carter Administration walked toward the exits of history, Lloyd Cutler suggested that movement along these lines was essential: "The separation of powers between the legislative and executive branches . . . has become a structure that almost guarantees stalemate today." Cutler proposed a quasi-parliamentary system by implementing several structural reforms: Have candidates for President, Vice President and Congress run as an entity ticket in all districts, thus linking their fortunes; require that half the Cabinet be sitting members of Congress; establish a six-year term for the President; and set up procedures for the President or Congress (or both) to be able to call for general elections when paralysis sets in.

Or consider two kindred 1980 proposals by Senate Republican leader Howard Baker. He proposed first that an official liaison "Presidential Office" be opened on Capitol Hill; second, he suggested that Cabinet officials should be brought before one or both houses of Congress at regular intervals to answer formally questions about executive policy. Earlier both President Carter and Vice President Mondale also endorsed the notion of requiring Cabinet members to appear before Congress to answer questions. In *Why Not the Best?*, Mr. Carter urged that the Cabinet "appear before the joint sessions of Congress to answer written questions," and Mondale, as a senator, actually sponsored legislation to implement the idea.

Little current poll information is available, but an early-1980 national survey, conducted by the St. Louis–based Civic Service, asked: "Would you favor having major new legislation worked out in close consultation between the President and congressional leaders before it goes to Congress to help reduce confrontation and stalemate?" Of respondents, 60.7 percent said yes, while 20 percent said no. Clearly, separation of powers commands little fidelity at the grass roots.

Let me also point out that some of the greatest enthusiasm for a divided American government is found in the Kremlin. A 1979 study by noted Soviet Americanologist Professor Yuri I. Nyporko, entitled "Constitutional Interrelationships Between the President and Congress of the U.S.A.," announced with satisfaction that "tensions now arise with greater frequency within the bourgeois governmental mechanism." Nyporko noted that the "intensifying struggle" between the legislative and executive branches had made checks and balances a reality. In his analysis, Soviet interests would be best served by a Republican President "balked" by a Democratic Congress, especially by the Senate. A Democratic President vying with a Republican Congress would rank second in favor, and least desirable would be an executive-legislative collaboration dominated by the same political coalition.

The presidential selection process also contributes to the flawed structure of the executive branch. Lone wolves tend to emerge, ensuring the sort of White House that fortifies itself against Capitol Hill. Beyond that, upon reaching the Oval Office, a President finds that the job simply has gotten too big. It must be reduced, spread or divided. If we can begin to move toward the quasi-parliamentary system advocated by Moynihan, Cutler and others, an enhanced role for the Cabinet would ease the burdens of the presidency. Cabinet government, pivoting on the department heads and on the major political and legislative leaders of the presiding coalition, could redistribute presidential responsibilities. Such a government cannot be compared to the occasional, half-hearted endorsements of "Cabinet government" made by various Presidents of the recent past. Genuinely reconstituted, the upper echelons of the White House would become less the purview of home-state cliques and more the ground for the mobilization of national talent.

A redefinition of the vice presidency is also essential. In the Gerald Ford and Ronald Reagan talks of 1980, such redefinition miscarried, but the basic idea of the Vice President assuming a role as chief operating officer of the government or being specifically responsible for certain areas of expertise should not be permanently set aside. After the Detroit deliberations, Ford's former presidential press secretary, J. F. terHorst, suggested that "a truly worthwhile [constitutional] amendment might be an enlargement of the role of the Vice President so that he could take up some of the duties of the executive branch . . . The aborted Reagan-Ford plan ought to spur some scholarly research into the feasibility of such an amendment."

If party realignment fails to occur and the return of national optimism fails to develop, effective reform of the federal government might be well served by instituting quasi-parliamentary modes of operation. A limited shift of the sort sketched, achievable without amending the Constitution, could set the scene for a stronger Cabinet and needed reform beyond ad hoc calls for better executive-legislative collaboration. It also would offer a possible vehicle for regrouping legislators and politicians in a time when the Republican and Democratic parties, both showing increasing signs of obsolescence, may no longer be able to revitalize themselves.

In this respect, we recently began to hear more and more about another institutional device most familiar but not limited to parliamentary systems: the coalition. It is my feeling that the two-party system can no longer produce ideological and political watershed elections, in part because the parties are obsolescent, but also to some extent because individual legislators have shaped themselves into communications-age ombudsmen—constituency servants who rise or fall too little on party tides to make party tides effective or meaningful. If so, reform must seek to bypass and finesse the problem using institutional means. During the mid-1970s a number of conservatives seriously contemplated a new party on the right, to which Gallup found 25–30 percent of Americans responding favorably. More recently, John Anderson's independent presidential candidacy led Gallup to poll the public on support for a new center party, and found 30–40 percent backing. Likewise, an early 1980 Opinion Research Corporation survey found 47 percent of those queried agreeing with the notion that a strong third party would revitalize our political system. But the issue of a strong third party is probably academic. Even though the public supports the idea, current federal election law is so stacked against the emergence of successful new parties that some strategists prefer something else—the coalition.

The idea of coalition is not something entirely new in our history. Bear in mind that Abraham Lincoln and the Republican party relied on a supraparty coalition, not straight Republicanism, first to organize Congress in the mid-1850s, then to win the wartime presidential election of 1864. The fledgling Republican Party would not have been strong enough on its own, given the political fragmentation that prevailed before and during the Civil War. Today's problem is different. Advocates favor using a coalition to transcend the old party labels that are linked to ineffective institutional arrangements.

A coalition is do-able in many ways. One approach is to use the implement concept contemplated briefly in June 1980 by the Reagan forces—choosing Georgia's Democratic senator, Sam Nunn (or some other Southern Democrat), as Reagan's running mate, producing the first political coalition at the national level since Abraham Lincoln picked Tennessee Democrat Andrew Johnson in 1864. But the Atlanta *Constitution,* reporting the plan, quoted one Reagan aide as saying the Nunn approach was abandoned because most GOP convention delegates had not yet perceived the extent of the institutional or national crisis: "We may indeed be reaching such a point, but the perception of the crisis has yet to take hold."

In times of turmoil and uncertainty, both parties have sometimes sought a degree of bipartisanship in Cabinet appointments. Prior to World War II, Franklin D. Roosevelt added Republicans Henry Stimson and Frank Knox as Secretary of War and Secretary of the Navy; in 1961, Democrat John Kennedy, after winning the election by the narrowest of majorities, appointed Republicans Robert McNamara and C. Douglas Dillon as Secretary of Defense and Secretary of the Treasury. Polls taken in early 1980 turned up 54 percent in favor of a similar move by Jimmy Carter, with 26 percent opposed; later that year several senior Reagan aides floated trial balloons on the possibility of naming some Cabinet members a few weeks before the election so that voters might consider them in casting their November ballots. Names included well-known Democrats to give the ticket the colors of coalition.

The most important form of "coalitionism," however, is likely to come on the legislative level. Party lines have already begun to fade into irrelevance at the state level. Accordingly, in the houses of seven legislatures—New Hampshire, New Mexico, Texas, Louisiana, Nevada, Alaska and Florida—organizational reins have been seized since 1979 by new supraparty conservative coalitions. Perhaps the most telling confrontation occurred in New Hampshire, where the conservative two thirds of the GOP state senators and the conservative one third of the Democrats outvoted liberals of both parties by a hair's-breadth margin, thereby taking control. The new Senate president, St. Anselm's College professor Robert Monier, subsequently told the press: "This was an election of philosophies. We no longer have a majority party and a minority party. We have a majority coalition and a minority coalition." The underlying sentiment in

New Hampshire and elsewhere was that Republican-Democratic divisions no longer represent groupings through which to mobilize governing coalitions.

Some conservatives believe the same thing is true in Washington. With the party system de-aligning, and with so many legislators turning into district errand-runners largely immune from national pressures, coalition advocates either have given up on the idea of electing a Republican House, or simply prefer a conservative coalition to a Republican majority. In the spring of 1980 the Washington-based Heritage Foundation released a nationwide Sindlinger poll showing that a 64 to 21 percent majority favored electing the Speaker of the House on issues, not party labels. A 71 to 10 percent majority said they would approve if their own congressman voted for the Speaker on that basis.

Coalitionism has been recognized as a *reformist* force in states like New Hampshire and New Mexico, in part because it broke up entrenched legislative interests and lines of communication–cum-influence. To the extent that a similar breakup might happen in Washington—at least on the non-Pentagon side of the river—the big losers would be liberals, which is why the major proponents are conservatives. Coalitionism could theoretically achieve what the party system and (non-) realignment seem unable to produce—an effective new governing majority.

My own feeling is that much of the impetus toward coalitionism in Congress must come—if it is to come at all—from the same quasi-parliamentary thrust and the same perception of the inadequacy of separation of powers described earlier. To overcome the current extreme separation of powers, congressmen and senators will have to be brought into the Cabinet; should that happen, the critical question becomes: In whose Cabinet, with what kind of President, would conservative Democrats serve? The election of 1976 (probably an aberration) aside, many white Southern Democrats vote for the Republican candidate for president and for conservative Democrats for Congress. If one implemented Lloyd Cutler's idea of having national and congressional candidates run together on a quasi-parliamentary ticket, metropolitan Houston, Tulsa, Shreveport, Jacksonville, Palm Beach, Winston-Salem and a dozen other cities would immediately shift to representation by conservative coalitionists.

The sad truth is that *most* of our institutions and processes—not just two or three—need reform. With the federal judiciary having overstepped so many bounds, perhaps Congress, as authorized by the Constitution, should cut back on the jurisdiction allowed to the federal courts. Public sentiment is strongly favorable.* Periodically, the National Governors Conference passes resolutions deploring the substantial inroads Washington has made on federalism and the perversion of that system when Congress dictates minutiae. Much, though not all, of the Reagan Administration's New Federalism is a worthwhile response. And there have been serious suggestions that the United States adopt some form of national initiative and referendum, in the beginning no more than advisory in nature, to give the public a larger role in policy making.

Chief Justice Warren Burger is a leading proponent of serious re-examination of the constitutional system. Speaking at a 1978 seminar on legal history, he summed up what should be the scope of our inquiry and concern:

> It may seem premature to be thinking about the next significant bicentennial celebration in our national life, but our experience with the bicentennial of 1976 demonstrates the desirability for long advance planning. It is not too soon to turn our minds to the two-hundredth anniversary of the document [the Constitution] signed in Philadelphia almost exactly 191 years ago. I submit that an appropriate way to do this will be to reexamine each of the three major articles of our organic law and compare the functions as they have been performed in recent times with the functions contemplated in 1787 by the men at Philadelphia.

Others have suggested a more formal re-examination: Delaware Senator William V. Roth and some of his colleagues would like to see a Second Constitutional Convention meet in this decade, and futurist Alvin Toffler goes so far as to urge "a widespread, public, political debate about future forms of democracy" to head off possible bloodshed and totalitarianism.

My own feeling is that top Washington policy makers would do well to harken back to 1980 and recall the deep skepticism many observers had about the system—about how the Reagan brand of Republicanism might be unable to surmount the obstacles it would

---

*According to a spring 1981 national survey done for the Heritage Foundation by Sindlinger and Company, "by overwhelming majorities, Americans are supporting sweeping changes in the appointment and authority of the federal judiciary—some of them bordering on major modifications of the constitutional doctrine of separation of powers."

confront. Such a re-examination would dispel a lot of false notions. There are no easy political answers—be they traditional party realignment or a sudden electoral reinvigoration of old institutions— any more than there are easy economic answers. In fact, the two problems are interrelated. Lester Thurow, in his 1980 book *The Zero-Sum Society,* correctly laid a portion of our economic difficulty at the feet of our outworn political modes of operation: "Some of our paralysis is due to irreconcilable differences, but some of it is also because of a political process that cannot make decisions when all decisions result in substantial income losses for someone."*

And if our political and institutional processes cannot handle tough economic decisions, neither can they handle difficult technological choices. In the wake of the Three Mile Island nuclear-power-plant accident, Dr. Lewis Branscomb, chief scientist at IBM and chairman of the National Science Board, noted the tensions between democracy and technology: "Each time the Congress and the executive are unable to/achieve a public consensus on a technologically complex issue, we witness other failures in the consensus process of our democracy. If this continues to happen with increased frequency, the pressures to alter the political foundations of our government inevitably grow." The argument many of these critics make—and which I, for one, find difficult to fault—is that governmental power is too diffused to make difficult and necessary economic and technical decisions; accordingly, the nature of that power must be re-thought. Power at the federal level must be augmented, and lodged for the most part in the executive branch.

To be sure, we sometimes seem to face a bankruptcy of ideological and economic policy imagination. Talk about a breakdown of the old ideas and a lack of new ones is widespread. The ideologies of liberalism and conservatism both seem to lack capacity for innovation. Some academicians are beginning to assert the need to recognize and heed new ideological categories like·populism and libertarianism.

Perhaps as ideological groups grow and become more diverse, our collective policy imagination will benefit. But as of the early 1980s, I am inclined to think that the biggest problem facing our economics and politics is *institutional.* "Procedure is policy," they used to tell

*In a spring 1981 *Atlantic* article, Thurow was more specific: "Our governmental system of checks and balances may have been right for the eighteenth century, but it does not permit the quick decisions necessary for survival in the twenty-first century. That system will have to be changed."

us in law school. And our governmental procedures are obsolete, skewing policy and adding to the socioeconomic woes that then aggravate other national tensions.

A few months after Ronald Reagan's inauguration, Common Cause, the Washington-based citizens' organization, also inaugurated a new president, and that official, Fred Wertheimer, suggested that government—its shape and its role in our lives—is likely to be *the* issue of the 1980s. The right may have first crack at giving government its new definition, but conservatives will have to get results. And I suspect that to do so, they will have to perceive that there are no soft landings, either at the end of Laffer Curves, creeping realignments or Coolidge restorations. With Fourth of July rhetoric unavailing, institutional revitalization is a necessary companion of economic revitalization.

17

THE PARTY SYSTEM: REALIGNMENT OR DE-ALIGNMENT?

> You're looking at the most massive shift of party identification that has occurred in the past twenty five years . . . a rolling realignment.
>
> —Reagan pollster Richard Wirthlin (July 1981)

THE ONGOING, LOW-KEY DEBATE OVER PARTY RE-alignment—and over the vitality of the current American party system—took on new dimensions in the spring of 1981, within months after President Reagan's inauguration. Even Republicans admitted that the 1980 election itself had not yielded a classic political realignment. However, as polls showed a narrowing gap between Democratic and Republican identification among voters, the President's own pollster, Richard Wirthlin, opined that for the first time in our history our politics might be experiencing a period of "creeping realignment." Some analysts agreed; more did not. Survey results, as usual, could be read both ways. Nevertheless, in the guise of a controversy over numbers and cycles, another important issue surfaced, namely: If a political system could not realign in the face of the upheavals and pressures of the 1960s and 1970s, what was the electorate really up to?

Hitherto, realignments have usually taken the form of a "big bang," a watershed election (like the one in 1932) in which the newly ascendant party swept to a massive victory up and down the ballot. The 1980 election was hardly one of those, not with the Democrats continuing to hold majorities of governorships and in the U.S. House and the state legislatures. That left three alternative interpretations: (1) continued, undisrupted New Deal coalition/Democratic Party majority status; (2) creeping realignment of the Republicans into majority status; and (3) de-alignment—the decomposition of the party system, with new minor parties springing up as the old ones prove incapable of maintaining or reassembling national majorities. This last scenario, alas, is what might be expected to flow from the other erosions—economic, institutional and psychological—that I have described.

I have never understood the thinking of those who, even in the late 1970s, espoused the first thesis. The New Deal coalition is dead, having given out audible noises of disintegration since the 1960s. The average Democratic share of the total vote in the last four presidential elections was just 43 percent, down from an average 49 percent in 1948–64, and an average 57 percent in 1932–44. Whole Roosevelt-era constituencies are milling at the partisan exits, while the principal credos of yesteryear's cohesion, the New Deal and Keynesian economics, are in substantial disrepute. Even if the Democratic Party pulls itself back together during the 1980s, the way it does that is unlikely to involve a further extension of the New Deal philosophy or coalition.* Scarcely anyone believes in more New Deal except a few aging Washington lawyers and employees of the Brookings Institution.

The theory of "creeping realignment" is somewhat more plausible. For more than a decade, our political system has been stumbling toward what in a bygone era would have been realignment—a new partisan majority. And since it has not come in a big bang, thanks to Watergate and the growth of ticket-splitting, some suggest it is creeping into existence. There was an element of "creep" back in 1972. Few polls were monitoring party trends on a week-to-week

*Some interpretations of the 1982 elections can be expected to suggest a resurgence of the New Deal coalition. For thirty years, Republican Administrations have been undercut in midterm elections—1954, 1958, 1970 and 1974—by recessions and unemployment. But the subsequent presidential elections, in which Democratic weaknesses resurfaced, produced two GOP landslides (1956 and 1972) and two hair's-breadth Democratic victories (1960 and 1976). The definitive proof of the collapse of the (1932–48) New Deal presidential-level coalition lies in the 1968–80 sequence of *presidential* election results—a massive reversal of old patterns.

basis from August to November 1972, but those that were found some intriguing shifts. As noted in Chapter 4, Pennsylvania pollster Albert Sindlinger, a close consultant to the White House, turned up a strong trend favoring the Republicans between August and mid-October, strong enough for the gap between the parties in voter self-identification to narrow to only a few percentage points. Then, in late October, as the Watergate scandal strongly suggested White House guilt, that shift ebbed and broke. Turnout intentions also plummeted. The Republicans may have lost a big-bang opportunity in 1972 or lost a potential for creeping alignment in 1973. No one will ever know.

As for the creeping realignment of 1981, the question was less about its magnitude than about its permanence. Not all polls agreed, of course, but most did show a GOP gain, with Democratic self-identification among voters dropping some 10 points into the 30–40 percent range, while Republican self-identification climbed 5 points into the 25–30 percent range. Skeptics made two rebuttals: first, creeping realignment can't occur, or at least never has yet—it's big bang or nothing; second, the great volatility of voter political self-identification, not just in 1980–81 but over the previous decade, militates against another firmly rooted realignment of the type that occurred in the period from 1860 to 1932. Instead, our current volatility suggests a process of *de-alignment*. Under that thesis, party decomposition continues in one way or another, though that broad trend does not gainsay short-term party gains.

Definitive answers must await the outcome of the elections of 1982 and 1984. Nevertheless, early evidence seems to favor the de-alignment thesis.* Polling data show great volatility. All too often, Gallup shows one thing and NBC News another. That degree of variation suggests not erratic survey planners but an erratic electorate.

That the Republicans chose in 1981 to hitch their wagons to a supply-side economic-policy star presents the big reason to be skeptical about any thesis of realignment. Bold promises of an economic renaissance helped elicit an enthusiastic early response from the electorate, but long-range success will be necessary to secure a full and extended commitment. Meanwhile, the European experience of past "price inflations" and our own experience of the present one

*A September 11, 1981 *Christian Science Monitor* poll of American Political Science Association members found an 85–15 ratio indicating that *de-alignment* rather than *realignment* was under way.

gives conservatives little to be optimistic about. Because the United States has never before experienced severe peacetime inflation, its politics have never before seen realignment while its economy was in the midst of a period of inflation. Moreover, it can be said that in Canada and Europe the conservative regimes elected since the 1970s have shown little success straightening out national economic difficulties their election rhetoric had blamed on previous left or liberal governments. The prime examples here include Canada, Britain, Holland, Sweden and Israel. Indeed, the principal reason for the ebb and reversal during 1981 and 1982 of the West's post-1975 "trend to the right" is the number of conservative governments unable to cope with stagflation. Conversely, the fall of France's center-right coalition in the spring 1981 elections underscored the extent to which voters were still ready to turn against conservative governments on issues of participation and income maldistribution—issues that some analysts on the right had proclaimed dead. Though Europe's *previous* price revolutions antedated the era of democratic elections, it still seems relevant to note that the later years of the Second Price Revolution (1550–1620) and the Third Price Revolution (1770–1820) were characterized by sheer political volatility. Ministers, parliaments and even rulers fell as they proved unable to deal with the pressure and turbulence induced by inflation. Contemporary politicians could encounter the same.

So whether we "creep" toward realignment or "de-align" depends on whether the new Republican economics can deliver a healthier economy. How much time is available for making good is not clear, but certainly by 1984. Absent success, the 1980s are likely to be a time of ongoing de-alignment in which the major parties prove unable to rally a new institutional majority while minor parties achieve increased success. Such a period would probably see considerable instability, as one might expect, given the debilitating legacies of the last two decades.

In *Mediacracy: American Parties and Politics in the Communications Age* (1975), I suggested that traditional realignment might be slipping beyond the realm of the possible, especially after Watergate confirmed the massive agenda-setting capacity of the news media. Political parties no longer serve the function of mobilizing and communicating to the electorate—a function they arose to serve, or at least took modern form to serve, back in the second quarter of the nineteenth century. Putting it a bit differently, the contemporary form of the political party is a creature of the Industrial Revolution and the rise of mass enfranchisement. Until the 1830s or so, they were unnecessary, and as of the last quarter of the twentieth century, one must again ask how necessary they are. The advances of information-age technology may soon lead to a "wired electorate," reducing the role of the traditional party still further. In such a climate, how can the dynamics of old-style, deep, long-lasting party realignment occur? One can argue by this logic that realignment is now simply impossible: no traditional parties, no realignment.

At this point some speculation is useful and perhaps even essential. If we *are* in a period of de-alignment nurtured by inflation, by a partial revolution in popular and elite ideologies and by the change wrought by electronic communications, what does the future hold? I would lay out four trends and developments, listed roughly in the order of how confident I am about their taking place.

Short Political Cycles. The New Deal Democratic era (1932–1968) may not go down as the last of our party cycles, but the odds are very good that it *will* be the last of the long 28–36-year cycles. Politics in a communications age can turn on a dime—or at least on the perception of the major media. Advanced information technology seems to speed up the evolution of political ideas and movements, as well as quickly consuming those who manage or merchandise them. The ideas of eight or ten years ago are far more remote to the political decision makers of 1982 than ideas of a similar vintage were to decision makers of 1882. The last two decades may have seen a transition. The years between 1968 and 1980, when political realignment was due but did not occur, can be considered an electoral "no man's land," featuring the first of a series of short regimes: a backlash, law-and-order Nixon-Wallace cycle from 1968 to 1972, followed by a period of national mortification from 1974 to 1980; then, since 1980, a nationalist time of "back to old values." More likely than not, we'll now begin to see regimes lasting from four to eight years, transient hegemonies having but shallow roots in fluid party situations.

A Multiplicity of Parties. The United States is the last major Western nation with a two-party system, to say nothing of a system based on two parties that happened to have received their economic, geographic and social definition one hundred and twenty-odd years ago. Other political-institutional arrangements—in Canada, Britain and

Germany, for example—allow third-party entry much more easily and possess substantial third parties. However, new-party entry into American presidential elections, although difficult, is by no means impossible. Post-Watergate election reforms now provide federal funding in the presidential election for any party or candidate managing to get at least 5 percent of the national vote in the one four years earlier. Thus, with 7 percent of the vote, John Anderson's 1980 independent candidacy qualified for 1984 return funding, and Anderson has given strong early indications of running again and turning his independent movement into a new center party of sorts. The Libertarian Party, which has run candidates in the last three presidential elections, drew 1 percent in 1980 and is determined to institutionalize itself not only at the national level but in most states. Some observers give the Libertarians a chance of electing a governor in Alaska and possibly elsewhere. Even leaders of the anticorporate Citizens Party, which drew only one quarter of 1 percent in 1980, with environmentalist Barry Commoner as its presidential candidate, feel that the times support its institutionalization. In 1981, several magazine articles discussed Citizens Party success in local races from Burlington, Vermont, to Santa Monica, California.[1]

Chart 17 profiles the principal Anderson, Libertarian and Citizens party support centers. Most European countries have minor parties with a centrist cast, as well as "Green" (environmentalist) parties, and it may well be that the American minor parties of 1980 will be able to stake out similar turf and roles. Here again, a lot depends on the new Republican economics.

Plebiscitary Parties and Presidencies. One of the more intriguing —and so far least understood—phenomena in Republicanism and New Right populist conservatism is the extent to which advanced communications technology is being used by both to pursue an increasingly plebiscitary politics. By this I mean five particular new practices and biases: First, we can see growing emphasis on the presidency as a vehicle to get the attention of the public and mobilize the electorate, especially since Ronald Reagan as "the Great Communicator" is uniquely able to use television to marshal national opinion; second, we can see unprecedented mobilization of grassroots communications and voter support to pressure senators, congressmen and interest groups to embrace a particular issue; third, we can note mushrooming and massive use of direct mail for issue agitation and fund raising; fourth, we can see a growing philosophic

Chart 17

Top Splinter Party States, 1980
(in percentage of total vote for President)

Top 10 Anderson States		*Top Ten Libertarian Party States*		*Top Ten Citizens Party States*	
Massachusetts	15.18%	Alaska	11.79%	Oregon	1.15%
Vermont	14.52	Montana	2.70	Vermont	1.09
Rhode Island	14.21	Wyoming	2.55	D.C.	1.05
New Hampshire	12.54	Oregon	2.19	Maine	0.84
Connecticut	12.22	Colorado	2.17	Virginia	0.75
Colorado	11.03	Arizona	2.15	California	0.71
Washington	10.62	Idaho	1.93	Washington	0.54
Hawaii	10.56	Nevada	1.76	Hawaii	0.51
Maine	10.20	California	1.74	New Mexico	0.48
Oregon	9.53	Washington	1.68	Colorado	0.47

Note: Overall, it's fair to say that the 1980 splinter-party vote was heavily concentrated in states—and especially in communities within those states—with heavy ratios of what could be called post-industrial, Third Wave, post-bourgeois or "Green" voters. The pre-eminence of New England, Colorado and the Pacific states —with their disproportionate numbers of universities, environmentalists, resort areas and high-tech concentrations—is the key. In New England, the splinter parties together pulled almost 15% of the vote, likewise in Colorado. Alaska was a bit higher because of its Libertarian strength. Splinter-party strength hit 13% in Washington and Oregon, 12% in Hawaii and 11% in California. It's notable that these concentrations include most of the states futurists usually look to as U.S. trend setters. Also, it's useful to bear in mind that in the United States, the growth and characteristics of splinter parties has usually signaled a major upcoming force in national politics.

embrace of plebiscitary mechanisms. In 1979 and 1980, conservative presidential candidates from John Connally to Philip Crane endorsed national plebiscites on the Panama Canal treaties and a balanced budget, while the Republican governors and/or parties in New Jersey, Texas, Minnesota and elsewhere plunked for state-level adoption of national initiative-and-referendum plebiscitary devices. Meanwhile, Congressman Jack Kemp and his "tax revolt" allies have called for adoption of a national initiative-and-referendum mechanism; and fifth, we can see GOP strategists making specific use of initiative and referendum as an ideological and institutional tool. Republicans in states like California have begun to use tax-cut, anti-crime and antibusing referenda as a device to mobilize political opinion. The GOP has also begun to use the initiative mechanism as a targeted political weapon—in states like Massachusetts, Ohio,

Oklahoma and California—to try to undercut Democratic legislatures by changing their organizational rules and by putting their redistricting plans on the ballot for public scrutiny and rejection.[2]

I think that this trend is enormously important. Moreover, there is nothing conservative about it in the traditional sense, and New Right populist conservatives are among the strongest proponents of the plebiscitary approach. Plebiscitary politics undercuts the role of party, putting increased emphasis on technology, the mood of the public and short-term issue-based coalitions. Such developments are entirely compatible with either a populist reinvigoration of atrophying institutions *or* a trend to Caesarism.

Supraparty Coalitions. As it became apparent during the late 1970s that the opportunity for party realignment was slim, conservatives —especially New Right populist conservatives—took the lead pushing supraparty coalitions based on shared philosophy. In a number of Southern states, the coalitions were neither unusual nor especially innovative—Republicans and conservative Democrats simply agreed to vote together against moderate and liberal Democrats to organize at least one legislative house in Texas, Louisiana and Florida. In New Mexico and New Hampshire, by contrast, the successful philosophic coalition enlisted conservatives of both parties to vote against liberals of both parties. Meanwhile, the New Right-linked Free Congress Foundation has staged several conferences around the country with an eye to getting a supraparty coalition to organize the House of Representatives. Intriguingly, similar arrangements of coalition were necessary to organize the House in the midst of the *last* major breakup of our party system. In 1855 a group of Whigs, Republicans and Free Soil Democrats voted to elect Nathaniel P. Banks Speaker. That sort of thing could happen again in the 1980s. The Reagan Administration successfully attracted conservative Democrats into issue-coalitions on tax and budget legislation; meanwhile, House Ways and Means Committee chairman Daniel Rostenkowski spoke openly in mid-1981 about the possibility of conservative Democrats going into coalition with the Republicans to organize the House in 1983. Which has a certain institutional logic. If de-alignment is to be the hallmark of party politics of the 1980s, then coalition may succeed yesteryear's mode of electoral realignment.

Whether we de-align or realign is the key question. My own sense is that both parties have been and still are in a process of long-term erosion. As of 1981, the Democrats elicited the loyalty of only 30–40 percent of Americans, down from roughly 50 percent in the mid-1960s and the years after Watergate and Nixon's resignation. The Republicans, with 25–30 percent, were back up to 1968–72 levels, but well below their Eisenhower-era percentages. The most enduring phenomenon of the years since the war in Vietnam and Watergate has been the rise in the ranks of *independents*.

Admittedly, a strong economic rebound in the 1980s could over-match the forces of de-alignment and create something resembling a traditional Republican realignment. And if the Republicans avoid erosion, that automatically eases pressure on the Democrats. The threat to the two-party system, the most plausible spur to accelerated de-alignment, is a 1981–84 failure of *Republican* economic policy in the wake of the 1977–80 failure of *Democratic* economic policy. Coming on top of all the political and social stresses of the last two decades, such double failure would create great strains—and new-party pressures.

The disintegration of the old Democratic coalition during the last two decades is now widely accepted. Failure now by Republicans in economic policy making could provoke a similar unraveling on their side of the aisle. The Sun Belt, fundamentalist-tilted forces of the New Right, and the GOP's lingering New England/Great Lakes/Pacific Northwestern social progressives are as hostile and incompatible as the McGovern/New Class and George Wallace Democrats were in the late 1960s and 1970s. Without the optimism of the early days of Reaganomics and a Republican realignment, their cohesion may not last the decade. In my view, the 1980 John Anderson constituency, though just 7 percent of the electorate, is fascinating, possibly foreshadowing a new center party not unlike the Social Democratic/Liberal grouping taking shape in Britain and the Free Democrats in West Germany. Heavily based in university towns, affluent resorts, moderate Yankee GOP strongholds, affluent suburbs and the new high-tech industrial areas, Anderson's is the first major American political splinter effort since the GOP in the 1850s to draw on a predominantly middle-to-high income, socioeconomic "cutting edge" electorate. Map 3 illustrates its Yankee (traditional GOP), suburban and high-tech geography. The usual appeal of a splinter party has been to alienated, less affluent peripheries. Should Reaganomics not pan out, the Administration would be obliged to intensify its appeal to populist lower-middle-income conservatives with pro-

Generalized Contours of the 1980 Anderson Vote

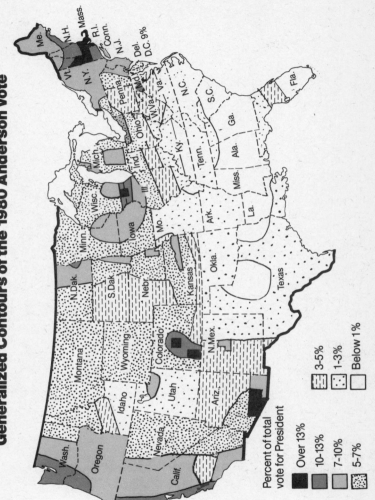

Percent of total
vote for President

Over 13%	3-5%
10-13%	1-3%
7-10%	Below 1%
5-7%	

Most top Anderson counties display one or more of seven major characteristics: 1) university; 2) ski area/arts-crafts orientation; 3) high-tech industry/suburbia; 4) smalltown Yankee/summer resort; 5) affluent suburban; 6) rural/urban Scandinavian; and 7) urban/suburban New England. So that you can assess the top fifty counties by characteristic, they've been categorized accordingly.

County (State)	Percentage	Characteristics
Nantucket, Mass.	21.7%	4
Winnebago, Ill.	21.5	6
Dukes, Mass.	21.0	4
Pitkin, Colo.	20.8	2
Barnstable, Mass.	19.4	4
Story, Iowa	19.4	1
Summit, Colo.	19.4	2
Windham, Vt.	19.1	2, 4
Johnson, Iowa	18.9	1
Chittenden, Vt.	17.9	1, 2, 3, 4
Tolland, Ct.	17.7	1, 4
Franklin, Mass.	17.2	4
Washington, R.I.	17.1	1, 4
San Juan, Colo.	17.1	2
Windsor, Vt.	17.1	2, 4
Hampshire, Mass.	16.9	1, 7
Douglas, Kansas	16.6	1
Latah, Idaho	16.6	1
San Miguel, Colo.	16.4	2
Cheshire, N.H.	16.1	4
Essex, Mass.	16.0	3, 4
Middlesex, Mass.	16.0	1
Newport, R.I.	16.0	4
Boulder, Colo.	15.8	1
Grafton, N.H.	15.8	1, 2, 4
Eagle, Colo.	15.6	2
Berkshire, Mass.	15.6	1, 4
Norfolk, Mass.	15.5	3, 5
Stephenson, Ill.	15.4	6
Plymouth, Mass.	15.3	4, 7
Champaign, Ill.	15.3	1

Bristol, R.I.	15.2	7
Lamoille, Vt.	15.2	2, 4
Kent, R.I.	15.1	4, 7
Addison, Vt.	15.0	1, 2, 4
DeKalb, Ill.	14.9	1
Washington, Vt.	14.9	2, 4
Los Alamos, N.M.	14.8	Atomic research
Orange, Vt.	14.6	4
Strafford, N.H.	14.5	4
Riley, Kansas	14.5	1
San Juan, Wash.	14.5	Puget Sound islands
Benton, Ore.	14.5	1
Bennington, Vt.	14.4	1, 2, 4
Clay, S.D.	14.3	1
Gunnison, Colo.	14.2	2
Middlesex, Ct.	14.2	4
Hartford, Ct.	14.2	5, 7
Albany, Wyo.	14.1	1
Kitsap, Wash.	14.1	5, resort

Other counties not quite making the list . . . Marin, Cal. (San Francisco hot-tub suburbia), 12.7%; Santa Clara, Cal. (Silicon Valley), 13.7%; Pima, Ariz. (Tucson and suburbs), 13.5%; Hennepin, Minn. (Minneapolis and suburbs), 11.2%; Montgomery, Md. (upper-income Washington, D.C. suburbs), 12.3%; Dane, Wisc. (Madison), 11.7%; and the two top Anderson counties/independent cities in the South—Orange, N.C. (Univ. of N.C.-Chapel Hill), 11.8%; and Williamsburg, Va. (restored Williamsburg and William & Mary College), 11.5%.

Source: The American Political Report, March 13, 1981

vocative social and foreign-policy themes. Whereupon the Anderson electorate could mushroom into an important 1984 independent political grouping. Moreover, if Vice President Bush should succeed to the presidency or win the Republican nomination in 1984, the New Right could bolt. *Both* ideological wings of the GOP are loose.

The major intraparty problem facing Reagan Republicanism, of course, can be found among the party's old Yankee and Northeastern establishment moderates. The problem's visibility, though quite obvious in 1980 election returns, was hidden in early 1981 as party moderates rallied around the Administration's tax and budget proposals. But that support was necessarily short-lived because Reagan Administration socioeconomic incompatibility with the old liberal GOP strongholds was inevitable. According to the Gallup poll, Reagan drew only 86 percent of the national Republican vote in 1981, the lowest of any party nominee since Barry Goldwater, who took only 80 percent. As Chart 18 shows, Reagan ran far behind Gerald Ford among liberal Republicans and somewhat behind the Michigander among moderate Republicans. Of course, Reagan more than made up for the slippage with sharp gains among Sun Belt voters, Protestant fundamentalists and conservative Catholic Democrats. But in the old Yankee GOP strongholds of New England—the best places to look for a reaction against a GOP Sun Belt, Southern or "Cowboy" strategy—Reagan in 1980 ran 30–45 points behind 1956 GOP presidential strength, and in some cases the former California governor barely ran ahead of Barry Goldwater's 1964 levels. Chart 19 illustrates the ebb. This ongoing GOP erosion in its ancestral territory, coupled with Democratic losses in Dixie, make for yet

Chart 18   *Liberal and Moderate Republican Trends, 1976–80*

Two-Candidate Preferences of Voters, 1976–80
(CBS News/New York *Times* Poll)

	1976		1980	
	% GOP	% Dem.	% GOP	% Dem.
Liberal Republicans	83	17	72	28
Moderate Republicans	89	11	86	14
Conservative Republicans	94	6	94	6
Conservative Democrats	35	65	44	56

Source: New York *Times,* November 8, 1980

Chart 19   *The Yankee Republican Ebb, 1956–80*

Republican Percentage of Total Vote for President

County*	1956	1964	1980
Barnstable, Mass.	83%	43%	51%
Dukes, Mass.	83	32	34
Nantucket, Mass.	83	33	41
Hancock, Maine	87	46	54
Lincoln, Maine	86	44	52
Orange, Vermont	84	41	50
Windham, Vermont	80	33	43
Lamoille, Vermont	84	46	47

*These counties, in 1956, were the Yankee Republican strongholds of their respective states.

another reason to think that the 1980s will not produce a 1930s-style traditional realignment, and another reason to think that a larger reshuffling and rearrangement of American politics is upon us.

If that sounds vague, it is. Trying to forecast the shape of our politics during a period of global upheaval is hard enough. In 1981 the nation also found itself in the midst of a possible electoral watershed under the aegis of a President who, having turned seventy years old just after his inauguration, was deemed by many observers unlikely to seek a second term in 1984. Previous watershed elections required the Presidents involved—Jefferson, Jackson, Lincoln, McKinley and FDR—to seek and win re-election to consolidate their party's new majority status. All five did.

To summarize: my sense is that the chances for a traditional realignment of the party system are slim. Instead, what we'll probably see are short-term political coalitions and supremacies based more on communications technology than on old-style parties. In the process, our politics will become increasingly prone to plebiscitary techniques and appeals. The American party system seems a long way from overcoming two decades of weakness. In fact, that weakness is probably moving front and center.

18

AMERICA AND
WORLD HISTORY

> Eventually we will have to face the fact of rot in our institutions and
> infrastructure: the inability of our schools to teach; slovenliness in
> standards of efficiency and precision; the decay of our railroads,
> bridges, harbors and roads; the aging of our industrial plants; the
> litigiousness of an overlawyered society; the decline of our political
> parties; the bland arrogance of the news media; the living-in-the-past
> of our labor unions; the irrelevance of our colleges; the short-term
> myopia of our industrial leaders; and the seeming inability of govern-
> ment to do anything efficiently and well.
>
> —Daniel Yankelovich, *New Rules* (1981)

NO FOURTH OF JULY SPEAKER IS LIKELY TO PLAGIA-
rize my attempt to profile the economic and historical vulnerabilities
of the United States during the 1980s. Our governmental system is
in trouble. A major convergence of problems faces obsolete party and
political mechanisms, and too few observers seem disposed to acknowledge the dangers. Calvin Coolidge, who made himself a folk
hero of sorts—and could become one once more—for terse repudia-
tions of intellectual Chicken Little-isms, liked to say that if you see
twenty troubles coming down the road, nineteen will never reach
you. Coolidge, of course, managed instead to get himself off the road
—out of the White House—before the twentieth trouble, the Crash
of 1929, hit. Nevertheless, his is the American way of looking at
things. Most troubles have, in fact, fallen off our national road. But
not all. Moreover, it has been a short historical road, only some two
centuries long.

Americans lack historical awareness. Which is not surprising,
since our national identity spans only one economic-political period

—the nineteenth- and twentieth-century era of industrialism. Even if the world at large experienced political and economic revolutions during the late eighteenth and early nineteenth centuries, the domestic institutional upheaval and the runaway price indexes of that time are easily explainable—those were the years of the birth of the new American Republic, and turmoil was to be expected. The bloody interlude of the Civil War, in turn, was too idiosyncratic in its origin and outcome to have much to teach anybody living in the twentieth century. But the force that really created the ahistorical American was the century of unalloyed American triumph during the years from 1865 to 1965. National achievement and good fortune were astonishing, and this success, especially in its final years, covered up a plethora of emerging weaknesses: an ebbing global economic competitiveness, a declining *civitas,* a Balkanizing society, a century-old party system and archaic national decision-making mechanisms.

The national penalty for that cover-up may be substantial. In the late 1960s and early 1970s, Americans knew they were being buffeted by unfamiliar political and economic winds: surging prices, political assassination and scandal, and the first lost war in our history. However, I think very few of us felt having come onto one of those great continental shifts of history, when the contours of global economies, politics and culture shake, yawn and crunch before slowly settling into a new shape. That is probably what the 1960s, 1970s and 1980s were and are: movement along a socioeconomic San Andreas fault.

The convergence of historical forces that have broken upon us has been especially quick and powerful. First, using the concept of America-as-empire, the United States achieved its greatest degree of relative global economic, political and military might in the 1940s and 1950s. And since the 1960s, the erosion of our power has been especially rapid, underscored by the events in Indochina. This decline has been a source of great frustration to us, even to those who say they harbor no imperial pretensions. Public reaction to the Panama Canal treaties was a good mirror. Moreover, that patriotic dislocation has been accompanied and aggravated after 1965 by the country's first long wave of peacetime inflation, Americans having no effective *national* memory of earlier price revolutions. Not surprisingly, the confluence of wartime cynicism and inflation helped escalate yet another upheaval—moral and sexual—which, in turn, helped to bring on what appears to be this nation's Fourth Great Awakening or religious revival.

Each of these national convulsions, by itself, would produce great tensions in our politics and society. When they struck together, a set of circumstances was created never before present in the United States, leaving the potential for volatility enormous.

The global overview is equally disturbing. The United States, a nation with no collective memory of an earlier price revolution, is now at the vortex of the most massive price revolution to date. By this argument, the pseudo-imperial defeat in Vietnam, the collapse of Pax Americana, inflation, and the cultural breakdown of the West are all part of a global socioeconomic upheaval, the fourth of its kind since A.D. 1000. Epochal turbulence has attended the rise of the Inflationary State, various forms of post-industrialism, the advance of information technology, and a host of allied developments. Moreover, as the most advanced political, economic and industrial power in the world from 1945 through the end of the 1960s, the United States was the prime architect of the global upheaval and later one of its most pained victims, as the internal system—created during our century of triumph, 1865 to 1965—could not cope with new demands and decision-making challenges.

If this overview is correct—and we have up to now shunned such thinking—the United States must confront its various problems as a polity and economy in decline and badly in need of institutional modernization. A substantial degree of reform seems imperative.

In this respect, history is not without its reassuring precedent. The United States is anything but a static society that willingly accepts Spenglerian decline; we have periodically revitalized ourselves by Western movement and geopolitical upheaval—and may be doing so again. According to the Census Bureau, the U.S. population center is moving south and west at the rate of three feet an hour, five miles a year. As Map 1 suggests (see Chapter 7), by the year 2000, domination by the Sun Belt will be far more advanced and complete than today, and therein lies a very critical aspect of the nation's future. No one can say what the politics of the Sun Belt will be then, but its enhanced national primacy seems indisputable. In the annals of the Republic—and before it, of the thirteen colonies—the new demography marks the first time the locus of national leadership will have shifted away from the Eastern seaboard.

This time the southward and westward movement may have unprecedented significance. The Northeast/Great Lakes bastion of the old industrial-political establishment is in decline, just as Britain is.

Simultaneously, however, the Sun Belt can be seen as a new nation rising to dominance within the political geography of the old. No European nation has anything like it. And to an extent greater and more intense than any other region of the country, the Sun Belt epitomizes the moods and forces resurgent in the United States of the early 1980s: nationalism, fundamentalist religion, but also high technology and "can do" entrepreneurialism. Thus the question: If the Sun Belt *is* a new American internal frontier, slapped together from cypress swamp and Southwestern desert, then maybe the country *can* handle the forces unleashed by stagflation, religious revivalism and patriotic frustration. After all, what seems like a politics of nostalgia in Minnesota, Maryland or Connecticut becomes much more vital and viable in the climate of central Florida or suburban San Antonio. Here the new entrepreneurialism is not a quest for the Fountain of Youth but the exuberance of economic and cultural adolescence itself.

The editorial writers of the San Diego *Union* put the optimistic case as well as anyone when they said that the regional shift

> isn't so much Sun Belt vs. Frostbelt as it is . . . America II emerging from the diminished promise of America I . . . Just over half of all Americans now live in the South and West, reversing a population tilt that prevailed for most of the nation's history. But what the new majority is doing is more important than where it lives. The citizens of America II, whether natives or transplants, tend to be innovators. They are building new kinds of cities less centralized and more livable than the congested urban centers of the North and East . . . Outmoded technology, inhospitable cities, intrusive government and a fading entrepreneuriship are more precise descriptions of America I than any of the regional boundaries so frequently cited.[1]

I suspect that the Sun Belt probably *is* the key to making America work again both as a polity and as economy. If the frontier Frederick Jackson Turner believed closed is economically and spiritually open once more, the United States may be able to steer itself through a great inflation, great national frustration and Fourth Great Awakening all at the same time. The social and economic safety valve would once more come into play. Opportunity and mobility would again save the day. Populism could succeed again. The specter of declining living standards, quasi-European social stratification and zero-sum interest-group combat could be avoided. At least on the national scale.

It goes without saying, boosterism aside, that many people in the Sun Belt believe that they *are* part of such a frontier, that their churches, their businesses and their patriotism demonstrate the ongoing vitality of old American credos and self-reliant ways of doing things. In this, their mindset and Ronald Reagan's were nicely matched in 1980. Richard Wirthlin, Reagan's pollster, has characterized the South by saying, "It is a land that is just beginning to enjoy the fruits of economic growth. The transfer of manufacturing capability to the South has created a buoyancy, an optimistic spirit, that does stand in contrast to the rest of the nation."[2]

But the chances that the Sun Belt can transmit that buoyancy to the rest of the nation seem slim. In the eras of Andrew Jackson, William Jennings Bryan and even Franklin D. Roosevelt, the forces of Southern and Western revivalism and populism lent themselves to political and institutional reform, but one wonders how that can happen in the 1980s. The Sun Belt is now the major axis of national power, no longer a peripheral, semicolonial assemblage of mining camps, cattle ranches and cotton fields. Social Darwinism is the credo among Sun Belt elites; if Cleveland, Detroit and Newark can't make it, the argument goes, Dallas and Houston can—a point President Reagan himself more or less made in one speech. If the Sun Belt is to carry things, it will find itself required to work through a national party system shaped one hundred and thirty years ago around a wholly different kind of sectionalism when California, Texas and Florida together had only five congressmen, one-seventh as many as New York. The Sun Belt may manage, may guide the successful emergence of the "America II." And perhaps carping Eastern elites are merely re-enacting *their* previous-era roles of denouncing vigor, innovation and progress. Nevertheless, there *are* reasons to be nervous about the character of a national renaissance captained by the Sun Belt. In 1968, my definition of the region in geographic terms also took note of a new culture:

> Long ago, in the hot valleys of the Tigris, Euphrates and other Near East cradles of civilization, human culture began in the warm womb of a land where people could live without technology, but during later millenniums far greater civilizations evolved in temperate zones where climate, like necessity, mothered progress and invention. Today, how-

ever, a reverse trend is afoot. Spurred by high pensions, early retirement, increased leisure time and technological innovation, the affluent American middle class is returning to the comforts of the endless summer, which they can escape at will in swimming pools and total refrigeration.

The persons most drawn to the new sun culture are the pleasure-seekers, the bored, the ambitious, the space-age technicians and the retired—a super-slice of the rootless, socially mobile group known as the American middle class. Most of them have risen to such status only in the last generation, and their elected officials predictably embody a popular politics impulse which deplores further social (minority group) upheaval and favors a consolidation of the last thirty years' gains. Increasingly important throughout the nation, this new middle-class group is most powerful in the Sun Belt. Its politics are bound to cast a lengthening national shadow.[3]

These two paragraphs have stood the test of time well, and I see no reason to change them. But during the intervening years, the Sun Belt has gone from an idea and a developing trend to perhaps the most powerful regional force in American politics. If the region is to dominate the nation, and that seems likely, we must think about it as a frontier of frustration as well as one of opportunity. Early-American frontiers were not settled by technocrats, by middle-class refugees from the cities or by retired people. The distinction is important. Today's Sun Belt represents a confluence of Social Darwinism, entrepreneurialism, high technology, nationalism, nostalgia and fundamentalist religion, and any Sun Belt hegemony over our politics has a unique potential—not present in the Jackson-to-Bryan frontier or the Adams-to-Taft Eastern establishment—to accommodate a drift toward apple-pie authoritarianism.

One can easily enough imagine the Sun Belt as the launch pad—indeed, it may be already—of a communications-based, high-technology, corporate-linked, frequently plebiscitary, intermittently populist conservatism. Corporatist policies would manage the economy more than is being done today, mobilizing a U.S.A. Inc. to cope with France Inc. or Japan Inc. The morality of the majority would be upheld and enforced, though with politically convenient lapses; "The Star-Spangled Banner" would wave with greater frequency and over many more parades; increased surveillance would crack down on urban outbreaks and extreme political dissidents. Walter Laqueur, the distinguished historian, is already projecting and to an extent even *proposing* somewhat the same thing for Western Europe. In *A*

Continent Astray: Europe 1970–78, he anticipates a swing toward regimes of strong leaders, and policies bordering on authoritarianism: "The reassertion of authority may be brutal, far-reaching, and costly, but it is equally possible that societies facing a crisis of survival will voluntarily surrender some of the freedom to which they have become accustomed and that gradually a new equilibrium will emerge between the rights of the individual and the interests of society."[4]

Instead of being a force for reform in yesteryear's frontier mold, then, the rise of the Sun Belt may instead constitute a force for a similar quest for order in the United States. However, that trend appears to be nationwide, supra-ideological; and progressives who associate a reassertion of civil and police authority with the mood of Miami, Dallas or Orange County must confront an equal tension and sentiment in the old Northern central cities. In 1981, for example, polls showed the most popular politician in New York to be the Democratic mayor of New York City, who was riding on a crest of support for the death penalty, antiminority imagery and use of police dogs to guard subway cars.

Contemporary populism may possess similarly precarious attributes. The agrarianism of William Jennings Bryan pursued relatively limited economic goals—at least in its early, presidential-campaign phase. But the middle-class populism of today has an agenda much more given to cultural, moral and end-of-empire issues; it also has a well-honed communications technology—on all sides. Post-industrial or communications-age "populism" may wind up rather authoritarian in substance, antigovernment rhetoric notwithstanding. The initiative device, for one, is a far more powerful tool in the 1980s—with a "wired electorate" near at hand—than it was when introduced by populists and progressives at the turn of the century.

The future always presents a gamble, of course. And in the United States, the future has usually belonged to optimists, with pessimists —save in the 1850s, and then again in the 1960s and 1970s—being gainsayed. Moreover, the great watershed periods of our history have rung with many an unjustified charge of dictatorship or fascism— directed toward Andrew Jackson, Abraham Lincoln and Franklin D. Roosevelt alike. As turbulent times, watershed periods have generated the boldest presidencies and the most notable and controversial changes of direction. Rhetoric was intensified (and exaggerated) accordingly.

That may be happening again. Yet during the 1980s, the risk seems to have doubled. We hope, first, for the success of a new economics, and we hope, second, that the United States can maintain its long tradition of rebuilding a vital and democratic politics through upheavals generated by various frontiers, populisms, restive anti-elites and religious revivals. The historical-versus-contemporary dichotomy is what remains troubling: to deny the past validity and effectiveness of these roiling forces is to deny the reality of American history, yet to reaffirm that faith and to trust those dynamics in present circumstances is not for the timid.

Two decades of political and economic trauma have brought this country to a point of considerable risk. Unrepentant liberalism having exhausted its credibility by the 1980s, the United States turned to a transformed, radicalized conservatism—and crossed its national fingers. The precariousness of the conservative experiment should not be understated. In an era of upheaval like this one, there is no going back, no way to recapture the past for more than a short period of time. Radical conservatism may succeed for a while, or it may metamorphose, or it may fail. But to future historians, the early 1980s are almost certain to mark a transition to a new politics, a new economics and a new philosophy of governance. It is my feeling that America has already become post-conservative as well as post-liberal.

Source Notes

1 Calvin Coolidge and the "Shadow Empire"

1. William Appleton Williams, "Empire as a Way of Life," the *Nation* (August 2, 1980), p. 104.
2. "Reagan's Optimism is Based on Nostalgia," Nashville *Tennessean* (June 1, 1980).
3. Objections to Conservatism: The Heritage Lectures (Heritage Foundation, Washington, 1981), p. 11.
4. "Reagan is Still on Automatic Pilot," New York Times Service, Denver *Post* (January 27, 1981).
5. "Reagan's Economics: Throwback to Coolidge," Knight-Ridder News Service, Hartford *Courant* (April 26, 1981).
6. Jules Feiffer, "Movie America—Or, The Past Recaptured," the *Nation* (July 11, 1981).
7. Jeffrey Hart, King Features Syndicate (November 2, 1979).
8. Frederick Lewis Allen, *Only Yesterday* (New York, Bantam Books, 1959), p. 129.
9. *Ibid.*, p. 130.
10. Carey McWilliams, *Southern California Country* (New York, Duell, Sloan & Pearce, 1946), p. 179.
11. TRB, "Heaven, Inc.," the *New Republic* (May 6, 1981).
12. See R. H. Tawney, *Religion and the Rise of Capitalism* (Gloucester, Mass., Peter Smith, 1962).
13. Arnold Toynbee, *A Study of History,* abridged ed. (Barre, Mass., Weathervane, 1972), pp. 245–246.
14. Milton Elleria and Ailsa Kesten, "The New Right," *USA Today* (March 1981), p. 15.
15. Leopold Tyrmand, "The Conservative Ideas in Reagan's Victory," *Wall Street Journal* (January 20, 1981).
16. *Human Events* (April 4, 1981), p. 7.
17. James Q. Wilson, "Reagan and the Republican Revival," *Commentary* (October 1981).

2 The Two-Decade Breakdown

1. Will and Ariel Durant, *The Lessons of History* (New York, Simon & Schuster, 1968), p. 40.
2. George Nash, *The Conservative Intellectual Movement in America* (New York, Basic Books, 1976), p. 325.

3 To the Nashville Station

1. Margaret Canovan, *Populism* (New York, Harcourt Brace Jovanovich, 1981).
2. Louis Hartz, *The Liberal Tradition in America* (New York, Harcourt, Brace & World, 1955).
3. Nash, *op. cit.,* p. 338.
4. Chilton Williamson, Jr., "Country & Western Marxism," *National Review* (June 9, 1978), p. 711.
5. Alan Crawford, *Thunder on the Right* (New York, Pantheon, 1980).
6. Peter Steinfels, *The Neoconservatives: The Men Who Are Changing America's Politics* (New York, Simon & Schuster, 1979).
7. Quoted in Sidney Blumenthal, "The Intelligentsia of the Right," the *Boston Globe Magazine* (March 15, 1981), p. 14.
8. Kevin P. Phillips, "The Neo-Conservatives," the *Washington Post (Outlook)* (August 26, 1979), p. 1.
9. Quoted in Jeffrey Hart, King Features Syndicate column (August 19, 1980).
10. Quoted in Blumenthal, *op. cit.,* p. 14.
11. Objections to Conservatism: The Heritage Lectures, *op. cit.,* p. 44.
12. French Catholic (Viguerie), German Catholic (Weyrich), Boston Jew (Phillips), Virginia Baptist (Falwell).
13. Harris poll release, November 4, 1980.
14. Richard Viguerie, "David Brinkley's Journal" (ABC Network, January 24, 1982).

4 The Emerging Republican Majority

1. Richard Nixon, *Memoirs* (New York, Grosset & Dunlap, 1978).
2. A. J. Reichley, *Conservatives in an Age of Change* (Washington, Brookings Institution, 1981), p. 335.

5 The Watergate Warp

1. Richard Whalen, "Time to Resume the Cold War," Washington *Post* (January 20, 1980).
2. Nicholas Von Hoffman, "The Breaking of a President," *Penthouse* (March, 1977), p. 48.
3. Robert Nisbet, *Twilight of Authority* (New York, Oxford U. Press, 1975), p. 44.

4. "Nixon as Dreyfus," *New York* (September 6, 1976), p. 59.

5. James Hougan, "The McCord File," *Harper's* (January 1980).

6. UPI. Atlanta *Constitution* (May 5, 1977), p. 11.

7. Chicago *Tribune* (June 23, 1976), p. 11.

8. H. R. Haldeman, *The Ends of Power* (New York, Times Books, 1978), pp. 121–164.

9. Raymond Price, *With Nixon* (New York, Viking, 1977), pp. 360–369.

10. John Dean, *Blind Ambition* (New York, Pocket Books, 1977), pp. 392–397.

11. John Ehrlichman, *The Company* (New York, Simon & Schuster, 1976).

12. Carl Oglesby, *The Yankee and Cowboy War* (New York, Berkley Books, 1977), preface.

13. Marcus Raskin, *Notes on The Old System: To Transform American Politics* (New York, David McKay, 1974).

14. Seymour Martin Lipset and Earl Rabb, "Watergate," *Psychology Today* (November 1973), p. 84.

15. "H. R. Haldeman's Watergate Story," Chicago *Tribune* (June 20, 1976), p. 21.

16. Associated Press (May 20, 1977).

17. Hougan, *op. cit.*, p. 37.

18. Nicholas Von Hoffman, King Features Syndicate (1976).

6 The Balkanization of America

No citations.

7 After the Sun Belt, What New Forces?

1. Harris poll release, November 4, 1980.

8 The Twentieth-Century Price Revolution

1. Marvin R. O'Connell, *The Counter-Reformation 1559–1610* (New York, Harper, 1974).

2. The pioneering work—E. H. Phelps-Brown and Sheila V. Hopkins, "Seven Centuries of the Price of Consumables, Compared with Builders' Wage Rates," *Economica,* XXIII (1956) pp. 296–314—came considerably ahead of the major upsurge of attention in the early 1970s. By the early to mid-1970s, a few analysts were beginning to review the previous price revolution dynamics and posit the probability that the West was in another such upheaval.

3. Fernand Braudel and Frank Spooner, "Prices in Europe from 1450 to 1750," *Cambridge Economic History,* IV, 447f.

4. George Gilder, *Wealth and Poverty* (New York, Basic Books, 1981), p. 195.

5. Earl J. Hamilton, *American Treasure and the Price Revolution in Spain, 1501–1650* (Cambridge, Mass., 1934).

6. Arthur Laffer, "Global Money Growth and Inflation," *Wall Street Journal* (September 23, 1975).

9 The Failure of Liberal Economics

1. Kuttner, *Revolt of the Haves* (New York, Simon & Schuster, 1980).

2. "Social Welfare Plans in W. Europe Pinched," Los Angeles *Times* (February 16, 1981).

3. *Ibid.*

10 The New Conservative Economic Theory

1. This and other counter–supply-side interpretations of Smith appear in John Hess, "The Compleat Adam Smith," the *Nation* (May 16, 1981), p. 589.

2. Gilder, *op. cit.,* p. 33.

3. Jude Wanniski, *The Way the World Works* (New York, Basic Books, 1978), pp. 125–141.

4. Allen, *op. cit.,* p. 244.

5. Caroline Bird, *The Invisible Scar* (New York, Pocket Books, 1967), p. 10.

6. J. K. Galbraith, *Money* (Boston, Houghton Mifflin, 1975), p. 184.

7. See Milton Friedman and Anna Schwartz, *A Monetary History of the United States, 1867–1960* (Princeton University Press, 1963) for the monetarist case against Federal Reserve Board aggravation of the early 1930s economic downturn.

8. Arthur Laffer. Los Angeles *Times* (June 2, 1981).

9. Quoted in Leonard Silk, New York *Times* (May 10, 1981).

10. *Agenda for Progress* (Heritage Foundation, Washington, 1981).

11. Michael Novak, "Toward a Theology of the Corporation" (Washington, American Enterprise Institute, 1981), p. 28.

12. Gilder, *op. cit.,* p. 24.

13. Los Angeles *Times* (June 10, 1981).

11 Political Economics of the 1980s

1. Lester Thurow, *The Zero-Sum Society* (New York, Basic Books, 1980), p. 11.

2. *Ibid.,* pp. 156, 199.

3. *Ibid.,* p. 15.

4. J. H. Plumb, "Inflation," *Horizon* (Spring 1975), pp. 46–47.

5. David Hackett Fischer, "Chronic Inflation: The Long View," *Journal of the Institute for Socioeconomic Studies* (Autumn 1980), pp. 82–103.

SOURCE NOTES

12 America in the 1980s

1. For European parallels, see Seymour M. Lipset, *Political Man* (New York, Anchor Books, 1963), pp. 127–179.
2. *American Political Report* (August 17, 1979), p.3.
3. Quoted in Kevin P. Phillips, "A Sense of Inevitability," King Features Syndicate (May 22, 1974).
4. Robert Cook, "American Weimar," *Worldview* (July 1980), pp. 11–14.
5. Quoted in the Chicago *Tribune* (April 23, 1978).
6. Jack Porter, "It Can't Happen Here," *Harvard Political Review* (Spring 1981), pp. 12–14.
7. Spencer Vibbert, "Punk, Boston Style," the *Boston Globe Magazine* (March 2, 1980), p. 8.
8. Nathan Glazer, "The Exposed American Jew," *Commentary* (June 1975), p. 25.

13 Vietnam: An Unexploded Bomb?

1. Washington *Post* (February 25, 1981), p. 2.
2. William C. Westmoreland, *A Soldier Reports* (New York, Doubleday, 1976)
3. Interview with General Westmoreland, Atlanta *Constitution* (August 1, 1977).
4. Quoted in Kevin P. Phillips, "Patterns of Postwar Recrimination," King Features Syndicate (June 4, 1972).
5. Douglas Kinnard, *The War Managers* (Hanover, N.H., University Press of New England, 1977).
6. Westmoreland, *op. cit.*, quoted in *Wall Street Journal* (February 24, 1976), p. 18.
7. Washington *Post* (June 10, 1967).
8. Peter Braestrup, *Big Story* (Westview Press, 1976).
9. Quoted in Edith Efron, "Massive Study Indicts Media Coverage of Vietnam," *TV Guide* (July 9, 1977), p. A-6.
10. *Loc. cit.*
11. Samuel Eliot Morison, *The Maritime History of Massachusetts* (Boston, Sentry Books, 1961), p. 208.
12. Frederick Jackson Turner, *The United States, 1830–1850* (Norton Library/New York, Norton, 1965), p. 562.
13. *Ibid.*, p. 562.
14. Otis A. Singletary, *The Mexican War* (Chicago, University of Chicago Press, 1962) p. 116.
15. *Ibid.*, p. 116.

16. Woods Gray, *The Hidden Civil War* (New York, Compass Books, 1964), p. 184.
17. *Ibid.,* p. 222.
18. Margaret Leech, *In the Days of McKinley* (New York, Harper & Brothers, 1959) p. 326.
19. *Ibid.,* pp. 408–409.
20. Eric F. Goldman, *The Crucial Decade* (New York, Random House; Vintage Books, 1960), p. 164.
21. *Ibid.,* p. 205.
22. National Platform of the Republican Party, Washington, 1980.
23. See especially "Revisionism: A New Look at Vietnam," Los Angeles *Times* (November 16, 1980), pp. 1, 20–23.
24. H. L. Mencken, *On Politics* (New York, Random House, Vintage Books, 1960), p. 44.

14 A Fourth U.S. "Great Awakening"?

1. Martin Marty, *A Nation of Believers* (Chicago, University of Chicago Press, 1976).
2. "A Religious Tidal Wave," Atlanta *Constitution* (September 10, 1977).
3. William G. McLoughlin, *Revivals, Awakenings and Reform* (Chicago, University of Chicago Press, 1978).
4. Kevin P. Phillips, *Mediacracy: American Parties and Politics in the Communications Age* (New York, Doubleday, 1975), pp. 54–56.
5. Jeremy Rifkin and Ted Howard, *The Emerging Order: God in an Age of Scarcity* (New York, Putnam, 1979).
6. Tom Wolfe, "The 'Me' Decade and the Third Great Awakening," *New York* (August 23, 1976), p. 26.
7. Tony Thomas, "Behind That New Time Religion," the *Washington Post (Outlook)* (May 4, 1980), p. 1.
8. *Ibid.,* p. 4.
9. Pat Horn, "The New Middle Class Fundamentalism," *Psychology Today* (September 1976).
10. "Great Reawakening in N.E.—Fundamentalist Religion Grows," Boston *Globe* (July 26, 1981).
11. "A Religious Tidal Wave," *op. cit.*
12. *Ibid.*
13. Knight-Ridder News Service (June 10, 1981).
14. *Intellect* (January 1978), p. 274.
15. Erling Jorstad, *The Politics of Doomsday: The Fundamentalists of the Far Right* (Nashville, Abingdon, 1970).
16. Quoted in Gordon L. Weil, "How Candidates Will Turn Evangelical

Glory Into Political Power," *Politicks & Other Human Interests* (December 6, 1977), p. 16.

17. Samuel Lubell, *The Future While It Happened* (New York, Norton, 1973), p. 61.

18. Albert J. Menendez, *Religion at the Polls* (Philadelphia, Westminster, 1977), p. 189.

19. *Ibid.*, p. 133.

20. *Ibid.*, p. 189.

21. Quoted in Lee Edwards, "Paul Weyrich, Conscience of the New Right," *Conservative Digest* (July 1981), p. 2.

22. "Ready on the Right," Washington *Post* (August 25, 1979).

15 Middle American Radicalism

1. C. Vann Woodward, "Who are 'the People'?" The *New Republic* (May 16, 1981), p. 32.

2. See Lipset, *op. cit.*, pp. 127–79.

3. *Ibid.*, p. 130.

4. *Ibid.*, p. 134.

5. Quoted in Kevin P. Phillips, "Extremism of the Center," King Features Syndicate (March 12, 1975).

6. Eugene Litwak, Nancy Hooyman and Donald Warren, "Ideological Complexity and Middle American Rationality," *Public Opinion Quarterly* (Fall 1973), p. 320.

7. Lipset, *op. cit.*, p. 139.

8. *Ibid.*, p. 132.

9. Fritz Stern, *The Politics of Cultural Despair* (Berkeley, University of California Press, 1961).

10. *Ibid.*, p. xvi.

11. Arthur Moeller van den Bruck, *Germany's Third Empire.* authorized English edition translated and condensed by E. O. Lorimer (London, Allen and Unwin, 1934).

12. "France's New Right Skirts Racism," Atlanta *Constitution* (August 30, 1979).

13. Alexander Yanov, "The Russian New Right: Rightwing Ideologies in the Contemporary USSR" (Institute of International Studies, University of California, Berkeley, 1979).

14. Abraham Brumberg, "Review of 'The Russian New Right,'" the *New Republic* (May 5, 1979), p. 32.

15. See "KKK Leader's Race Stirs Dismay," Los Angeles *Times* (May 29, 1980) and "White Supremacist's Vote-Getting Talent Stuns His GOP Detractors," Washington *Post* (November 15, 1980).

16. See "Ku Klux Klan on the Rise Again, This Time on Campuses," Chicago *Tribune* (June 9, 1981).

17. See *Congressional Record,* February 19, 1981, p. H525.

18. "Officials Alarmed by Growing Militarism," New York *Times* (December 21, 1980).

19. "Watergate Sphinx: An Unrepentant Liddy is Campus Hero," Washington *Post* (November 17, 1980).

16 Soft Landings and Other Institutional Myths

No citations.

17 The Party System

1. Richard Walton, "Citizens Party," the *Nation* (May 16, 1981).

2. The most innovative Republican use of the initiative in 1981–82 involved party efforts in Oklahoma and California to put the reapportionment plans passed by Democratic legislatures on the ballot to be voted up or down.

18 America and World History

1. San Diego *Union* (September 13, 1981).

2. Quoted in "Newcomers to South and West Reinforcing Reagan's Strength," New York *Times* (May 30, 1980).

3. Kevin P. Phillips, *The Emerging Republican Majority* (New Rochelle, N.Y., Arlington House, 1969), p. 437.

4. Walter Laqueur, *A Continent Astray: Europe 1970–78* (New York, Oxford U. Press, 1979).

Index

Index

Falwell, Jerry, 23, 47, 88, 141, 163–64, 190–91
fascism, 196, 197
Fay, John, 124
federalism, 13, 139, 217
Federalists, War of 1812 opposed by, 172–73
Federal Reserve Board, 118, 135, 137, 138
feminism, 74, 77
Finch, Robert, 56
Fischer, David Hackett, 151
Fitzgerald, F. Scott, 3, 11
Ford, Gerald R., 15, 38, 39, 60, 61, 70, 91, 159, 190, 195, 210, 213–14, 232
France, 126
New Right in, 202
Friedman, Milton, 14, 50, 130
frontier theory, 40–41, 237–38
fundamentalists, 22, 47–48, 49–50, 90, 91, 94, 97, 180–92, 196
church membership data on, 182–84
confluence of conservative economics and, 141
defined, 184
"great awakenings" of, 180–82, 235
humanism and secularism deplored by, 185–86
political mobilization of, 189–92
popular extremism and, 161
populism linked to, 180–81
as pro-Zionist, 163–64
voting patterns of, 186–89, 191, 195

Galbraith, John Kenneth, 7, 129, 133, 136–37
Gallup, George, 181, 184
geopolitics:
Goldwater and, 34–35
of Republican Party, 37–40, 57, 232
shift in, 35–37
Germany, revolutionary conservatism in, 200–201, 202
Germany, Weimar, see Weimar analogy
Germany, West, social spending in, 121–22, 124

Gilder, George, 13, 14, 45–46, 115, 131, 135, 140–41
Glazer, Nathan, 44, 163
Godwin, Mills, 59
gold standard, 50–51, 122, 138–39, 142, 181
Goldwater, Barry, 15, 102, 156, 170
in election of 1964, 34–35, 36, 37–38, 39n, 45, 50, 180, 232
on New Right, 49n–50n, 191
Goodhart, A. L., 64, 71
Graham, Billy, 187
Gray, Woods, 174–75
"great awakenings," 180–82, 235
Great Britain:
consumer demand in, 121
economic policies in, 124, 137, 144–45
rightist youth movements in, 156, 162, 202
Great Depression, 11, 19
causes of, 130, 133–37
Great Gatsby, The (Fitzgerald), 3, 11
Great Society, 19–20, 21, 22, 32, 34, 121, 122
Greece, ancient, moral breakdown in, 86

Hacker, Andrew, 53, 74
Haldeman, H. R., 38, 59, 66–67, 70–71, 81
Harding, Warren G., 133
Harris, Fred, 194
Harris, Louis, 49, 85, 91, 93, 102, 191
Hart, Jeffrey, 11, 42
Hartz, Louis, 40, 43, 46
Harvard Political Review, 162
Hawley-Smoot Tariff Act, 135
Health, Education and Welfare Department, U.S., 22
Hendricks, Steve, 182–83
high-technology workers, 98, 99
Hispanics, 80, 98, 99–100, 103
historical awareness, Americans lacking in, 207, 234–35
Hitler, Adolf, 156, 157, 159, 161, 164, 197, 199
Holmes, Oliver Wendell, 210

INDEX

INDEX

About the Author

KEVIN P. PHILLIPS, author, lawyer, commentator and publisher, was born in New York City in 1940 and educated at Colgate, the University of Edinburgh and the Harvard Law School. In 1968 he served as the chief political/voting patterns analyst in the Republican presidential campaign and thereafter published *The Emerging Republican Majority*. He is currently editor and publisher of *The American Political Report* and *Business & Public Affairs Fortnightly*, a syndicated political columnist and a commentator for CBS (Spectrum). He and his wife and two children live in Bethesda, Maryland, and West Goshen, Connecticut.